Four Chapters on Freedom

With kind regards, ॐ and prem

Swami Niranjan

Four Chapters on Freedom

Commentary on the Yoga Sutras of Patanjali

Swami Satyananda Saraswati

Yoga Publications Trust, Munger, Bihar, India

Published by Bihar School of Yoga
First edition 1976
Reprinted 1979, 1989

Published by Yoga Publications Trust
Reprinted 2000, 2002

ISBN: 81-85787-18-2
Price: Indian rupees one hundred only

Publisher and distributor: Yoga Publications Trust, Ganga Darshan, Munger, Bihar, India.

Website: www.yogavision.net
E-mail: ypt@yogavision.net

Printed at Thomson Press (India) Limited, New Delhi, 110001

SWAMI SIVANANDA SARASWATI

Swami Sivananda was born at Pattamadai, Tamil Nadu, in 1887. After serving as a medical doctor in Malaya, he renounced his practice, went to Rishikesh and was initiated into Dashnami sannyasa in 1924 by Swami Vishwananda Saraswati. He toured extensively throughout India, inspiring people to practise yoga and lead a divine life. He founded the Divine Life Society at Rishikesh in 1936, the Sivananda Ayurvedic Pharmacy in 1945, the Yoga Vedanta Forest Academy in 1948 and the Sivananda Eye Hospital in 1957. During his lifetime Swami Sivananda guided thousands of disciples and aspirants all over the world and authored over 200 books.

SWAMI SATYANANDA SARASWATI

Swami Satyananda was born at Almora, Uttar Pradesh, in 1923. In 1943 he met Swami Sivananda in Rishikesh and adopted the Dashnami sannyasa way of life. In 1955 he left his guru's ashram to live as a wandering mendicant and later founded the International Yoga Fellowship in 1963 and the Bihar School of Yoga in 1964. Over the next 20 years Swami Satyananda toured internationally and authored over 80 books. In 1987 he founded Sivananda Math, a charitable institution for aiding rural development, and the Yoga Research Foundation. In 1988 he renounced his mission, adopting kshetra sannyasa, and now lives as a paramahamsa sannyasin.

SWAMI NIRANJANANANDA SARASWATI

Swami Niranjanananda was born at Rajnandgaon, Madhya Pradesh, in 1960. At the age of four he joined the Bihar School of Yoga and was initiated into Dashnami sannyasa at the age of ten. From 1971 he travelled overseas and toured many countries for the next 11 years. In 1983 he was recalled to India and appointed President of Bihar School of Yoga. During the following 11 years he guided the development of Ganga Darshan, Sivananda Math and the Yoga Research Foundation. In 1990 he was initiated as a paramahamsa and in 1993 anointed preceptor in succession to Swami Satyananda. Bihar Yoga Bharati was founded under his direction in 1994. He has authored over 20 books and guides national and international yoga programs.

SWAMI SATYASANGANANDA SARASWATI

Swami Satyasangananda (Satsangi) was born on 24th March 1953, in Chandorenagore, West Bengal. From the age of 22 she experienced a series of inner awakenings which led her to her guru, Swami Satyananda. From 1981 she travelled ceaselessly with her guru in India and overseas and developed into a scholar with deep insight into the yogic and tantric traditions as well as modern sciences and philosophies. She is an efficient channel for the transmission of her guru's teachings. The establishment of Sivananda Math in Rikhia is her creation and mission, and she guides all its activities there, working tirelessly to uplift the weaker and underprivileged areas. She embodies compassion with clear reason and is the foundation of her guru's vision.

Contents

Introduction

Two pandits entered the ashram to attend satsang. It was a cool, refreshing evening and a large mat had been laid out on the lawn. The pandits were the first to arrive and they sat on the mat directly in front of the guru's seat. Soon many other people arrived and when the guru took his seat, the satsang began.

Initially, the satsang was concerned with asana, pranayama and other yogic practices, but after some time the pandits said to the guru, "We've come here to discuss more important things; we have come to ask you about the philosophical implications of samadhi according to Patanjali." The debate began. One pandit insisted, "Asamprajnata samadhi is surely the same as nirbeeja samadhi." The other disagreed, "No, no you are totally wrong, they are different." Each began to quote widely from various scriptures to prove their point of view and soon they were having quite a furious argument.

The guru could not get a word in edgeways so he sat in silence. The pandits became oblivious to him, though at one stage one turned to him and asked, "What do you think? Is samprajnata different to nirbeeja samadhi, or not?" But before the guru could reply, the same pandit continued, "The books that I've read say that they are definitely different." The guru remained silent and the pandits continued their discussion. Eventually they started yelling at each other and almost came to blows.

The heated discussion continued for about half an hour. Then a big, fat, contented cow casually strolled onto the mat as though it owned the place. Everyone was amused at the arrival of the new visitor, everyone that is except the two pandits who were so involved in their debate that they did not see it. People moved out of the way and the cow quietly sat down behind the pandits. The cow seemed to be intently interested in the debate and seriously contemplating the meaning of every word that was spoken.

Suddenly the cow bellowed, "*M-o-o-o-o-o-o-o*," with full approval. The two pandits jumped with fright. For the first time in half an hour they were lost for words. Everyone laughed and the cow slowly arose and lumbered away, perhaps to find another interesting satsang elsewhere.

The cow uttered the wisest words in the satsang. Unknowingly, or perhaps knowingly, it told everyone, including the pandits, that the *Yoga Sutras* of Patanjali were not written for intellectual debate and speculation. They were written to explain the process and practical methods of raising levels of awareness, gaining deeper wisdom, exploring the potential of the mind and eventually going beyond the mind. The text is primarily practice-orientated; it is not intended to be an intellectual exercise on samadhi. Surely Patanjali himself would have smiled at the appropriate wise words of the humble cow.

Many of the verses indicate things that are beyond the range of normal mundane experience and comprehension. This is not done to bring intellectual understanding; it is so that a *sadhaka* (aspirant) who practises the yoga of Patanjali or any other system will progressively gain insight and understanding of the deeper aspects of his being. He will gradually understand Patanjali's cryptic verses through his own experience. The verses tell him if he is going in the right direction or not and also help him to proceed further. The verses can never be understood intellectually, nor are they intended to be understood in this manner. The verses were written as a map, a guide for the journey from mundane levels to higher levels of consciousness and eventually to liberation. The text shows the path to perfect freedom through sustained yogic practice.

Everything that needs to be said is contained within the verses of Patanjali and in the commentary. The purpose of this introduction is to:

- Give basic background information.
- Highlight the incredible consistency and perfection of the verses so that the reader can more easily and clearly see the yogic, scientific and psychological truths contained within the main text.
- Point out the things that you should notice, but which you may otherwise so easily miss in the simplicity of the verses.

Structure of the text

This book is a commentary on the *Yoga Sutras*, a scripture of 196 sutras (verses) written by the sage Patanjali. In English the text can be called 'Verses on Yoga', but actually the word *sutra* means 'thread'. The word implies that the written words carry an underlying continuous thought; the various ideas connect together like the beads on a mala to form a complete philosophy.

The scripture is also called *Yoga Darshana*, which is widely translated as 'Philosophy of Yoga', but actually the word *darshana* has a much deeper meaning. Literally, it means 'to see'. It is derived from *drish*, meaning 'to see' and is related to the word *drashta*, meaning 'the seer'. Darshana is the process of seeing. Therefore, *Yoga Darshana* means 'a process of seeing through yoga', but it does not mean seeing with the eyes, nor does it mean seeing with any other senses in the outside world. It means to see something beyond the senses and beyond the mind. It is a process of seeing with the eyes and other senses closed, and with the mind under complete control. *Yoga Darshana* is a method of higher perception; it is a means 'to see the invisible' or 'to see with spiritual insight'.

The scripture is regarded as the most precise and scientific text ever written on yoga. It is divided into four chapters:

1. Samadhi Pada

Chapter on samadhi consisting of 51 verses. This chapter is concerned with the following subjects:

Definition of yoga
Purpose of yoga
Vritti (mental modification)
Practice and detachment
Samprajnata and *asamprajnata samadhi*
Means of attaining experience
Ishwara (pure consciousness)
Aum
Obstacles to progress
Methods of harmonizing the mind
Sabeeja and *nirbeeja samadhi*

2. Sadhana Pada

Chapter on practice consisting of 55 verses. It discusses the following subjects:

Klesha (basic tensions of life)
Removal of klesha
Purpose of destroying klesha
The knower and the known
Awareness and lack of awareness
The path to *prajna* (intuitive knowledge)
The eight limbs of Patanjali yoga
Yama (social code)
Niyama (personal code)

Method of controlling negative thoughts
Results of perfecting yama and niyama
Asana (sitting position)
Pranayama (control of prana)
Pratyahara (sense withdrawal)

3. Vibhooti Pada

Chapter on psychic powers consisting of 56 verses. It discusses the following subjects:

Dharana (concentration)
Dhyana (meditation)
Samadhi (superconsciousness)
Samyama (concentration, meditation and samadhi)
Parinama (transformations of consciousness)
Nature of external appearance
Psychic powers

4. Kaivalya Pada

Chapter on onlyness consisting of 34 verses. It discusses the following subjects:

Means of attaining psychic powers
Cause of individuality
The individual and the cosmic mind
Karma (predestined actions and thoughts)
Unity of all things
Theory of perception
The mind as an unconscious instrument
The path to *kaivalya*
Kaivalya

All the verses are in methodical sequence; each has its place for a specific purpose. Patanjali moves from one verse to the next, from one topic to the next, with faultless logic.

Each Sanskrit word has an exact meaning in the context of the scripture. Many technical words are precisely defined within the text itself. This minimizes misunderstanding and confusion that can arise through words changing their colloquial meaning over the course of time. Many words have no exact equivalent in English; occasionally, two or more Sanskrit words have the same literal meaning in English, but have vastly different implications in the context of yoga practice and experience. The translation has overcome these problems whilst retaining the meaning and flow.

The text is a masterpiece of brevity and clarity. Patanjali has removed all unnecessary words for the following reasons:
- To allow easy memorization by disciples; remember, there were no printing presses at that time.
- To allow the verses to be the object of enquiry; too many words would confuse.
- To prevent misquotation and misinterpretation.

Though brief to the utmost, the verses contain the essence of *Patanjali yoga* from start to finish, for they contain maximum information in minimum words.

The verses are sheer poetry combined with sublime scientific precision. To gain the best understanding from this book, we suggest that you first of all carefully read both the verses and commentary together, then slowly read the verses alone, one after the other. This will allow you to follow the wonderful sequence and flow of Patanjali's exposition.

Definition

Patanjali called his system *yoga.* He did not give it a specific title to differentiate it from other yogic paths. Since the time of writing the *Yoga Sutras*, however, his method has come to be called *Patanjali yoga* (the yoga of Patanjali).

Patanjali yoga is widely identified as being the same as *raja yoga* (the royal path of yoga). We, however, prefer to define Patanjali yoga as a specific system within the wider framework of raja yoga. According to our definition, raja yoga includes the following systems:

- Kundalini yoga; also called laya yoga
- Kriya yoga
- Mantra yoga
- Dhyana yoga as described in the *Bhagavad Gita*
- Patanjali yoga

Raja yoga (including Patanjali yoga) is the science of the mind. Instead of exploring the outer world like other sciences, raja yoga is concerned with exploring the inner world and unleashing the power and knowledge contained within. It is the science of mental discipline and includes various methods of making the mind one-pointed. Patanjali himself defines his method of yoga as 'the elimination of mental fluctuations'. We prefer to call the mind 'the visible tip of pure consciousness', which encompasses the conscious, subconscious and unconscious layers of being. Therefore, we translate Patanjali's definition as follows: "Yoga is the control of the patterns of consciousness."

Specifically, Patanjali yoga is that system which consists of eight stages: yama, niyama, asana, pranayama, pratyahara, dharana, dhyana and samadhi. It is therefore widely called *ashtanga yoga* (the yoga of eight stages).

The basis and date of the Yoga Sutras

One tradition says that *Hiranyagarbha* (Brahma) formulated the *Yoga Sutras*. Maybe, but for the sake of simplicity we can say that he formulated them through the agency of a man called Patanjali.

Some experts say that Patanjali lived in the 4th century AD; others say about 50 AD; some say that he definitely lived about 400 BC and still others say that he existed 5,000 years ago. A widely accepted date, though not certain, is about 400 years before Christ. This date is estimated by various methods. One method is to compare the practices and philosophy of the *Yoga Sutras* with those contained in other texts, such as the early Upanishads and the scriptures of Samkhya and

Buddhism. The main flaw is that the ancient texts cannot be reliably dated. Furthermore, it is difficult to really say who influenced who and which text came first. Moreover, a scripture does not by any means fix the date of a philosophical system; a scripture may be written hundreds of years after the formulation, development and proliferation of a specific philosophy.

A man called Patanjali seems to have written two other texts on Sanskrit grammar and on medicine, called the *Mahabhashya* and *Charakapratisanskrita*. It is not really certain whether this is the same Patanjali who wrote the *Yoga Sutras*. If it was, then it suggests that the *Yoga Sutras* were written at about the same time or a little after Buddha and the great grammarian Panini, that is, about 500 BC.

The basis of the *Yoga Sutras* certainly lies in Samkhya philosophy, which is said to have been formulated by rishi Kapila. This system existed before the rise of Buddhism; in fact, Buddha himself studied Samkhya at an ashram called Alarkalam early in his search for enlightenment. Samkhya was a very popular philosophy at that time in India. The Samkhya system dispenses with all theories of God; it says that the existence or non-existence of God is irrelevant to personal *sadhana* (spiritual practice). Buddha said the same thing; he taught neither belief nor disbelief in God. In this respect, the influence of Samkhya on Buddha's teachings can be clearly seen. Patanjali, on the other hand, differs from both Samkhya and Buddhism as he introduces the concept of God, but he does this very cleverly and as a powerful means of sadhana for those who are inclined towards the path of bhakti yoga. None of this information, however, really fixes the date of the *Yoga Sutras*.

Some say that Patanjali was influenced by the Jains, others say that he influenced the Jains. Some say that Buddhism is partly based on the *Yoga Sutras*, whilst others say that Patanjali has based much of his text on Buddhist beliefs and practices.

It is probably more a case of 'six of one and half a dozen of the other' for no system grows in isolation. Each and every system has been influenced by previous systems and contemporary systems.

Any person with some knowledge of Buddhism can clearly see close resemblances between the teachings of Buddha and Patanjali, especially in such basic rules as yama and niyama and in the basic philosophical concepts, but whether the *Yoga Sutras* come before or after Buddha is not certain. The influence of the *Yoga Sutras* can be clearly seen in later Buddhist texts, such as the *Vishuddhi Magga*, but still this does not fix the date of the *Yoga Sutras*.

It is interesting to note that Patanjali does not directly quote or refer to any other texts. This tends to suggest that they were formulated before many of the well-known scriptures and religious systems of India. On the other hand, the language used in the *Yoga Sutras* is later than that used at the time of Buddha. This seems to conclusively fix the date at the widely accepted date of approximately 400 BC, but again there are many other factors to consider. The language of the *Yoga Sutras* may have been updated after the original manuscript was written, the original having been lost, or the *Yoga Sutras* may have existed in non-written form long before it was put on paper.

Our opinion can be summarized by saying that all the techniques of raja yoga existed long before Patanjali, even if in a latent seed form within the collective unconscious mind. The *Yoga Sutras* are probably a compilation of previously known verses handed down from guru to disciple by word of mouth. It was the genius of someone called Patanjali who put the system into a comprehensive written whole.

If you are interested in the history of Patanjali and the *Yoga Sutras*, we suggest that you study it further. We are not really interested in the identity or date of Patanjali, for he (or she?) is merely a spokesman for the timeless wisdom that is the heritage of all mankind. It does not really matter whether his name was Patanjali or Buddha, Singh or Smith; whether he was Indian, Chinese or Aboriginal. It does not even matter when the text was written because it contains wisdom that is eternal and which belongs to no specific era. It is applicable to all ages and all people, no matter what the background. It is the content and application of the *Yoga Sutras* that is important.

Commentators

Many commentators have written about the meanings hidden within the verses of the *Yoga Sutras*. The most well-known are:

- *Yoga Bhashya* by Vyasa (date uncertain)
- *Tattva Visharadi* by Vachaspati Mishra (about 9th century)
- *Bhojavritti* by Bhoja Raja (11th century)
- *Yoga Vartika* by Vijnana Bhikshu (14th century)
- *Raja Yoga* by Swami Vivekananda (19th century)

All of these commentaries are widely available. There are many other traditional commentaries, and even commentaries on commentaries. For example, Ganesha Bhatt wrote an explanation of the commentary *Yoga Vartika*. Many commentaries have been written in this century, including this commentary.

The eight stages

Patanjali gives a wide range of techniques that slowly harmonize the mind and gradually induce more subtle perception. However, the main path of Patanjali is contained within eight fundamental stages. The first five are:

1. *Yama* (social code)
2. *Niyama* (personal code)
3. *Asana* (sitting pose)
4. *Pranayama* (control of prana)
5. *Pratyahara* (sense withdrawal)

These first five stages are the esoteric or *bahiranga* (external) practices of yoga. They progressively prepare the body-mind for the last stages:

6. *Dharana* (concentration)
7. *Dhyana* (meditation)
8. *Samadhi* (superconsciousness)

These last three stages are the esoteric or *antaranga* (internal) practices of yoga. The first five stages negate consciousness, whilst the last three stages expand consciousness. The more advanced stages can only be practised successfully after prior practice of the earlier preparatory stages. The stages up to pratyahara gradually remove external distractions, whilst the practices from dharana onwards eradicate the disturbing thoughts and psychic manifestations so that the mind ceases to function. The *ida* (inner world) is balanced with the *pingala* (outer world) so that the *sushumna* (transcendental world) begins to function in samadhi.

The eight stages progressively steady the five *koshas* (sheaths) of man: *annamaya* (physical); *pranamaya* (pranic or bioplasmic); *manomaya* (mental); *vijnanamaya* (intuitive) and *anandamaya* (blissful). Eventually the aim is to transcend the limitation of these sheaths. The movement is from the gross to the more subtle. Let us briefly discuss each of the eight stages in turn.

Yama and niyama: The five yamas are *satya* (truthfulness); *ahimsa* (feeling of non-violence to all things: human, animal or whatever); *asteya* (honesty); *brahmacharya* (sexual control or abstinence) and *aparigraha* (non-possessiveness). The niyamas are also five in number: *shaucha* (cleanliness); *santosha* (contentment); *tapah* (austerity); *swadhyaya* (self-study) and *Ishwara pranidhana* (surrender to the cosmic will). The yamas are designed to harmonize one's social interactions and the niyamas are intended to harmonize one's inner feelings. All the rules, yamas and niyamas, are designed to reduce friction between one's outer actions and inner attitudes. There is a two-way relationship: the mind stimulates external actions and external actions stimulate the mind. If the external actions are not harmonious, then the mind will be disturbed. Conversely, a disturbed mind will tend to produce disharmonious acts. It is a vicious circle, where inner turmoil leads to outer turmoil and where, in turn, external turmoil leads to further inner turmoil. The yamas and niyamas aim to break this vicious circle and thereby calm the mind by sensible actions and sensible attitudes towards oneself, towards one's life and towards one's surroundings.

Though the yamas and niyamas consist only of ten vows, they encompass a wide range of human activity. They tackle the problem of mental disturbance from the outer edge, the periphery, but it is also a start to more profound changes that can arise from deeper exploration of the mind. The rules are not easy to apply, but even limited application will lead to greater peace of mind. Perfect application can only arise with self-realization.

Asana is defined by Patanjali as a steady and comfortable sitting position. In theory, it can include many of the asanas of hatha yoga, but practically it includes only a few, such as padmasana, siddhasana, etc. The purpose of an asana in Patanjali yoga is to balance the different nerve impulses, feelings of pain and pleasure, heat and cold and all other opposite sensations.

Pranayama is practised to concentrate all the pranic forces of the human structure. This leads to control and one-pointedness.

Pratyahara means 'to gather inwards'. The practice is concerned with checking and curbing the outgoing tendencies of the mind so that awareness can be directed inwards. It is impossible to explore the inner realms of the mind if one is addicted to, disturbed and distracted by external sense experience. Therefore, the sense experiences, such as sound, smell, etc. are cut. All meditative techniques such as antar mouna, ajapa japa, trataka, etc. are initially concerned with inducing this stage of pratyahara. Pratyahara, in a higher sense, also includes the cutting of inner psychic and mental sensations.

Dharana means concentration of mind. It is the step before meditation and is concerned with fixing awareness on one object to the exclusion of all others. If the state of pratyahara has been achieved, then all outer disturbances should have been eliminated, yet the mind is still full of inner chatter in the form of memories of the past and projections of the future. The mind thinks of and tries to relive past pleasant experiences, is obsessed by unpleasant experiences, or is planning or fearing the future.

Various methods can be used to induce mental one-pointedness. Religions in general try to induce it through rituals, church service, *pooja* (worship), chanting, kirtan, prayer and so forth. Patanjali yoga utilizes a psychic symbol as a focal point for internal concentration. It can be one's guru, a deity, a mantra, an enquiry; it can be almost anything. It must be something that spontaneously attracts the attention of the individual and must be chosen to suit the inherent nature of the mind and personality. The psychic symbol, projected in front of the closed eyes, must be so overwhelming that one's whole being is consumed and absorbed by it. There must be spontaneous attraction, otherwise one's psyche will remain scattered.

Dharana needs regular and persistent practice. Gradually one will perceive deeper aspects of the symbol; its archetypal nature will start to reveal itself. One will spontaneously flow into dhyana.

Dhyana is merely an extension of dharana. It arises when one is able to maintain a smooth, unfluctuating flow of concentration towards the inner symbol for a period of time. The mind becomes moulded around one pattern in the form of the psychic symbol. The flow of awareness is often compared to a smooth flow of oil. Eventually this leads to an elimination of duality; the seer, seen and seeing merge into unity and one's being fuses into the state of samadhi.

Samadhi: Patanjali lists different levels of samadhi, but a good definition in the *Katha Upanishad* (111:10) is as follows:

> *When the five senses of perception together with the mind are at rest, when even the intellect has ceased to function, that, say the sages, is the supreme state.*

This is the state where there is complete absence of both external and internal mental modification; all that remains is awareness. Samadhi brings self-realization.

In the *Bhagavad Gita* (2:53), it says:

> *When the intellect, having been perplexed by hearing the words of the scriptures, stands immovable in samadhi, then you shall attain self-realization.*

The most bland explanation and definition of samadhi is given in the *Yoga Chudamani Upanishad* (111–113):

> *Twelve (protracted rounds) of pranayama lead to pratyahara. Twelve (extended durations of) pratyahara lead to dharana. Twelve such dharanas lead to dhyana and twelve such dhyanas result in samadhi.*

The eight steps are for advanced aspirants

The *Yoga Sutras* are well known, yet the eight steps are really advanced techniques for those people who have exhausted most of their mental problems and conflicts. They are not really for the average person. In the very beginning it says, "Now, therefore, complete instructions regarding yoga." The words 'now, therefore' mean that one will be able to practise the eight steps after vast amounts of preparation. The *Yoga Sutras* are a sequel to previous more basic texts and teaching. In the *Hatha Yoga Pradipika* it says:

Prostrations to Shiva who taught hatha yoga as a ladder to climb to the peak of raja yoga. Because of confusion and misconceptions, most people are unable to practise raja yoga; in compassion, Swatmarama (the author) describes hatha yoga as a torch to remove ignorance.
(1:1,2,3)

Hatha yoga in the form of asanas, pranayama and other practices should be mastered until one is ready for raja yoga. (1:67)

Without this preparation, one makes no headway with Patanjali yoga.

Why are the eight steps called advanced? One reason is that they ask people to restrain their thoughts. For most people, who have disturbed minds, this would do more harm than good. It is only when the fluctuations of the mind are small that one can restrain the thoughts. One can easily crush and destroy small cockroaches that disturb the cleanliness of a yard, but it is much more difficult to tame a wild elephant. It is definitely *not* advisable to try to suppress the compelling thoughts and desires that still exist in the mind of the average person.

The basic rules of yama and niyama are also very difficult for the average person. These rules are really for those people who have exhausted most of their *samskaras* and *karmas* (mental turmoil and desires). For example, if most people try to practise *brahmacharya* (continence), then they will become neurotics; it can only be practised by people who have worked out most of their desires and have already purified their mind.

The eight stages of Patanjali yoga are for advanced aspirants, *not* for beginners. First of all, one should take steps to purify the mind through hatha yoga, karma yoga, bhakti yoga and general meditative techniques that involve awareness more than concentration. One can also practise some of the associated techniques that Patanjali suggests in the text. These methods will prepare one for the practice of the eight steps and to meet the guru who can teach them personally.

Associated yoga techniques

The path of yoga formulated by Patanjali is not confined only to the eight stages. It is an integrated system that brings in many other yogic practices. Patanjali lists and suggests a wide range of techniques which help to harmonize one's mind and life; however, his explanations and description of the techniques are very brief and terse, to say the least. It is very easy to miss the significance of Patanjali's statements without the expert guidance of a guru.

Swami Satyananda, with his intimate knowledge and his personal experience of yoga, clearly points out the hidden implications behind many obscure verses. For example, verses 1:32–39 describe the basis of most meditative techniques, including yoga nidra, antar mouna, khechari mudra, and so on. Mantra or japa yoga is clearly indicated in verses 1:27–29. The commentary clearly explains and highlights these concealed meanings.

The human personality can be divided broadly into four fundamental categories: emotional, active, intuitive and volitional. Patanjali has clearly understood this fact and that each person has a different temperament and inclinations according to a predominance of one or more of these categories. He therefore knew that the yogic path had to be designed to suit the specific characteristics of an individual. Therefore, he suggests:

Bhakti yoga for those who are emotionally and devotionally inclined (refer to 1:23; 2:1; 2:23, 2:45; etc.).

Jnana yoga for those who are intuitive by nature. He recommends reflection and enquiry into the real meaning of *Aum* (1:27–29) and also explains much of Samkhya philosophy (2:20,21 etc.) as a means to higher realization. He also makes it clear that all mental knowledge is limited.

Raja or **Patanjali yoga** for those with strong willpower; this is the theme of the entire scripture.

Karma yoga for those who are active by nature is not specifically mentioned, but certainly it is implicit in many verses. For example, the yamas and niyamas imply the practice of karma yoga in daily actions and duties. Karma yoga is also implicit in the verses on bhakti yoga.

Patanjali knew that success in bhakti yoga leads automatically to success in raja yoga; jnana yoga leads to perfection of raja yoga, and so forth. He knew that a person on the path of raja yoga must integrate his whole being. Petty-mindedness and egoism have to be removed by any available method. All negative and limiting functions of the mind have to be erased.

> *The stopping of the vrittis (mental modifications) can be achieved by vairagya (detachment) and abhyasa (practice of yoga).* (1:12)

This statement includes all paths and techniques of yoga. None are excluded. They all lead to success in yoga.

Viyoga leads to yoga

Most people know that the word *yoga* means union, but in the *Yoga Sutras* Patanjali refers to yoga as a process of separation. How can this contradiction be explained? It can be explained in terms of Samkhya philosophy, which is the basis of the *Yoga Sutras*.

Samkhya divides existence and individual being into two aspects: *purusha* (consciousness) and *prakriti* (nature, energy, manifested being). Remember that it is only a philosophy and like all other philosophies, no matter how sublime, can never truly represent reality. Existence and the individual being arise when purusha and prakriti come together. The purusha implies the *drashta* (seer) and prakriti implies the *drishya* (seen). The purusha means subjective being and prakriti means objective, external existence.

The process and practices of yoga are concerned with *viyoga*, separating the purusha from prakriti, the seer from the seen; that is, separating awareness from identification with the mind-body vehicle. This separation and difference between awareness and the mind-body can only be understood by personal experience. No amount of reading or talking will convince one of the truth and reality of this difference – only personal, overwhelming, staggering experience. This personal experience will transform one's life; it will provide a platform on which to reassess and understand one's life and being. One will see a new dimension, never before suspected, in one's own being. The process of yoga is designed to bring viyoga, separation between the seer and the seen; this leads to yoga, union, as the culmination. First of all the purusha and prakriti have to be separated and then, when this is achieved, they are seen to be the same thing. Thus viyoga (the practice of yoga) leads to yoga at a higher level.

Another way of explaining the same thing is to say that pure consciousness (purusha) is tied down to levels of awareness through wrong identification with the mind-body (prakriti). The purpose of yoga is to liberate purusha from prakriti. Swami Satyananda defines yoga as:

> *(A method) by which consciousness is disconnected from the entanglement with mind and the manifested world. Yoga (union) is the result.*

Experience of the difference, and separation of pure consciousness from the mind and body, leads to realization of the oneness of all things. All yoga paths and techniques utilize this process of removing limitations of the mind and body so that *jnana* (transcendental knowledge) can shine through in its full glory. Perfection of mind leads to spontaneous illumination of pure consciousness.

Nature of the mind

Modern psychology tends to regard the mind as the source of awareness and consciousness. Patanjali clearly states the yogic point of view when he says that the mind cannot be the source of consciousness because it too can be perceived as an object (4:19). The mind does *not* illuminate itself.

Modern science tends to regard both mind and consciousness as the expression and manifestation of matter. Yoga, on the other hand, says that matter is really the gross form and manifestation of mind; matter is controlled by mind, not mind by matter. The material world that we see around us is really an expression of the more subtle mental aspects of existence.

Apart from these two fundamental differences, yoga and modern thought agree on many factors concerning the mind. According to Jung's psychology, the mind can be classified into three different dimensions: conscious, subconscious and unconscious. These can be related to yogic terminology as follows:

1. **Conscious mind**, *sthula* (gross dimension)
   jagrit (waking state)
   surface thought and perception of the outside world
2. **Subconscious mind**, *sukshma* (subtle dimension)
   swapna (dream state)
   individual memory
   samskaras (mental tendencies)
3. **Unconscious mind**, *karana* (causal dimension)
   sushupti (deep sleep state)
   cosmic collective samskara and memory

These realms contain the instinctive, intellectual, psychic and intuitive aspects of man. The purpose of Patanjali yoga is to explore these different mental spheres so that they become known. The aim is to proceed from the conscious to the subconscious and then to the unconscious.

Few people understand or even slightly appreciate the incredible depth of the mind. No modern psychological system has attempted to define its contents; yet Vyasa, one of the most profound commentators on Patanjali's *Yoga Sutras*, who possibly lived two thousand years ago, has actually divided and classified the subconscious and unconscious mind into seven aspects. These are as follows:

1. Inhibited samskaras (mental impressions, caused by individual repression).
2. Samskaras which cause one to act in a specific manner. These memories may be prenatal and determine actions, illnesses, talents and so forth. This is the hereditary aspect of man.
3. Latent unexpressed data memories of past events. These are hidden and stored in the collective unconscious beyond the normal limitations of individual awareness.
4. Instinctive reflexes that control the vegetative functioning of the physical and pranic body. We do not learn to digest food; the ability is already pre-programmed in the individual mind.
5. Prana (bioplasmic energy). The mind itself, no matter how subtle or gross, is composed of prana. Prana is also the means for the mind to carry out actions in accordance with thoughts.
6. Innate fluctuations of the mind. The mind by its very nature is designed to change with cosmic rhythms.
7. Psychic powers. Supernormal powers tend to take place in the domain of the collective unconscious or cosmic mind.

This is a very comprehensive list and is certainly thought provoking. It gives an indication of the scope and nature of the mind. These different aspects progressively manifest on the path of yoga.

All the secrets of the universe are in the mind. It contains all knowledge that has existed, now exists and which will exist in the future. It has layer upon layer of expression from the most subtle to the most gross. The purpose of Patanjali yoga is to progressively remove existing restrictions and veils of the individual mind, to explore and unfold its inherent potential, and to gradually shape the individual mind into a perfect instrument and reflector of the cosmic mind of which it is a part. The aim of Patanjali yoga, and all other paths of yoga, is to go further and take a jump into the chasm of no-mind – superconsciousness.

Psychic or supernormal powers

Psychic powers are called *siddhis* in Sanskrit. They include telepathy, clairaudience, clairvoyance, premonition and a vast array of less well-known powers. They take place through the mediumship of super-individual realms of the mind. The siddhis arise in the collective unconscious where every person, every individual mind and every thing is linked intimately to everything else. They can take place in the past, in the future and even in the realms beyond time-space, yet no matter how wonderful they may seem, they are still merely expressions within the mind. Scientific experiments in Russia and elsewhere have measured various psychic phenomena with instruments, but these experiments are not really necessary, for one will discover some of them personally on the path of yoga.

Many of the verses of the *Yoga Sutras* describe a large selection of well-known and obscure siddhis. However, the text clearly warns that one should not aspire to achieve these powers or dabble with them. They can be dangerous for oneself and others if they are used for selfish purposes. The purpose of yoga is *not* to develop siddhis, but to bring realization of one's real nature. The siddhis are merely passing scenery which will surely arise as the mind becomes more one-pointed and purified. There should be ruthless detachment towards them.

On the yogic path, temptations become more and more subtle. It is difficult to resist the temptation to dabble with psychic powers, yet if you do, then you will crash and pay a heavy penalty for your indiscretion. All of the great saints, yogis, etc. tell of their battle against temptation; these include Buddha and Christ. Luckily, these siddhis rarely arise in an egotistical mind. If they did, then there would be total chaos in the mind and in the more subtle realms of the psyche. So do not practise yoga to gain siddhis; first of all satisfy your desires in the safer physical world.

The sublime psycho-psychiatric system

Most modern psychiatric systems are mainly concerned with bringing about 'normality' in an individual, whatever this term means. Patanjali yoga also tries to achieve this normality, but goes much further. It aims to enable an individual to explore all layers of the mind to bring about self-realization and then perfect freedom. Patanjali yoga can be called the ultimate psycho-psychiatric system towards which all others will eventually look for guidance, yet it contains less than two hundred verses and was written thousands of years ago.

As you read the text and commentary you will see the method that is used to tackle the problems of the mind. The following are a few examples.

Patanjali has briefly enumerated the basic techniques that modern psychiatry applies in therapy. These are given in verses 1:32–39. Verse 32 suggests the cultivation of intense interest in one thing; this can be a hobby or work and constitutes occupational therapy. Verse 33 suggests the cultivation of positive attitudes to others. This involves some autosuggestion, which can be imparted by a psychiatrist to his patient. Verse 34 suggests breath control. The relationship between mental disturbance and irregular breathing is well-known; deep breathing can be used to induce mental tranquillity. Verses 35 and 36 advise that one should concentrate on sense perception. This can include music therapy, massage, etc. and can quickly bring calmness into the mind. Verse 37 suggests that one should reflect on a person who has achieved higher states of awareness. This specifically means a yogi or guru but it can also apply to the psychiatrist; in fact, most modern therapies are almost totally dependent on the trust that a patient has in the therapist. Without this trust there can never be successful treatment. Verse 38 suggests dream therapy, which is almost the foundation of some modern psychiatric systems. Finally, verse 39 recommends meditation; modern psychiatry has recently grasped the significance of this form of therapy. All these methods help to purify the mind and allow memories to bubble to the surface and be exhausted.

The symptoms of mental disturbance are also enumerated in verse 1:31, as suffering, which includes illness, depression, nervousness and heavy or unrhythmical breathing.

Unhappiness is the universal problem of mankind. In a few short but penetrating verses Patanjali defines the cause of human unhappiness and its cure; he has explained what thousands of other books, philosophies and psychological systems, old and modern, have tried to do with little success. He sums up the whole situation in a nutshell without getting lost in verbose jargon and details. Because these verses are so explicit, comprehensive and logical, we will briefly discuss them here though they have been fully explained in the commentary. We have slightly changed the translation for the sake of emphasis.

Firstly, Patanjali says:

> *The basic tensions of the mind (which bring unhappiness) are ignorance of truth, egoism, attachment, aversion and fear of death.* (2:3)

This verse sums up the entire cause of unhappiness. The next verses define the implications behind the basic tensions:

> *Ignorance of reality is the root tension from which all other tensions arise; the tensions can be dormant, slight, scattered or manifest.* (2:4)

Patanjali explains that the root cause of unhappiness, whether conscious or subconscious, is ignorance of one's real nature. Until one knows the essence of one's being there will always be tension and unhappiness in some form or another.

Patanjali defines the tensions as acting at different levels. They are either:

1. **Dormant** (*prasupta*) – rooted deep in the subconscious mind, which you are not yet aware of. They will be confronted as perception becomes deeper through yoga practice.
2. **Slight** (*tanu*) – minor, insignificant tensions.
3. **Scattered** (*vichchhinna*) – tensions that bring neuroses, phobias, depression and so on in life. Yoga will eventually resolve these tensions by allowing you to accept yourself and harmonize your drives.
4. **Manifest** (*udara*) – conscious tensions that can be clearly recognized in daily interactions.

These tensions thus span the spectrum from the gross to the most subtle. What is this fundamental tension called ignorance? Patanjali explains in the next verse:

> *Ignorance can be defined as regarding the perishable as the imperishable, the impure as the pure, unhappiness as happiness and the non-self as the self.* (2:5)

This ignorance is the lack of knowledge of *swaroopa* (one's real nature). This is the core of the cause of unhappiness.

This ignorance is slowly broken down by the light of understanding that comes from regular and persistent practice of yoga. The mind itself is a source of ignorance, since it works on the principle of separation and differences. Ignorance is slowly dissolved by gaining more insight into the nature of the mind and then eventually going beyond the mind. It is the mind that results in false identification of consciousness with the mind-body. When *viyoga* (separation) of awareness from the mind-body is achieved, then one is moving towards breaking down basic ignorance and in turn all the other lesser causes of unhappiness. Ignorance leads to egoism. This is explained in the next verse:

> *Egoism can be defined as wrong identification of purusha (the seer) with the instrument of the mind-body.* (2:6)

People falsely identify with their mind-body; this produces a strong sense of individuality. Every person tries to impose his will on others for selfish gain. He seeks personal gratification at all costs. The cost is generally frustration and unhappiness, since the ego can never be fully satisfied.

The sense of ego leads to aversion and attachment to the things of the world:

> *Attachment can be defined as absorption in the pleasures of the world. Aversion can be defined as repulsion for things of the world.* (2:7,8)

These two tensions of attachment and aversion, likes or dislikes, lead one to conflict and unhappiness in life, for actual life situations rarely, if ever, meet one's needs and expectations.

These likes and dislikes lead to fear of death, since one wishes to continue the status quo of pleasure and individuality. Patanjali says:

> *The fear of death is an inherent and dominating force in all people, even in those who are very learned.* (2:9)

This causal chain of tension and unhappiness is very rational. Ignorance leads to egoism; egoism leads to likes and dislikes and these lead to fear of death. The removal of this basic ignorance and all the other tensions leads to perfect happiness. How is this to be done?

> *These causes of unhappiness can be annihilated by resolving them to the source and by removing the associated mental states through meditation.* (2:10,11)

Thus the tension can be removed by exploring the mind through meditative techniques.

These few brief verses sum up the nature of mental problems, tensions and unhappiness and the method of eliminating them. An entire encyclopaedia could be written to elucidate them. A whole psychiatric system could be developed around them. Patanjali yoga tries to tackle the very source of human dissatisfaction; any other approach can only scratch the surface of human suffering. Patanjali gives insight into the basic cause; without this insight how can unhappiness be cured? Therefore, the sutras define the causes and then indicate how to remove them. It is only in this manner that one can find the happiness that lies beyond one's wildest dreams.

Patanjali has written a wealth of knowledge in a few thousands words. As far as we are concerned, it should be the standard reference book for all psychiatrists. It should be the 'Bible' of psychology and psychiatry. Such is our reverence for this masterpiece of practical wisdom.

The necessity of this commentary

Patanjali, or whoever wrote the *Yoga Sutras*, was a mastermind. He was more scientific than most scientists, more logical than most logicians. He was strictly and drastically economical with words. He avoided repetition. Sometimes his sentence structure is incomplete, yet each and every word contains a wealth of information and significance, some obvious but some hidden. It is very easy to miss or misunderstand the implications behind the verses. The cryptic meanings can only be revealed by a living master; furthermore, the verses have to be explained in terms that modern man can understand. It is for this reason that this commentary had been produced, based on the practice and personal experience of a modern master, our guru, Swami Satyananda Saraswati.

Chapter One

Samadhi Pada

(51 Sutras)

Sutra 1: Introduction to yoga

अथ योगानुशासनम् ॥ १ ॥

Atha yogānuśāsanam

Atha: now therefore; *yoga*: (regarding) yoga; *anuśāsanam*: complete instructions

Now, therefore, complete instructions regarding yoga.

Atha: We shall pause and try to find out why the author has used the word atha. He could have used atra yoganushasanam, which means, 'here are instructions on yoga', but he used the word atha. *Atha* means 'now therefore', which means that these instructions on yoga are in connection with some previous instructions. The word atha is used here to denote that, after having purified oneself by karma yoga and after having unified the mental tendencies by bhakti yoga, the aspirant is being given instructions on yoga. By this, it is meant that those instructions on yoga which follow will become intelligible, fruitful and also palatable to those whose hearts are pure and whose minds are at rest, otherwise not. Those who have impure minds and wavering tendencies will not be able to practise what has been instructed in this shastra. Therefore, the word atha has been used in order to emphasize the necessity of qualifying oneself in karma yoga, bhakti yoga and other preparatory systems.

Yoga: The meaning of yoga follows in a subsequent sutra.

Anushasanam: The actual word is shasanam, *anu* being a prefix to emphasize its completeness. *Shasan* is a word which means giving a ruling, command, order, instruction. The word shastra is developed from the word shasan. Shastra does not literally mean scripture. *Shastra* literally means a process of instructions and rulings. From the same word, another word has evolved – Ishwara, meaning ruler, governor, commander, and which is commonly used for God.

So, you will understand that *anushasanam* means instructions. You may have read other commentaries on the yoga sutras where the word anushasanam is translated as restatement, exposition, explanation. If you analyze the word properly, you will find that the translations are totally incorrect. They are not at all appropriate to the text because the yoga sutras themselves are so simple, so concise, so short-worded that they can be neither an explanation nor an exposition; they can only be instructions.

Yoga is this; this is how you practise yoga; these are the conditions of mind; this is how the individual experiments; this is the place of God in yoga – such and other similar matters are dealt with in this book. There are, of course, expositions, short notes, explanations, commentaries, criticisms, etc. on yoga by great scholars like Vyasa, Bhoja, Vijnana Bhikshu and others. So, ultimately, we can take it that the word anushasanam means complete instructions.

Sutra 2: What is yoga?

योगश्चित्तवृत्तिनिरोधः ॥ २ ॥

Yogaschitta vṛtti nirodhaḥ

Yogah: yoga; *chitta*: consciousness; *vṛtti*: patterns or circular patterns; *nirodhaḥ*: blocking, stopping

To block the patterns of consciousness is yoga.

The sutra is a composition of four words: yoga, chitta, vritti and nirodhah. We will not explain the word yoga now, as it will be better understood after studying the 195 sutras.

Chitta is derived from the basic idea of *chit*, which means to see, to be conscious of, to be aware. Hence *chitta* means individual consciousness, which includes the conscious state of mind, the subconscious state of mind and also the unconscious state of mind. The totality of these three states of individual mind is symbolized by the expression chitta. Chitta has been differently accepted in Vedanta, but here chitta represents the whole of the individual consciousness, which is comprised of three stages: the sense or objective consciousness, the subjective or astral consciousness, and the unconsciousness or mental state of dormant potentiality. These three states of pure consciousness should be understood as the chitta referred to in this sutra.

In the *Mandukya Upanishad*, the four states or dimensions of consciousness are dealt with in a very lucid form. If you read this Upanishad or a commentary on it, your personal consciousness will become clear to you. In this sutra, chitta represents all the four dimensions of consciousness, but it is a symbol of three dimensions of consciousness. These three dimensions of consciousness are spoken of as chitta, and the fourth dimension is spoken of as atman. In brief, we can say that atman plus chitta is jivatman, the individual awareness; jivatman minus chitta is atman. This is merely an indirect explanation of the word.

What do we mean by blocking? Does it mean that we block and stop our thoughts, visions, respiration, desires and personality complexes? If that is so, then Patanjali is introducing suppression. This is true only so long as chitta is taken in the light of mind, the instrument of general knowledge, but when the chitta is understood to be the total consciousness in the individual, giving rise to various manifestations in the mental or astral realms, then the doubt regarding the act of suppressing will be rent asunder.

The expression *nirodha* in this sutra apparently means a process of blocking, but it should not mean an act of blocking the fundamental stuff of awareness. In fact, it is clear in this sutra that it is an act of blocking the patterns of awareness, not the awareness itself. As a practitioner of yoga, you will certainly agree with this apt expression in the sutra, that the patterns of awareness become blocked in the yogic state of meditation. A little later in this chapter you will learn more about the fundamental structure and the nature, action and reaction of chitta, but in this sutra it is hinted that a different and fundamental state of consciousness can be achieved by blocking the flow of consciousness.

When you go to bed at night and enter the unconscious state of awareness, what happens to your sense awareness, your body and brain? Do they die, or is it a process of blocking the flow of sense awareness and mental awareness? Certainly it is a state where the psychological functions are cut off from the realm of individual awareness. The flow of vrittis changes and therefore you experience a different plane, different objects, events, persons, places and processes. All that is the vrittis, pertaining to a different state of awareness due to the process of blocking the normal vrittis. If you analyze all such states where individual awareness manifests in different modes, forms and dimensions, you will come to the realization that the process of vrittis is different from awareness and that one can block this flow of vrittis and transcend the limitations of awareness or, rather, put an end to this ever-incarnating flow of vrittis.

This again brings us to the fact that there is a definite process, unconcerned and different from all that relates with the body, mind, senses and prana, and it is that awareness which keeps on changing from state to state. This process is consciousness, a state of constant and unbroken awareness.

There is in us the existence of consciousness which is irrespective of this body; which is with the body and at the same time it can be without the body, or outside it. It is that which is to be blocked. It is not the ordinary thoughts that we have to suppress. These thoughts are just nothing, a mere handful of our awareness. There seems to be a fantastic area of consciousness, unimaginable, beyond this body, with this body, but sometimes outside this body, and it is infinite. We call it *ananta*, unending, infinite. So, by certain practices which we will learn about in the next chapter, there can and there will take place an event in which this invisible process of consciousness can be blocked.

Let us understand it correctly. The flow of consciousness that we are talking about is not the flow of your mind and thoughts; it is not the flow of your feelings, passions and desires; it is not the stock of your emotions and experiences. The word chitta means the consciousness as a whole, in and outside the body, with and without it. In brief, the consciousness is like a thread connecting many lives and incarnations. Therefore, the word nirodha does not mean blocking thoughts, desires, ambitions, passions and so forth, but it means the act or acts of blocking the process of consciousness responsible for remanifestation.

Vritta means a circle and *vritti* means circular. When you throw a stone into a pond, the movements of the water spread outward in the form of circles. In the same manner, the consciousness has its circular patterns; these are neither horizontal nor perpendicular, but circular and so it moves in a circular pattern. Therefore, the attitudes of chitta, the modes of mind, are called *chitta vritti*.

Nirodhah is from the basic word rodha, which means an act of blocking. We have words developed from this root – rodha, avarodha, nirodha, virodha. Avarodha is obstruction, nirodha is blocking, virodha is opposition. So the idea of blocking is clarified. To come to the final point – what is yoga? The sutra replies that yoga is the blocking of the patterns arising in all the dimensions of consciousness. It is not only shutting yourself off from the external experiences which you face every morning and evening, but it is setting aside the vision you have in deep meditation and higher samadhi. When the expressions of individual awareness arising in different planes are transcended, the state of yoga manifests. This is the order or sequence of evolution of your consciousness.

Mental states and kundalini yoga

Evolution of consciousness in man is classified according to five stages. Human consciousness will finally develop itself when it becomes free from the clutches of prakriti, or the three gunas, which will be fully discussed in the second chapter. In discussing the word chitta vritti, we mentioned the five stages of mind. When we compare these five stages with the awakening of kundalini, it can be safely said that the moodha state, dullness of mind, belongs to mooladhara chakra, where the individual consciousness is sleeping or dormant. In Sanskrit, it is said that the kundalini is dormant, the serpent power is sleeping. After you have done certain practices, this becomes so stimulated or agitated that the agitation continues up to manipura chakra. The associated state of mind at this stage is known as kshipta.

Up to manipura, or the navel centre, there is every possibility for a spiritual aspirant to be thrown back to mooladhara. The consciousness wakes up, goes to swadhisthana, then up to manipura, but it comes back to mooladhara again, because that is its nature. However, when the consciousness has reached manipura and has stayed there for some time, and has gone through or transcended it, then the consciousness becomes steady in the sense that the vikshipta stage continues up to ajna chakra, and from ajna chakra onwards, the state of concentration takes place. Sahasrara, the highest chakra, is the seat of nirodha. It is beyond the three gunas.

All functions of the body, mind and world are dependent on the interplay of the three gunas. Much has been written on the gunas and no better explanation can be had about the gunas than in Samkhya philosophy. The cosmic nature has the threefold characteristics in its nature; in this sense every action, thought and event is created due to the interaction of the three gunas.

The mind, too, is greatly influenced by their interaction. When sattwa guna predominates, the mind remains quiet, the vrittis remain concentrated and nothing causes disturbance. When tamas predominates, then nothing in the world can keep you active, spiritual or blissful; you will always find your mind dull, inert and tense. Such is the effect of tamas over the consciousness.

One guna alone does not influence the personality. There is always a combined influence of all the three gunas. When tamas guna predominates and is suppressing the two other gunas, the mind enters into an inactive state. As a result there is a process of slow thinking; at times thinking also ceases to manifest. When this state deepens, the mental inactivity becomes acute, manifesting in a state of deep neurosis. This is the dull state of mind, known as the moodha condition of chitta.

When rajas is predominant, with sattwa and tamas suppressed, the mental condition is scattered, dissipated, broken into pieces; intending to commit suicide, trying to murder, and developing a split in the personality. This is the kshipta state of mind.

The vikshipta state of mind is an oscillating state of mind. In this particular state of mind, the individual consciousness operates between steadiness and distraction. This is the usual condition of all spiritual aspirants when they sit for pooja, meditation, concentration or antar mouna. This is the state of mind of a good student who, though keen and deep in his studies, is subject to temporary unsteadiness, due to the interplay of the gunas. When the flow of concentration, born of sattwa, is interrupted by unsteadiness, born of rajas, one is said to be in the vikshipta state of consciousness.

In this state of consciousness one has inner visions. The aspirant is very sensitive and subject to moods. You will find him meditating for hours and suddenly leaving everything for days together. This is a very important stage; here yoga begins. All the gunas have complete freedom here to express themselves individually.

When sattwa has free expression, one-pointedness dawns. When rajas is overpowering, the mind is dissipated. When tamas comes into play, there is neither one-pointedness nor dissipation; there is only dullness and inactivity.

It is very important for a spiritual aspirant to analyze the predominance of the three gunas and to find out the guna in power at the moment. It is a rare moment when all the gunas have an equal influence on a person. One guna always holds sway over the others and rules, even though the other gunas have an equal chance of operation. For example, when rajas is in power there is always a countermovement of the other gunas, resulting in a state of concentration and dissipation following each other. Therefore, one has to realize which particular guna is in absolute power at the moment and how countermovements are taking place. If there is more dissipation and less concentration, then it is rajas. If there is less concentration and less dissipation but more snoring and sleep, it means tamas is predominating. If there is more concentration and less dissipation and less sleep, it means sattwa is predominating.

After having analyzed the influence of the three gunas over consciousness, one should find out ways to eliminate the negative influence of a particular guna and to develop the influence of a positive guna. For instance, if after observation and analysis of the thoughts, you have discovered the influence of tamas during meditation, you should try to find out ways and means to reduce that influence and develop the opposite guna by any appropriate method. The technique of developing the positive influence is more important than trying to suppress the negative influence of the guna. In this context, one should employ asanas, pranayama and certain practices of hatha yoga. It does not matter whether tamas is constitutional or mental, habitual or a temporary physical change, asanas and hatha yoga will eliminate the pressure of tamas to a very great extent. Physical work is also a great power to exterminate the very existence of tamas, not only during meditation, but from the very structure of life.

If you are overpowered by the force of rajas, during meditation in particular and your daily life in general, so much so that you are unable to concentrate on anything due to mental troubles, samskaras, desires, life's problems and depressions, you should stop fighting with yourself and employ all those practices that reduce the element of rajas from the very root of life itself. Such practices, for example, are bhakti and japa yoga. Karma yoga should be practised; you should also do physical work, not because you need it, but because it is a necessity in your spiritual life.

Suppose you find that raja guna is very powerful at the time of meditation and as a result you are unable to concentrate your mind and after a while you go to sleep, then the mind starts wavering, thinking about many different things; you cannot control it. What should you do? At this time you have to employ the practices by which you can reduce rajo guna, and please remember that rajo guna can be reduced by the practices of bhakti and the monotonous rotation of japa.

Sometimes you find that sattwa guna is powerful, although the other gunas are also operating one after the other. Of course, you do not have to eliminate sattwa guna; you will have to strengthen it because sattwa is desirable. Tamo guna is undesirable and you will have to reduce it. Rajo guna is also undesirable and you will also have to reduce it. While tamo guna is predominating, you have to reduce it; when rajo guna is predominating, you have to reduce it, but when sattwa is predominating and at the same time rajas and tamas are present, you have to intensify the power of sattwa guna by different methods, as enunciated in yogic texts. You need to think for yourself by which method you can strengthen your sattwa guna – maybe through dharana, maybe through satsang, maybe through studying books, maybe through adjustment of diet.

Every spiritual aspirant has to analyze the influence of the three gunas for at least some time during the twenty-four hours. So, when you find that, for one full month, the mind was full of concentration and in between there was a little bit of wavering, it is the oscillating state or vikshipta state of mind. Now, for example, your state is unsteady. You have not established it, but you are establishing it. Which particular guna is more powerful? If tamo guna is more powerful, you will go down; your sadhana will be reduced. If sattwa is predominating, you will be concentrated and go into meditation. Thus, in general, you have to read your condition during meditation and the means will have to be employed according to that.

It is said that yoga begins when the vikshipta state of mind is arrived at. Kshipta and moodha, the two previous stages, are unyogic. They are what we call the worldly stages of mind. Moodha is far from any yogic concept.

Now we come to the word ekagrata. *Ekagrata* means one-pointedness and in this rajo guna and tamo guna are absent; only sattwa guna is present. When the mind attains a one-pointed state, at that time rajas and tamas are both totally absent; sattwa alone prevails. When this stage is arrived at, then the last one to be achieved is nirodha, complete cessation. In this, neither tamas, nor rajas, nor sattwa guna functions. That is a state of mind called *trigunatita*, beyond the three gunas, when the consciousness is rendered absolutely free from the clutches of the three gunas. When your individual consciousness is rendered free from the clutches of the three gunas and when your consciousness stays alone, without any friendship or without any alliance with these three gunas, that state of consciousness is called nirodha.

This is the comparison between the awakening of kundalini consciousness and the yogic terminology as detailed here.

Sutra 3: The culmination of yoga

तदा द्रष्टुः स्वरूपेऽवस्थानम् ॥ ३ ॥

Tadā draṣṭuḥ svarūpe'vasthānam

Tadā: then; *draṣṭuḥ*: seer; *svarūpe*: one's own essential nature; *avasthānam*: establishment

Then the seer is established (abides) in his own essential nature.

Self-realization can only take place when the chitta vrittis cease their activity, when the mind or chitta is no longer affected by the play of the three gunas and varying moods, and there is no longer a feeling of identification with the objective world. With our very limited understanding, we are not able to know or understand the state of *kaivalya*, self-realization, or even begin to comprehend the higher states of consciousness which unfold in samadhi. Realization comes from within and cannot be comprehended by our present level of awareness of the mind, coloured and conditioned as it is by likes and dislikes, false beliefs, erroneous conceptions, false thinking and so on, which are our usual patterns of thought and which are all related to *asmita*, the ego or 'I'-principle.

Purity of mind, complete sense-control, desirelessness and so on, are all necessary before one is competent to reach the goal of yoga, which is kaivalya or self-realization. The word avasthanam is indicative of restoration to its original state, and this will be discussed in the fourth chapter.

Sutra 4: What happens otherwise to purusha?

वृत्तिसारूप्यमितरत्र ॥ ४ ॥

Vṛtti sārūpyamitaratra

Vṛtti: modification, pattern; *sārūpyam*: identification; *itaratra*: in other state

Or there is identification with the modifications of chitta.

What happens to purusha, the self or soul, when it is not abiding in its essential nature is being stated here. When the chitta vrittis are not in the state of nirodha, then the patterns or modifications of chitta are superimposed on purusha.

We are all familiar with this type of wrong identification. When we watch a movie or stage play, we tend to identify ourselves with what is portrayed, and experience corresponding emotions of sorrow, joy, fear, like, dislike, etc. Although the actors are only playing a role, we tend to identify with them and forget that we are mere spectators of what is taking place. In the same way, purusha is only a witnessing consciousness, but it has forgotten its true nature, and is identifying with the chitta and its patterns or modifications to such an extent that it is very difficult to extricate itself.

The science of yoga as propounded by Patanjali recommends different techniques to cater for the differing temperaments of all individuals so as to bring the mind-stuff, or chitta, into a state of nirodha. In that state, the purusha becomes aware of its true nature.

Sutra 5: Vrittis – main classification

वृत्तयः पञ्चतय्यः क्लिष्टाक्लिष्टाः ॥ ५ ॥

Vṛttayaḥ pañchatayyaḥ kliṣṭākliṣṭāḥ

Vṛttayaḥ: modifications of mind; *pañchatayyaḥ*: fivefold; *kliṣṭā*: painful, lit. hard, difficult; *akliṣṭāḥ*: not painful

Modifications of mind are fivefold; they are painful or not painful.

This whole sutra is a combination of four words. The word vritti has become known to you, yet still needs a thorough explanation. From this sutra onwards, a detailed explanation of vritti follows. The sutra says that the vrittis of mind are fivefold, of five kinds. The modifications are fivefold and these fivefold modifications are either painful or not painful. This means that the modifications of the mind are ten in all; five of these are painful and five are not painful. To illustrate, the mind sees a flower; with the help of the eyes, it assumes the shape of the flower, and it likes the flower. This is called *aklishta*, or pleasant. Then your mind sees the crushed, decomposed body of a dog over which the wheels of a vehicle have passed. Your mind looks through the eyes and assimilates the perception, but it does not like it. That is called *klishta*, or painful. So, the particular modification of mind in the case of the flower was unpainful, or pleasant. In the case of the crushed dog, it was painful, or klishta. The modification is the same; the perception is through the eyes, the vision is twofold: klishta and aklishta, painful and not painful.

In the same way, the mind has or assumes, in general, fivefold modifications or manifestations. What are these five vrittis? We shall discuss them in the following sutras, but before we proceed to that topic, you need to understand very carefully what Patanjali means by everything. It is the manifestation of mind in different spheres of life. When you look at a tree, a person or a landscape, you are doing it through the eyes, but it is one of the manifestations of your mind. When you listen to music or to a lecture, that is also one of the modifications of your mind. When you close your eyes and think of the past, present or future, about your relations, friends or enemies, that is one of the modifications of mind, one of the formations or patterns of mind. When you are worried, anxious or full of anger or passion, or full of grief, jealousy, compassion, love for your fellow humans, love for God, that is also one of the patterns of your mind. This particular modification is called a vritti.

According to the yogic system, every dimension of knowledge, every kind of thought and every field of awareness is one of the vrittis of the mind. In yoga, even the state of sleep is considered to be one of the conditions of mind. It is a mental state, a mental condition. Dream is also a mental condition. Similarly, doubt, illusion, mistakes in thinking, such as mistaking a rope for a snake, are also mental conditions or vrittis.

In Sanskrit and more so in yogic and Vedantic texts, the word vritti occurs again and again. It is such a confusing term that sometimes philosophers and thinkers have not been able to explain it properly. There was a great scholar in the seventh century named Goudapadacharya. He was the guru of the guru of the great Shankaracharya. He wrote a detailed commentary on a small Upanishad, namely the *Mandukya Upanishad*. In his commentary, the great scholar writes: "The whole world seems to be nothing but one of the forms of mental modifications of a supreme consciousness."

Not only the earth but the entire cosmos may be unreal; it may be just an expression of your mental thinking, the mental thinking of a supreme being, a cosmic thinking force.

So, when we use the term mental modification, we mean the different patterns or personalities of the mind, the different stages, spheres or dimensions of personality.

In a play, the same person may come on the stage as a beggar, a king, a robber, a sannyasin, a man or a woman, and so on. In the same manner, it is a single stuff, called awareness or consciousness in human beings, which appears to be manifesting itself in the form of waking, dreaming, sleeping, thinking, liking or disliking. It is one consciousness which seems to be playing different roles, and these are the different vrittis.

Sutra 6: Five kinds of vrittis

प्रमाणविपर्ययविकल्पनिद्रास्मृतयः ॥ ६ ॥

Pramāṇa-viparyaya-vikalpa-nidrā smṛtayaḥ

Pramāṇa: right knowledge; *viparyaya*: wrong knowledge; *vikalpa*: fancy, imagination; *nidrā*: sleep; *smṛtayaḥ*: memory

The fivefold modifications of mind are right knowledge, wrong knowledge, fancy, sleep and memory.

We have been talking about the word vritti in the last three sutras. It is important for a student of yoga to understand this word properly. After a lot of thought, you will realize that the final aim of yoga is nothing but the total destruction of the patterns of the manifestation of consciousness. To illustrate: different idols or patterns of form can be made of mud and when these forms are destroyed, they become mud again. Similarly, a goldsmith prepares different ornaments out of gold which are known by different names and forms, but when these ornaments are destroyed or melted down, they become gold again. In the same manner, different things and structures come out of the mind and are variously named in the cosmic process of nature. The mind or consciousness has to be divested of all its forms so that the consciousness remains nameless and formless, which is the ultimate aim of yoga.

It is not only the cessation of the world which is a part of yoga, a point which is misunderstood by many aspirants. They close their eyes and ears, forget all outer sights and sounds, and then see wonderful visions inside. They think they have arrived at the final goal of yoga, but even that has to be destroyed. Anything that is of the nature of mind must be finished with. Therefore, before you start practising yoga, you must understand the significance of what you are going to do, and here Patanjali is helping you.

Sometimes we are told to withdraw our consciousness, but what is consciousness? You withdraw your consciousness from outer sounds, but can you withdraw it from sleep? No, because you do not even believe that sleep is a mental condition; you think that sleep is not a mental condition. Yoga says that sleep is also a mental condition. Further on in the sutras, Patanjali says that even samadhi is a mental condition which has to be thrown out. The lower savikalpa samadhi is also a modification of mind and has, therefore, to be transcended.

The ultimate goal of yoga is a refining process and for this purpose Patanjali is helping us. The fivefold vrittis are carefully classified. All that you see, hear and experience, all that the vrittis do through the mind and the senses, is classified into five groups, namely, right knowledge, wrong knowledge, imagination, sleep and memory.

These five modifications constitute consciousness of mind. They form the three dimensions of individual consciousness. These constitute the mental factory of man. Every mental state is included in these five modifications, such as dreaming, waking, looking, talking, touching, beating, crying, feeling, emotion, action, sentiment; in fact, everything is included in these five.

Sutra 7: (i) Pramana – sources of right knowledge

प्रत्यक्षानुमानागमाः प्रमाणानि ॥ ७ ॥

Pratyakṣānumānāgamāḥ pramāṇāni

Pratyakṣa: direct cognition, sense evidence; *anumāna*: inference; *āgama*: testimony, revelation; *pramāṇāni*: the sources of right knowledge

Direct cognition, inference and testimony are the sources of knowledge.

In this sutra, the rishi is trying to explain right knowledge, *pramana*. It has already been included in the previous sutra as a manifestation of mind. The mind does not always take the form of right knowledge alone; it sometimes manifests wrong knowledge also. This sutra explains what is meant by right knowledge. Right knowledge can be gained from three sources: sense evidence, inference and testimony. Sense evidence is the knowledge produced by the contact of a sense organ with an object of knowledge; for example, we see a flower, we smell it, we hear someone crying, and so on.

If your senses, indriyas, are intact, if none of them are defective, then sense evidence is one of the sources of right knowledge. It should be remembered that this is not the only source of right knowledge because sometimes our senses deceive us; for example, the mirage produced in a desert due to hot air. In this case there is actually no water, but our eyes make us believe the appearance of water to be a reality. The sense evidence in this case does not constitute right knowledge, for we can become aware of our illusion if we try to get to the water.

Anumana, inference, becomes a source of right knowledge when it is based on sound reasoning. We see smoke on a distant mountain and immediately infer that there must be fire on the mountain. This inference is based on the experience which has never failed us, namely, that whenever we came across smoke, we also found the presence of fire. This is called invariable concomitance. When two things or events are invariably found to go together, we can infer the presence of either of them whenever we see the other.

Agama means testimony. It is useful in such circumstances where no sense evidence is available, as well as if there are not sufficient grounds for inference. Here we have to depend simply on what others say, but there is one important condition. The other person whose authority may be taken as a sufficient source of right knowledge, and who is called an *apta*, has to fulfil two conditions. First, he should have right knowledge himself and, secondly, he should be able to impart that knowledge without any mistake. When these two conditions are fulfilled, we can take agama as right knowledge.

In yoga the authority is called a guru. What he hands over to the disciple is simply on faith but, nevertheless, it is right knowledge because a guru is a person who knows correctly. The scriptures are known as agama because they are the revelations of the rishis who have experienced at first hand the topics discussed therein. Moreover, the statements of the scriptures are not amenable to either sense evidence or inference.

Sutra 8: (ii) Viparyaya – misconception

विपर्ययो मिथ्याज्ञानमतद्रूपप्रतिष्ठम् ॥ ८ ॥

Viparyayo mithyājñānamatadrūpapratiṣṭham

Viparyayah: misconception; *mithyā*: false, illusory; *jñānam*: knowledge; *atat*: not its own; *rūpa*: form; *pratiṣṭham*: based

Wrong conception is false knowledge which is not based on its own form.

Patanjali is dealing here with the second type of chitta vritti which we have to block. He defines *viparyaya* as false knowledge which is not based on or does not correspond to a real object. This is opposed to right knowledge. Right knowledge is based on the correspondence between a real object and our knowledge of it. For example, we see the colour of a flower, we smell it, feel the softness of its petals, and the knowledge that it is a flower arises in our mind. This is right knowledge because it is *tadrupaprathistha*, that is, there is a real object on which our knowledge is based. In the case of viparyaya there is really no object existing on which the knowledge may be based, therefore, it is called *atadrupaprathisttham*. For example, when we mistake a rope for a snake, our knowledge is incorrect, because the thing that actually exists before us, which we take to be a snake, is a rope. This false knowledge can be corrected by creating conditions, such as enough light, for correct knowledge to arise.

Viparyaya is also called avidya, for all our knowledge is based on a misunderstanding of the real nature of purusha and prakriti. Wrong knowledge is ultimately replaced by viveka, which involves the correct understanding of the true nature of purusha and prakriti.

Sutra 9: (iii) Vikalpa – unfounded belief

शब्दज्ञानानुपाति वस्तुशून्यो विकल्पः ॥ ९ ॥

Śabdajñānānupātī vastu-śūnyo vikalpaḥ

Śabda: word, sound; *jñāna*: cognition; *anupāti*: following upon; *vastu*: object; *śūnyaḥ*: empty; *vikalpaḥ*: fancy, imagination

Following upon knowledge through words but empty of an object is fancy.

Vikalpa is imagination without the basis of an object. It does not mean that it has no object, but the object mentioned in the statement is non-existent. For example, when we read wonderful stories of fairyland or about Lilliput in *Gulliver's Travels*, we find words which can be used properly in sentences, but actually there are no real objects corresponding to them at all. These are examples of vikalpa, imagination or fancy. Vikalpa is a creation of our mind. It is, however, not completely devoid of experiential material. We take ideas from our experiences and combine them to form new ideas of things that actually do not exist.

The trouble with many of us, even in the case of spiritual aspirants, is that sometimes the mind becomes full of fancy and idealism. There are many spiritual aspirants throughout the world who seek to attain an imaginary goal. They are living in a world of ideas which are nothing but vikalpa.

In meditation, dhyana, there is sometimes a flight of imagination. It is so delightful and interesting and gives pleasure and satisfaction to the meditating mind, but according to Patanjali, this form of vikalpa is also to be set aside. Similarly, in India we find a branch of fanciful meditation which is called conscious day-dreaming. It is a separate sadhana by itself, but according to Patanjali it is in essence a dull state of mind and must be overcome through right knowledge. This sadhana is very helpful for a beginner in as much as it can make an aspirant capable of going deeper and deeper in the state of concentration. However, it should not be forgotten that this sadhana, although helpful for a beginner, has to be discarded afterwards.

In the states of dharana, antar mouna, dhyana, the aspirant imagines certain objects and qualities. They may be unreal and fanciful notions in the ultimate analysis, but they are very helpful in the beginning and a student of yoga must use their assistance until he goes forward to master the deeper states. It is declared by many great thinkers that up to nirvikalpa samadhi, the different experiences an aspirant goes through are nothing but the planes of one's mental consciousness.

Right knowledge, wrong knowledge and imagination are equally processes of consciousness, but they differ insofar as right knowledge has a true object, wrong knowledge has a false object, whereas imagination or vikalpa has no object at all. This difference should be carefully understood.

Sutra 10: (iv) Nidra – state of sleep

अभावप्रत्ययालम्बना वृत्तिर्निद्रा ॥ १० ॥

Abhāva-pratyayālambanā vṛttirnidrā

Abhāva: absence; *pratyaya*: content of mind; *ālambana*: support; *vṛttih*: modification; *nidrā*: sleep

Sleep is the vritti of absence of mental contents for its support.

This is a very important sutra. As compared with the first three vrittis mentioned previously, this vritti is characterized by no awareness, consciousness or unconsciousness. Sleep is also one of the states of mind. It is very important to understand it, because if we are able to analyze the sleep condition of the mind, we can easily understand the state of samadhi. Sleep is a condition of mind which hides or conceals the knowledge of the external world. In the *Mandukya Upanishad*, it is said that in sleep one does not desire anything, nor is there dream or any other perception. All the vrittis of the mind are concentrated together and the energy process fuses into one. The capacity of the faculty of perception is introverted; outer objects are not seen or heard, nor is there any feeling whatsoever. It is an unconscious state of mind.

This is exactly the idea which Patanjali wants to emphasize in this sutra. He says that in sleep there is no object before the mind – it does not see, hear, touch or feel anything. Every form of knowledge, every content of mind has become silent.

When we have a mental experience of an object, that experience is called a *pratyaya*, content of mind. We can have a pratyaya with or without the senses coming in contact with an object. We can, for example, see a rose inside our mind either in the form of a vision, a dream, or an ideal. The content of mind in all these states is called pratyaya.

When the very idea of an object, the very content of mind is removed through a certain process, the mind becomes supportless. Sleep is a vritti in which the content of mind is absent. In this state there are thoughts but they are not present before the mind, so the mind does not see, touch, think, hear, feel or have any sense or mental experience. Psychologically, in that state the brain and the mind are disconnected and thoughts are suppressed temporarily. Similarly, in dhyana we sometimes become unconscious when the activity of the mind stops.

The state of sleep is comparable with the state of samadhi inasmuch as in both there is absence of consciousness of the external world. The only difference between sleep and samadhi is that in the latter state the notion of 'I' persists to a certain extent, whereas in sleep there is no awareness of the 'I' notion. In the state of samadhi, the awareness of separate existences and qualities, such as an individual's nationality, one's own name and form, ceases completely, yet a kind of awareness still persists. This awareness is devoid of all the peculiarities belonging to the external world. The awareness we have in the waking state is exactly like the one in samadhi. The difference is that in samadhi the objects are absent, but the awareness is there. There has been much misunderstanding, misconception, misruling and misinterpretation. It is supposed that samadhi is a state of absolute unconsciousness, whereas it is actually the opposite.

Sutra 11: (v) Smriti – memory

अनुभूतविषयासम्प्रमोषः स्मृतिः ॥ ११ ॥

Anubhūtaviṣayāsaṃpramoṣaḥ smṛtiḥ

Anubhūta: experienced; *viṣaya*: objects of sense perception; *asampramoṣaḥ*: not letting escape; *smṛtiḥ*: memory

Not letting the experienced objects escape from the mind is memory.

Memory is the fifth vritti of the mind. It is of two kinds: conscious memory and subconscious memory. Conscious memory involves the recollection of things already experienced, recall of past experiences. Subconscious memory is dream. Here one does not consciously remember, but remembers unconsciously. This memory is also of two kinds: one is imaginary, the other is real. In dreams, one sometimes has fantastic experiences which are not in any way relevant to actual life. One may thus see oneself cut down under the wheels of a train, or see oneself dying. This is a fancy of mind and hence it is called imaginary subconscious memory. However, we must remember that every dream has some basis and that no dream is baseless. In the case of real subconscious memory, one remembers in dream something that actually happened in the past without distortion of facts. This memory, which brings out the impressions of the preconscious and unfolds them on the conscious plane, is one of the faculties of our consciousness. It is one of the modifications of consciousness and is therefore classed as a vritti.

The objects of experience are of five kinds, such as those which can be perceived through the eyes, ears, skin, tongue or nose. When we experience these objects, our mind comes in contact with them through the indriyas. When next there is a similar contact, memory of the past experience arises if the experience is not allowed to escape from the mind. If the experience does escape, then memory fails us. So, Patanjali has used the word *asampramosha* to emphasize the fact of not letting the experience escape from the mind. The meaning of the word is as follows: *a* – no; *sam* – completely; *pra* – high or great; *mosha* – releasing, escape. Thus, literally, the word means not allowing to escape.

Thus we can summarize the five vrittis mentioned by Patanjali in the following manner. The first vritti involves right knowledge; the second, wrong knowledge; the third, imaginary knowledge; the fourth, no knowledge; and the last one, past knowledge. This covers the entire field of our consciousness. While defining yoga, Patanjali has already said that the essence of yoga is contained in blocking or stopping all the vrittis. He describes the means which are to be used for this purpose in the next sutra.

Sutra 12: Necessity of abhyasa and vairagya

अभ्यासवैराग्याभ्यां तन्निरोधः ॥ १२ ॥

Abhyāsavairāgyābhyāṃ tannirodhaḥ

Abhyāsa: repeated practice; *vairāgyābhyāṃ*: by vairagya; *tat*: that; *nirodhaḥ*: stopping, blocking

The stopping of that (five vrittis) by repeated practice and vairagya.

In this sutra, Patanjali describes two methods for stopping the flow of the chitta vrittis. They are abhyasa and vairagya. *Abhyasa* means repeated and persistent practice. *Vairagya* is a very controversial word. From time to time, from country to country and from brain to brain, it has had different meanings. We may say that it is a mental condition of non-attachment, or detachment, which is freedom from raga and dwesha, attraction and repulsion. When the mind becomes free of these, that state is called vairagya. In India, vairagya traditionally means an order of sannyasa. Patanjali has described raga and dwesha in a further chapter. *Raga*, we may say, is the attitude of liking for any object of our choice. On the other hand, *dwesha* is an attitude of the mind which involves dislike for an object. Freedom from these two is called vairagya.

We come across many spiritual aspirants who try to concentrate their mind without first practising abhyasa and vairagya, without first conquering raga and dwesha. It is futile to make the mind silent without first removing the disturbing factors, namely raga and dwesha, which make the mind unsteady. Patanjali tells us that abhyasa and vairagya are the means one should first master so that meditation will follow easily.

Sutra 13: Abhyasa means constant practice

तत्र स्थितौ यत्नोऽभ्यासः ॥ १३ ॥

Tatra sthitau yatno'bhyāsaḥ

Tatra: there, out of the two; *sthitau*: being fixed, established; *yatnah*: effort; *abhyāsaḥ*: practice

Of the two (mentioned in the previous sutra) 'to be established in the endeavour' is abhyasa.

Patanjali explains the meaning of abhyasa in this sutra. The word *tatra* literally means there, but with reference to the context of the sutra, the word tatra means of the two. Abhyasa means to be perfectly fixed in the spiritual effort (sadhana). The effort here involves the practice of chitta vritti nirodhah. It may include meditation or karma yoga or bhakti or self-introspection and other practices. It should be remembered that just practising something for some time is not abhyasa. Abhyasa means continued practice; you cannot leave it at all. It becomes a part of your personality, a part of your individual nature. To emphasize this, the rishi has used the word *sthitau*, which means being firmly fixed or firmly established.

The next word – *yatna*, effort – indicates all effort, whether it is kriya yoga, hatha yoga or meditation. There is one important point concerning abhyasa which must be understood. When abhyasa becomes natural, firmly rooted and complete, it leads to samadhi. So, every student must pay utmost attention to regular and continued practice which, when perfected, leads to the complete blocking of the vrittis.

Sutra 14: Foundation of abhyasa

स तु दीर्घकालनैरन्तर्यसत्कारासेवितो दृढभूमिः ॥१४ ॥

Sa tu dīrghakāla nairantaryasatkārāsevito dṛḍhabhūmiḥ

Sah: that (abhyāsa); *tu*: but; *dīrgha*: long; *kāla*: time; *nairantarya*: without interruption; *satkāra*: reverence; *āsevitaḥ*: practised; *dṛḍha*: firm; *bhūmiḥ*: ground

It becomes firmly grounded by being continued for a long time with reverence, without interruption.

There are three conditions for the practice of abhyasa: it should be practised with complete faith; it should continue uninterrupted and it should go on for quite a long time. When these three conditions are fulfilled, abhyasa becomes firmly established and a part of one's nature. It is often observed that many aspirants are very enthusiastic in the beginning, but their faith dwindles away later on. This should never happen with a student of yoga who wants to achieve the goal in this very birth. A spiritual aspirant must continue his sadhana until he is able to receive something very concrete and very substantial, but very few aspirants can do this.

The word nairantarya is very important. It means practising without interruption. *Antar* means difference; *nairantarya* means absence of this difference. It means continuity. This is very important because if the practices are interrupted now and then, the student cannot get the full benefit from his practices. This means spiritual maturity. The aspirant must have attained spiritual maturity when he begins his practices, and the practices must continue for a long time. Sometimes we observe a misconception in many people that the task of spiritual evolution can be completed within a few months, but this is wrong. It may take many births to achieve. The aspirant should not be impatient; there should be no hurry or haste. Our ancient literature is full of stories wherein it is declared that it may take many births for an individual to attain the highest goal of yoga. What is important is not the length of time but the fact that one has to continue the practices without any interruption and until the goal is achieved, whatever time it may take to reach there. One should not lose heart; one should continue the practices with faith. Faith is the most important factor, for it is only through faith that we have the patience and energy to continue the practice against the odds of life. If the aspirant has complete faith in the fact that he will surely achieve the goal through his practices, then it matters little to him when he reaches the goal.

The next important point is that one should like sadhana to the highest extent. Just as a mother becomes disturbed if her child does not return home on time, so the aspirant should become disturbed if he does not do his daily practices. He should love his practices as much as he loves his body. He should be as attracted towards the practices as he is towards a sweet dish of his choice. The practices can produce the desired result only if they are done with love and attraction. There should be no feeling of compulsion, but one should do the practices willingly. This is the meaning of *satkara*. It means earnestness, respect and devotion. If one has these qualities, good results are assured. Attachment to the practices can be developed through constant self-analysis and satsang.

Patanjali declares that if we practise abhyasa with faith and conviction continuously for a long time, it will definitely bring about a blockage of the fivefold vrittis of the mind.

Sutra 15: Lower form of vairagya

दृष्टानुश्रविकविषयवितृष्णस्य वशीकारसंज्ञा वैराग्यम् ॥ १५ ॥

Dṛṣṭānuśravika-viṣayāvitṛṣṇasya
vaśīkāra-sañjñā vairāgyam

Dṛṣṭa: seen; *anuśravika*: heard; *viṣaya*: object; *vitṛṣṇasya*: of the one who is free of desire (*tṛṣṇā*: craving, desire); *vaśīkāra*: control; *sañjñā*: awareness; *vairāgyam*: absence of craving

When an individual becomes free of craving for the sense objects which he has experienced as well as those of which he has heard, that state of consciousness is vairagya.

When a person is without craving, without thirst, without hankering for all the objects of pleasure and so on that he has heard or seen for himself in his life, this state of mind – cravinglessness, thirstlessness – is known as vairagya. Drishta includes the pleasures of pleasurable objects experienced through the senses. All experiences within the range of personal sense knowledge are called drishta. *Anushravika* objects are those which one has not experienced but of which one has heard from other persons and from books. Thus vairagya is completely a process of buddhi; it is not a sect by itself. If one thinks that for the practice of vairagya one will have to change one's life, then one is mistaken. Vairagya is the final assessment of everything that one has undergone in life.

It is possible to attain vairagya even when one undergoes all the responsibilities of family and society. It is not at all necessary to give up one's duties. What is needed is not to give up the different acts, but rather to completely give up raga and dwesha, which cause the subconscious agony. This is explained very well in the *Bhagavad Gita*, which says that an individual can be free in this life itself even while performing the various necessary acts in life, if only he can detach himself from the good or bad effects of his actions. What is important for meditation is not what one does or does not do in the outer life; it is the inner life, the life of inhibitions, suppressions and complexes, the life of mental and psychic errors, that plays a decisive role in meditation. For this there must be vairagya, so that the proper attitudes come into being.

The practice of vairagya starts from within and never from without. It does not matter what clothes you wear or what kind of people you live with. What really matters is what kind of attitude you have towards the various things, persons and events you come across in life. Vairagya makes for a balanced attitude and integrated approach, a feeling of love and compassion for all, yet a sort of detachment which works in everything that one does. Vairagya is thus a manifestation of the purity and peace of one's mind. It bestows upon the sadhaka an undisturbed happiness and silence which remains unchanged, whether the sadhaka is confronted with events that please him or events that would be unpleasant.

An important question arises here. It may be argued that a student can purify the mind and make it silent in the state of samadhi even without the practice of vairagya. It may be said that the other techniques of yoga such as pranayama, meditation, etc. are quite sufficient for taking a student to the higher state, but this is not a correct belief. If you observe your mind impartially, you will be aware of the fact that at the deeper level of consciousness and of the subconscious, every one of us has certain desires, cravings, ambitions and wishes we want to fulfil. These unfulfilled desires give rise to conflicts and tensions. In our daily life we may not be aware of these conflicts and tensions, but a person who wants to meditate finds it impossible to make his mind steady unless the underlying urges and tensions are resolved.

As Patanjali will explain in a further chapter, there are five types of these basic urges, which may be described as subconscious agonies or afflictions. They must all be got rid of, for unless that is done, a student cannot make his mind steady in samadhi, and vairagya is the only way through which the subconscious agonies can be done away with.

There are three stages of vairagya. In the first stage, all the likes and dislikes towards the objects of the world are active in the mind. An effort is made to control the natural passions and cravings, such as the tendencies of hate, violence, etc. This stage is characterized by the struggle to overcome the effects of raga and dwesha. In the second stage, some items of raga and dwesha come under the control of the mind, but there are some items which have not yet been controlled. In the third stage, the conscious aspect of raga and dwesha is completely evolved and the mind becomes free of raga and dwesha. Thus we see that in the first stage there is effort without much success, in the second stage there is partial success, and in the third stage the aspirant completely succeeds in the extermination of raga and dwesha, although their roots may still be there.

Sutra 16: Higher form of vairagya

तत्परं पुरुषख्यातेर्गुणवैतृष्ण्यम् ॥ १६ ॥

Tatparaṃ puruṣakhyātergunavaitṛṣṇyam

Tat: that; *paraṃ*: highest; *puruṣakhyāteh*: true knowledge of purusha; *guṇavaitṛṣṇyaṃ*: freedom from the desire for gunas

That is highest in which there is freedom from the desire for gunas on account of the knowledge of purusha.

There are two varieties of vairagya: one is the lower state and the second is the higher state of vairagya. In the lower form the aspirant transcends the attachments for sense objects, but these still remain in a subtle form. This has been explained also in the *Bhagavad Gita*. The lower form of vairagya involves a process of suppression in the sense that there is discrimination and control through the development of religious consciousness and satsang. There is conscious control by the mind and the desires and cravings are kept under control. *Paravairagya* involves not only giving up the enjoyments, but even the deep-rooted taste for enjoyment. There is a possibility of going back from the lower vairagya, but when one attains to paravairagya there is no return to the life of cravings and passions. Paravairagya is characterized by the absence of desire in all its forms. There is no desire for pleasure, enjoyment, knowledge or even sleep. This happens when there is awareness of the real nature of purusha. The spiritual aspirant becomes aware, in meditation or in samadhi, of the purusha in himself. He has a direct intuitive cognition of purusha and this gives rise to paravairagya. The aspirant overcomes all attractions and remains unshaken, even when the pleasures of the world are offered to him.

There is a story in the *Kathopanishad* which describes how Natchiketa, filled with the desire to know what happens to the soul after death, rejected all the worldly pleasures offered to him by Yama, the god of death. He ultimately got true knowledge because he proved himself to be fit to receive the highest knowledge by rejecting all worldly pleasures. This state of paravairagya cannot be reached through reading books or through satsang or any practice. It comes to you when you have intuitive direct knowledge of the purusha.

We must clearly understand what *purushakhyateh* means. The word purusha is formed out of two words: *puri*, which means 'town' and *sha* which means 'sleep'. In philosophical language, our physical body is considered to be a town having nine gates. The mental body is considered to be a town having four gates. There is also a third body called the pranic body. The awareness of the world is supposed to be a function of the subtle body. Purusha is nothing but consciousness which is dormant, unmanifest in the bodies. When purusha comes into relationship with prakriti, there is a beginning of the universe. Prakriti consists of the five primary elements (*panchabhuta*), five karmendriyas, five jnanendriyas, the fourfold functions of the mind, five pranas, three bodies and five objects of sense pleasure. All these put together form the basic tattwas in Samkhya philosophy. They are the components of prakriti. According to Samkhya, the universe came into being with the relation of purusha with prakriti. According to yoga, purusha is the awareness which is devoid of the contents of the mind. It is free from any content of mind. It is a manifestation of consciousness without any of the five kinds of vrittis.

In yoga, purusha is looked upon as the highest manifestation of consciousness, which is free of the vrittis as well as free from any entanglement with prakriti. Usually our consciousness functions through the senses, mind and buddhi. In meditation it functions at a deeper level, but there is a pratyaya or content of mind present in that state. However, there is only one entanglement, namely the 'I' notion, the feeling that 'I' am. Ultimately, beyond meditation, that feeling of 'I' also vanishes; what remains is the consciousness called purusha. This supreme awareness of the purusha gives rise to freedom from the three gunas, which are termed respectively sattwa guna, rajo guna and tamo guna. By sattwa guna we mean knowledge, peace or light; by rajo guna we mean greed, anger, tension; by tamo guna we mean procrastination, laziness, dullness and so on. Freedom from the gunas means that the mind is not influenced by the three gunas when the awareness of purusha takes place.

Sutra 17: Definition of samprajnata samadhi

वितर्कविचारानन्दास्मितानुगमात् सम्प्रज्ञातः ॥ १७ ॥

Vitarka-vichārānandāsmitānugamāt samprajñātaḥ

Vitarka: reasoning; *vichāra*: reflection; *ānanda*: bliss; *asmitā*: sense of individuality; *anugamāt*: by association; *samprajñātaḥ*: samadhi with prajna

Samprajnata yoga constitutes association respectively with reasoning, reflection, bliss and sense of individuality.

Samadhi is the goal of yoga. It is the positive aspect. The negative aspect is laid by chitta vritti nirodha. There is a lot of misunderstanding about this important topic of samadhi. We may define samadhi by saying that in that state, the aspirant arrives at the pointless point of consciousness beyond which no consciousness remains. It is to reach the deepest level of consciousness where even the sense of individuality does not function. The ancient authors described samadhi as a state of higher awareness where the mental bodies do not function. The atmic vehicle alone functions in that state. There is no need for a content or basis for knowledge.

Samadhi begins only after your consciousness has become free from the physical sphere. The boundary line of the sense world, or maya, ends where pure mental awareness begins. If one is able to withdraw the physical as well as the pranic sense of awareness, but remain aware of mental awareness, that is the beginning of samadhi. This samadhi begins when the consciousness has gone deep into the manomaya kosha, the mental body, where there is no trace of physical or pranic awareness. Here we may mention three spheres of mind, namely manomaya kosha, vijnanamaya kosha and anandamaya kosha. Atman is subtler and finer than all of these. Atman is not a sphere, but pure awareness.

There are, in all, five spheres of consciousness; we have already mentioned three of them. The other two are the annamaya kosha, which is the gross body, and pranamaya kosha, which is finer than annamaya kosha. Then we have the manomaya, vijnanamaya and anandamaya koshas, which are finer and finer. The anandamaya kosha is the finest sphere of consciousness, which is nothing but bliss. There is no physical content. Beyond these five spheres of consciousness there is ultimate awareness, known as purusha. Samadhi is achieved when the consciousness goes deeper and deeper to finer states and transcends the spheres of object, motion, thought, instinct and ultimately reaches the sphere of awareness. In this process the consciousness frees itself from the physical, pranic and other spheres. All the five spheres of consciousness are entangled with prakriti, but when the consciousness reaches anandamaya kosha, it becomes practically free from the clutches of prakriti.

The whole range of samadhi is classified under two categories: namely, *sabeeja*, with seed, and *nirbeeja*, without seed. Sabeeja is the lower state and nirbeeja is the finer state. In sabeeja samadhi we have a basis or content or a centre or a symbol. In sabeeja samadhi the mind is fixed on a symbol, either gross or subtle, and there is a pratyaya, that is the content of the symbol in the mind. A beginner has to use a certain basis for fixing the mind. There are four kinds of basis, according to which there are four kinds of samadhi. The notion of pratyaya is extremely important for understanding the state of samadhi. There is a great misunderstanding throughout the world about this pratyaya. Some people talk in favour of it, some people talk against idols, but both these views are partial and not perfect.

It is said in yoga philosophy that the pratyaya depends on the three gunas and accordingly there are sattwic, rajasic and tamasic pratyaya. Thus samadhi is a particular range in which the spiritual aspirant begins with minimum pratyaya, minimum objects on which to rest the mind. Gradually he goes deeper and deeper and there comes a time when he discards the pratyaya. Even the last basis for consciousness to rest and dwell upon is dropped and the mind becomes free from pratyaya. In the beginning one has the japa mantra or roopa, form, as the pratyaya for meditation, but later on that is dropped. Thus one may have a chakra, or a lotus, or a sound, or a mudra, or pranayama, or a smell, or a sensation in mooladhara, or a light in bhrumadhya, or one's own guru for the pratyaya, but when ultimately the pratyaya is thrown away through a process of refinement of consciousness, one reaches the state of samadhi.

Sutra 18: Definition of asamprajnata samadhi

विरामप्रत्ययाभ्यासपूर्वः संस्कारशेषोऽन्यः ॥ १८ ॥

Virāmapratyayābhyāsapūrvaḥ saṃskāraśeṣo'nyaḥ

Virāma: stopping; *pratyaya*: content of mind; *abhyāsa*: continued practice; *pūrvaḥ*: coming before; *saṃskāraśeṣa*: in which only the traces remain; *anyaḥ*: the other samadhi

The other samadhi (asamprajnata) is preceded by a continued study of stopping the content of mind. In it the mind remains in the form of traces.

There is a misconception created by intellectuals regarding this type of samadhi. We should remember clearly that every depth of samprajnata samadhi is intermixed with a state of asamprajnata samadhi and that asamprajnata samadhi is not nirbeeja samadhi. Asamprajnata samadhi belongs to the category of sabeeja samadhi. Nirbeeja samadhi is the highest samadhi and therefore both samprajnata and asamprajnata are varieties of sabeeja samadhi.

When the spiritual aspirant departs from the field of dhyana and enters into samadhi, that particular state is known as vitarka samprajnata. If it is perfected, it will be followed by asamprajnata. The next stage is vichara samprajnata, which is again followed by asamprajnata. Similarly, with ananda and asmita samadhi. Asmita samprajnata samadhi finally culminates in nirbeeja samadhi.

In this sutra, virama means stopping or putting a full stop. Pratyaya is the content of mind. Our consciousness has something to dwell upon during concentration. That support, which may be a symbol or a particular idea, gross or subtle, is called pratyaya. When you meditate on Aum, the form Aum is the pratyaya for the mind; similarly with other symbols. It is sometimes argued that no symbol is necessary because the supreme being is formless, but this is simply a kind of theological and philosophical confusion created by individuals. It is true that God or the supreme being has no form or shape, but the aspirant's mind must have something to rest upon during the process of meditation. The difference between samprajnata and asamprajnata is therefore made clear by Patanjali.

In asamprajnata samadhi there is no awareness of any symbol. This is called virama pratyaya, the cessation of awareness of a symbol, but the mere absence of awareness of a symbol does not mean asamprajnata. Asamprajnata has behind it a dynamic state of consciousness. This state of laya which comes between vitarka and vichara, vichara and ananda, etc. is not free from samskaras. The consciousness is not static there, although there is absence of the symbol. Even during the laya state, there is an underground dynamism called samskara. When the samskara is completely finished, the consciousness is completely dissolved; that state is nirbeeja samadhi because there is no need of consciousness. Thus in asamprajnata there are two distinct characteristics: one, dropping of the pratyaya and two, the presence of samskara.

This state is preceded by practice. Practice includes the states of vitarka, vichara, etc. In vitarka samadhi, the aspirant is aware of an object only, without there being an awareness of anything else. When this practice continues, the consciousness of this symbol, pratyaya, also ceases and that is the state of laya. From this state of laya, the aspirant is either thrown up into the next higher state, or he may again revert to a state of awareness of the symbol. It may even happen that he reverts to the state of dhyana or dharana. The state of asamprajnata is similar to the state of nirodha. From it, one may either ascend to a deeper state of consciousness or one may revert back to a grosser state. This is very important.

It is important to note that when one steps into the vitarka stage, the personal conscious willpower stops functioning and the entire range of operation is held by samskara; that is, the dynamic consciousness which carries the aspirant further on. It is this same dynamic consciousness which again brings the aspirant back to the state of dhyana, dharana or vikshepa.

The word samskara may be translated in English as latent impression, or dormant or past impressions, but this is perhaps not the correct meaning. *Samskara* is the seed of consciousness which survives up to the state of samprajnata samadhi. After that state it comes to an end, giving rise to nirbeeja samadhi. Nirbeeja samadhi is not a state at all; it is a state devoid of awareness, devoid of consciousness. According to yoga, consciousness or awareness is in the form of motion or vibration, but nirbeeja samadhi is not a state of motion or vibration. It involves stillness. Thus asamprajnata samadhi, according to this sutra, is there when only samskara remains and awareness of object drops, due to practice (abhyasa).

A confusion which is prevalent amongst scholars who do not practise samadhi but only look at it intellectually, needs to be cleared up. The confusion lies in the belief that the objective consciousness, samskara, is ultimately dropped, but actually it is not so. Consciousness of the object does not vanish completely; it only changes layers of our past experiences. We usually experience the symbol through these layers, but when they are dissolved through practice, the object can be clearly seen.

This is what happens as a student passes from vitarka to vichara, etc. In dharana the object appears as the formulated pattern of gross consciousness; in dhyana there is the concentrated pattern of consciousness; in vitarka samadhi there is a supramental pattern of consciousness; in vichara it is a contemplative pattern; in ananda it is the bliss pattern, etc., but pratyaya remains until the end. It only drops intermittently, when it is called virama pratyaya. In asamprajnata samadhi, the pratyaya or awareness of the symbol drops, but only temporarily. It again revives itself, but not in the same state of awareness. The state of awareness now may be either deeper or grosser. Asamprajnata samadhi is not a permanent state; it is only an intermediate state in which the consciousness is trying to transcend into a different plane. It is like alighting from a car and boarding a plane. It is a transient period, the going over from one plane to another.

It may be said that most of us do experience the vitarka and other stages as well as the asamprajnata stage, but the only difficulty is that these stages are not stabilized; they are fluctuating. So we should never give up the object or symbol, whatever it may be – a cross, or a shivalinga, or any object for that matter. We should, through continued practice, try to go to deeper states until at last the asmaprajnata state is reached, but that is indeed extremely difficult.

Sutra 19: Past merits needed for asamprajnata samadhi

भवप्रत्ययो विदेहप्रकृतिलयानाम् ॥ १९ ॥

Bhavapratyayo videhaprakṛtilayānām

Bhavapratyayah: birth is the cause; *videha*: disembodied yogis; *prakṛtilayānām*: the yogis who are merged into prakriti

The videha and prakritilaya yogis have birth as the cause of asamprajnata samadhi. (This is bhavapratyaya asamprajnata samadhi.)

Usually samadhi is attainable through faith, by courage, memory and a higher form of intelligence. It is through these different methods, according to the intensity of application and urge, that the student can attain samadhi sooner or later. However, we find many people who have practised nothing reaching the state of samadhi very easily. This is because at the time of birth they got all the traces of their past karma. Thus there are examples of persons going beyond the barriers of the lower consciousness at a very young age; for example, the great saint Jnaneshwar and, similarly, Ramana Maharshi of Arunachala, who attained samadhi when he was in his teens.

In this sutra, Patanjali says that the two types of yogis, namely, those who are disembodied and those who are merged into prakriti, can attain asamprajnata samadhi right from birth. They do not have to practise any preliminary stages like dharana, dhyana or vitarka, vichara, etc.

Sutra 20: Otherwise, merits needed for asamprajnata samadhi

श्रद्धावीर्यस्मृतिसमाधिप्रज्ञापूर्वक इतरेषाम् ॥ २० ॥

Śraddhāvīryasmṛtisamādhiprajñāpūrvaka itareṣām

Śraddhā: faith; *vīrya*: energy, strong will; *smṛti*: memory; *samādhiprajñā*: intelligence arising from samadhi; *pūrvaka*: preceded by; *itareṣām*: of others

Others (other than those disembodied and merged into prakriti) attain to asamprajnata samadhi through the stages of faith, strong will, memory and intelligence derived from samprajnata samadhi respectively.

The two types of yogis, namely videha and prakritilaya, as we have already seen, attain to samadhi right from birth, but such yogis are rare. The vast multitude of aspirants have to go through regular practice of different techniques, which are described in this sutra.

The word shraddha is made of two parts: *shrat* meaning 'truth', and *dha* meaning 'to hold'. Thus *shraddha* means 'that which holds the truth'. The word faith is perhaps not a correct translation of the word shraddha. Faith is usually blind, belief is always firm, but it is not so with shraddha which comes only after understanding the truth. Shraddha arises from true experience. Belief is always learned from other people; it is not an outcome of realization of truth, but shraddha never fails. Shraddha is the first essential principle required by a student of yoga. It is different from mere belief. Shraddha can be had only after having a glimpse of truth, just as Swami Vivekananda and Swami Yogananda had a glimpse of truth when they came in contact with their gurus. It is, however, not the whole of truth, but only a glimpse; it is just the beginning of the path of yoga. The guru induces in the disciple an experience of truth or samadhi through his own power and thus shraddha arises.

The next essential quality is called *veerya,* that is, energy, physical as well as mental. In the context of samadhi, it means courage through which we can overcome the many impediments on the path of yoga. It involves strong will and determination. One must continue on his path at any cost. The mind is to be properly controlled, and a controlled mind is full of courage, veerya. In the Vedas there is a prayer in which the rishi asks for veerya and ojas for achieving courage and energy.

The third factor is memory. The word smriti here actually means dhyana, in which the aspirant remembers the symbol. Through smriti we can bring the realization of consciousness into the conscious field.

Next we come to samadhi prajna. It is very essential for attaining asamprajnata samadhi. According to yoga, intelligence is of two types: worldly intelligence, which we require for being successful in daily life, and a higher type of consciousness which develops as a result of samprajnata samadhi. This kind of intelligence is not present in most of us, but it can be developed through regular practice. When once developed, the aspirant can make tremendous progress in a very short time. It may be described as a particular or favourable angle of vision. It presupposes spiritual realization.

It may be said that Swami Vivekananda had this faculty in him and due to it he could make very swift spiritual progress, in spite of various conflicting ideas in his mind regarding religion, God, human destiny, etc. So, this samadhi prajna is a peculiar faculty; it is the spiritual attitude or spiritual vision that one develops by constant satsang and by constant self-purification.

Sutra 21: Quicker is intensity of eagerness

तीव्रसंवेगानामासन्नः ॥ २१ ॥

Tīvrasaṃvegānāmāsannaḥ

Tīvra: intense; *saṃvega*: urge; *āsannaḥ*: quite near

Those who have an intense urge attain asamprajnata samadhi very soon.

Sutra 22: Three degrees of eagerness

मृदुमध्याधिमात्रत्वात् ततोऽपि विशेषः ॥ २२ ॥

Mṛdumadhyādhimātratvāt tato'pi viśeṣaḥ

Mṛdu: mild; *madhya*: medium; *adhimātra*: extremely strong; *tvāt*: due to; *tatoapi*: also, more than that; *viśeṣaḥ*: special, peculiar

With the intensity of urge rising through the mild, medium and strong conditions, asamprajnata samadhi can be achieved sooner.

The general meaning of this sutra is that samadhi which is attainable through effort is quite easy for those whose speed or urge is intense. It is observed that out of a number of aspirants practising the same type of sadhana, some reach the goal quickly and others linger on. Intensity of speed depends upon one's earnestness and sincerity. Earnestness is a mental attitude. It should be as intense as that which was exemplified by Dhruva, the great devotee of Lord Vishnu. He reached God because of his sincerity and intense urge. Similarly, an aspirant must have these mental qualities.

Earnestness does not mean hard or difficult sadhana. Even the easiest sadhana can bring you nearest to realization, provided you have intense samvega. Nor is intensity of speed to be confused by impatience. That is very different from eagerness of urge. Patanjali declares that for those who are earnest, samadhi is quite close.

In the next sutra, increasingly intense stages of earnestness are described. They are called respectively mild, medium or extremely strong. Many aspirants are found to be very enthusiastic in the beginning, but their urge is rather weak and so they do not have very promising results, even if they practise their sadhana for a long time. In the course of time their interest fades away and they lose the courage and energy with which they had started. They may carry on in that state without much hope. They are examples of mild intensity of earnestness. The medium type of aspirants are no doubt earnest, but they are not ready to go through intense sadhana to reach samadhi quickly. The adhimatra intensity of earnestness is a rare thing, but if it is there, it makes the aspirant so intent upon achieving his goal at once, that he does not rest until the goal is achieved.

These three classes of aspirants have three different sadhanas, according to the intensity of their eagerness. Usually the teachers who give spiritual lessons judge the intensity of the aspirants and guide them accordingly. A good student should not demand a higher sadhana in the beginning. He should practise with earnestness whatever sadhana he receives from his guru, for, in fact, there is no such differentiation of higher or lower sadhana that should matter in the beginning. It is the earnestness which is more important.

Sutra 23: Or by devotion to Ishwara

ईश्वरप्रणिधानाद्वा ॥ २३ ॥

Īśvarapraṇidhānādvā

Īśvara: Lord; *praṇidhānāt*: devotion; *vā*: or

Or by devotion to the Lord (asamprajnata samadhi can be attained).

Usually Ishwara is translated by the word God, but by God we should mean not a person but a superior spiritual consciousness. It is neither physical nor mental, but purely spiritual. If an aspirant experiences that he is incapable of going through the stages of faith, energy, etc., then he may use another means for reaching the highest goal, which is intense devotion to the Lord. Some yogis attain samadhi by birth, others have to make the effort, a very earnest effort of great intensity, to achieve that goal. There are many aspirants who cannot put in the required effort because they lack the necessary faculties. Yet for them there is hope. Patanjali recommends intense devotion to God as an equally sure way of reaching the goal.

The word *va* in this sutra indicates that an optional method is being described. The word *pranidhana* means placing completely, absolutely, thoroughly. It is the complete placing of one's awareness, one's mind, one's thought and consciousness into Ishwara.

This sutra has been explained in different ways by different authors. It is said, for example, that the meaning of this sutra is that samadhi is obtained by self-surrender to God, or it is said that samadhi is obtained by fixing the mind on the Lord. Some say that it is the awareness which is to be placed in God. To understand the sutra correctly, we must have a clear idea of God. In all the different religions, the word is used differently. Some religions believe in a personal God, some look upon it as the ruler or creator of the universe. Some people feel that there is no God, but there is only universal consciousness. We must note in this connection that yoga philosophy is an offshoot of Samkhya, which is an atheistic doctrine. Similarly, there is no God in Buddhism.

It is really a wonder that here Patanjali, who took his philosophical ideas from Samkhya, should speak of God and of devotion to him. Perhaps he brought in the concept of the Lord for the spiritual welfare of mankind. We should note that a yoga teacher should not teach atheism, even if he is himself an atheist, because the average person in all countries of the world finds great solace in the idea of God. Patanjali must have brought the idea of God into his yoga sutras knowing full well that it did not fit in with the atheism of Samkhya, because he knew that the principal purpose of his yoga was to give a practical way of life to mankind, in which one was allowed to make progress on the spiritual path according to one's beliefs, limitations and suppositions. He was fully aware that a spiritual teacher should not bring in his own experiences while giving instructions to the beginner and, therefore, he must have allowed the idea of God to be included in his philosophy, although he himself might have been an atheist.

There are three conceptions about God. Firstly, philosophical thinkers in India have viewed him as not different from man, but they have said that atman is Paramatman. Secondly, it is believed by some that God is in the heart of man and that one does not have to go out to seek for him. Thirdly, the greatest number of people believe in the duality of God and man.

Sutra 24: Definition of Ishwara

क्लेशकर्मविपाकाशयैरपरामृष्टः पुरुषविशेष ईश्वरः ॥ २४ ॥

Kleśakarmavipākāśayairaparāmṛṣṭaḥ puruṣaviśeṣa Īśvaraḥ

Kleśa: afflictions; *karmavipāka*: fruits of acts; *āśaya*: store of the traces of past karma; *aparāmṛṣṭaḥ*: untouched; *puruṣaviśeṣa*: special kind of soul; *Īśvaraḥ*: God

God is a special soul untouched by afflictions, acts, their traces and their fruits.

The nature of God has been made clear in this sutra. Patanjali does not believe in a personal God. His idea of God is that of spiritual consciousness which is so pure that it is completely free of any relation with karma and its effects. An understanding of this sutra would require a clear understanding of the basic spirit of Indian sadhana. There are many varieties of yoga included in Indian sadhana, such as raja yoga, hatha yoga, mantra yoga, karma yoga, laya yoga and tantra, but the fundamental basis is surrender to the supreme reality. It is true for a layman and it is equally true for highly intellectual Indian philosophers.

An individual can surrender to God only if one is aware of one's limitations. When one knows one's limitations, one will not be led astray and can surrender to God completely. As long as one believes that one has some important qualities, one cannot be a real bhakta. Bhakti starts when you know yourself truly, when you know your nature and are sure about it. Man is weak as he is, but through ignorance, he thinks himself to be strong and capable. Ishwara pranidhana does not only mean going to a temple; it requires complete surrender by a continuous process of self-analysis for quite a long time.

In addition to Ishwara pranidhana, an aspirant should do his other sadhana. Surrender to God is one of the quickest ways to realization. Ishwara is a particular purusha who remains untouched by the five afflictions, three kinds of action, three kinds of fruits of action and the seeds of karmas. The afflictions are five: ignorance, I-feeling, raga, dwesha, and fear of death. These afflictions are rooted in everyone's mind, but God is free of them. Actions or karma are of three types: good, bad and mixed. They have good, bad and mixed fruits, such as span of life, enjoyment and kind of birth. God is free from all these aspects.

It is due to our past karma that we are born in favourable or unfavourable circumstances. Our health, enjoyments, mental development and span of life are the effects of our past deeds. With these we go on accumulating new traces of our deeds. Thus the store of the traces, which is called *karmashaya*, goes on increasing and we have to enjoy its good or bad effects in future births. God is completely free from this karmashaya.

According to Samkhya, there are many purushas in the universe and Ishwara is the most superior of them. Just as a king, although he is a human being like other human beings, has a special status by virtue of being the ruler, similarly, God is a special kind of purusha, inasmuch as he is completely free of the aspects which are found to bind the other purushas. The other purushas are also free of prakriti by nature, but they come in contact with prakriti and due to this contact, they go through various births and rebirths. Ishwara is ever-free. *Purushavishesha* is a special state of consciousness which is beyond the things mentioned above, yet it manifests itself in every human being on earth. Therefore it is possible for every individual to attain the supreme being which is purushavishesha, but for that one must have direct conception or experience of Ishwara, because the intellectual conception which we usually have is not enough.

Sutra 25: Attribute of Ishwara

तत्र निरतिशयं सर्वज्ञबीजम् ॥ २५ ॥

Tatra niratiśayaṃ sarvajñabījam

Tatra: there (in God); *niratiśayaṃ*: limitless; *sarvajña*: omniscient; *bījam*: principle, seed

In Ishwara there is the seed of limitless omniscience.

Sutra 26: Ishwara is the jagatguru

पूर्वेषामपि गुरुः कालेनानवच्छेदात् ॥ २६ ॥

Pūrveṣāmapi guruḥ kālenānavachchhedāt

Pūrveṣām: of those who came before; *api*: even; *guruḥ*: greater, teacher; *kālena*: by time; *anavachhedāt*: because unlimited by time

Not being limited by time he is the guru of the earliest gurus.

Sutra 27: Pranava is verily Ishwara

तस्य वाचकः प्रणवः ॥ २७ ॥

Tasya vāchakaḥ praṇavaḥ

Tasya: of it; *vāchakaḥ*: designator, indicator; *praṇavaḥ*: Aum

Aum is the word denoting God.

Sutra 28: Sadhana for Ishwara

तज्जपस्तदर्थभावनम् ॥ २८ ॥

Tajjapastadarthabhāvanam

Tat: that; *japa*: repetition of the word; *tat*: that; *artha*: meaning; *bhāvanam*: dwelling upon mentally

That (the word Aum) should be recited repeatedly while dwelling mentally on its meaning.

The nature of Ishwara and Ishwara pranidhana has been made clear in these four sutras. *Ishwara* is the highest manifested consciousness in man. In it there is the seed of all knowledge. The ultimate point of consciousness of divinity in us is samadhi. We have already seen that purusha is the manifestation of consciousness in the course of evolution, and that there are infinite stages in this process, inasmuch as there are infinite purushas in the universe. When we enjoy life's different experiences our mental consciousness of the outer world is described in Vedanta as *vaishvanara purusha*. The consciousness in the state of dream is called *tejomaya purusha*. In sleep it is called *prajna purusha*. God is the supreme purusha which presides over the infinite purushas.

Purusha should not actually mean spirit as is usually thought, but it should mean a particular manifestation of consciousness. The supreme purusha is Ishwara. He is not in the realm of manifestation but in the realm of the unmanifested state of things (*avyakta*). That is called *Parabrahman*, the transcendental being. In it there is the seed of limitless knowledge. It is called *sarvajna*, because there is nothing in the universe which is outside its sphere.

The highest state of evolution includes knowledge that knows no limitation. It is knowledge of everything, but that knowledge is not gained from outside. Ishwara manifests that knowledge, and an aspirant who has attained the highest state of consciousness is in touch with all knowledge, although it is not necessary that all that knowledge is brought down to sense knowledge. In normal working life everyone exhibits only a trace of that knowledge.

Ishwara is the guru even of the ancients because he is not conditioned by time. He is the master of masters. Even the great seers and sages, prophets and teachers are later in time than Ishwara. The state of consciousness which is supposed to be the highest and which is still in us, but which never dies with the death of the body, is timeless.

The difference between man and Ishwara is that man is the manifest state of consciousness, while Ishwara is the highest state of consciousness. The manifest state goes on manifesting in different births, in different incarnations, taking the medium of different bodies: human, animal and so on. Ultimately, it takes a finer and higher body when it reaches the highest point of evolution. Therefore, Ishwara, being unconnected with birth and death, timeless and beginningless, is said to be the guru even of these past prophets and masters.

Ishwara is the ultimate point of supreme consciousness. It is not possible to reach him through thinking alone. We cannot reach him either through speeches, discourses, nor through intellect, nor by learning about him through great people or the scriptures. Thinking and experience are two different things. The whole structure of Indian philosophy is divided into tattwa chintana and tattwa darshan. *Tattwa chintana* means contemplation and reflection on supreme consciousness, while *tattwa darshan* means perception of the supreme consciousness. Tattwa chintana gave rise to the six systems of Indian philosophy. It is a rational approach to the understanding of the supreme consciousness, but that remains incomplete. Therefore, tattwa darshan developed through yoga, bhakti, mystic and occult practices, etc. Chintana is knowledge, while darshan is experiencing.

Patanjali has mentioned a scheme for going from the state of knowledge to the state of perception or experience. He says Aum is the word which indicates Ishwara; Ishwara is described by Aum. We have seen that supreme consciousness, or Ishwara, is formless, it has no form, but there should be some vehicle which expresses it. This is described by yantra, mantra and tantra. These three are the expressions of the formless consciousness, just as in mathematics various formulas are developed for expressing various processes; for example, the formula $E=mc^2$. This equation was given by Einstein. It is the expression of matter in energy, which we cannot see, but it expresses itself in the process. It is the meaning of vachaka. Like the formula used in science, we have mantras, or tantras, as well as yantras, used in the tantra shastra.

Just as a scientist gives an expression to the principle of energy which he sees or experiences through intuition, similarly Patanjali has given an expression, a designation of the supreme consciousness of Ishwara. That may be in the form of mantra, yantra or tantra. Mantra means designation in the form of sound. Supreme consciousness is designated by a sound formula. In tantra there is symbolism in the form of human or animal figures, such as the figures in human shape or in animal shape. Yantra is a psychic symbol. Aum is both mantra and yantra. It is not tantra, because tantra must have a human symbol. People in different countries have always formulated certain symbols to signify the finer forces, such as thought, anger, passion, vision or supreme knowledge. Aum is a mantra and every mantra has two forms: it has a sound and a form. Aum has a form which is visible to the eyes, and at the same time it has a sound. So, Aum as a mantra is subject to perception and hearing. Yantra also has the diagrams and sounds, but tantra has no sound. It can only be seen, not heard. In yantra a beeja mantra is also added and thus a yantra is a combination of sound and form with a beeja mantra.

We cannot perceive Ishwara with the eyes or with the ears, but we can have experience of him with the help of a mantra. Aum is the mantra which designates Ishwara.

Patanjali recommends that the mantra Aum must be repeated and its meaning should be contemplated upon. This is perhaps a complete departure from the Samkhya position, because the Samkhya system does not believe in any supreme being. It believes that the highest knowledge can be achieved only through properly understanding the twenty-five basic tattwas. Patanjali must have realized that this was only possible for a few highly developed persons, so he evolved this sadhana of mantra japa of Aum. This is an altogether new approach which is introduced, namely, the approach of bhakti. Instead of asking you to meditate directly on a formless thing, he has provided a support in the form of Aum.

By constant repetition of the word Aum and dhyana on its meaning, meditation becomes complete. Japa alone is not sufficient. Japa and meditation must go together. Patanjali recommends that while doing japa of Aum, the student should become aware of the japa and put his mind to understanding its meaning. For this, we must understand the meaning of Aum. We find this clearly mentioned in the *Mandukya Upanishad*. It is in terms of supreme consciousness of cosmic being.

The word Aum is made of three letters, namely, A, U and M. A should be understood in relation to the world of the senses, body, objective enjoyments and vishva purusha. The syllable U should be understood in relation to the subconscious mind, subjective enjoyments, or the tejas state of purusha. The syllable M should likewise be understood in relation to the unconscious, mindlessness, no enjoyment, or prajna state of purusha. This is only a glimpse of the *Mandukya Upanishad*. It explains that the syllables A, U and M are to be understood in relation to the state of consciousness. In this way the student transcends the three states of manifested consciousness and ultimately reaches the fourth state, called the turiya state, which is the unmanifested, unheard and unexpressed state of purusha.

Sutra 29: Result of this sadhana

ततः प्रत्यक्चेतनाधिगमोऽप्यन्तरायाभावश्च ॥ २९ ॥

Tataḥ pratyakchetanādhigamo'pyantarāyābhāvaścha

Tataḥ: from that (practice of meditation on Aum); *pratyak*: turned in, in opposite direction; *chetanā*: consciousness; *adhigama*: attainment; *api*: also; *antarāya*: obstacle; *abhāva*: absence; *cha*: and

From that practice the consciousness turns inward and the obstacles are overcome.

Two things happen as a result of doing japa of Aum: the consciousness or awareness is introverted and the obstacles disappear. When a student tries to go ahead on the path of yoga he comes across many obstacles which block his way. Patanjali will give a list of these obstacles in the next sutra. Thus we have a complete sadhana described for the average person in sutras 23 to 29. This sadhana, called Ishwara pranidhana, is meant for those who are neither videhas nor prakritilayas and who do not have shraddha, virya and the other qualities. It is meant for those who have an unsteady, vacillating mind, who have attachment to the lower things of life. Patanjali has been very kind to them in describing the preliminary type of sadhana in sutras 23 to 29. By practising this, the average person will ultimately obtain higher intelligence and keenness of mind, so that he can follow the higher and deeper courses of sadhana and thereby reach the highest spiritual goal.

Sutra 30: Obstacles in the path of yoga

व्याधिस्त्यानसंशयप्रमादालस्याविरतिभ्रान्तिदर्शनालब्धभूमिकत्वानवस्थितत्वानि
चित्तविक्षेपास्तेऽन्तरायाः ॥ ३० ॥

Vyādhistyānasaṃśayapramādālasyāviratibhrāntidarśanālabdhabhūmikatvānavasthitatvāni
chittavikṣepāste'ntarāyāḥ

Vyādhi: disease; *styāna*: dullness; *saṃśaya*: doubt; *pramāda*: procrastination; *ālasya*: laziness; *avirati*: craving for enjoyment; *bhrāntidarśana*: erroneous perception; *alabdhabhūmikatva*: inability to achieve a finer state; *anavasthitatva*: instability; *chittavikṣepāḥ*: obstacle to the mind; *te*: they; *antarāyāḥ*: obstacles

Disease, dullness, doubt, procrastination, laziness, craving, erroneous perception, inability to achieve finer stages and instability are the obstacles.

We have seen that the practice of japa causes the mind to be introverted and the obstacles to be removed. The obstacles are enumerated in this sutra. These are the nine disruptive forces of consciousness. Spiritual aspirants would do well to know the way to remove them through japa, so that progress on the spiritual path is unhindered. It should also be noted that these obstacles are no different from consciousness, they are a part of it. They are definite points in the framework of consciousness.

A sincere spiritual aspirant should realize that during the course of his practice these obstacles are bound to come. Ailments will come at some time or another, usually stomach disorders or those pertaining to the brain or other organs. We know from the science of glandular secretions that when the consciousness is drawn inward, the metabolism and other functions of the body are altered and modified. When you sit for meditation, sometimes you fall asleep. In the same way, when sadhana is practised for a long time, there is sometimes a state of erroneous perceptions.

The spiritual aspirant is often observed to be careless about his personal life, family duties and other obligations. There may be doubt in his mind whether a particular sadhana is right, or whether he would reach the goal at all. Doubt is bound to be there.

Sutra 31: Other obstructions

दुःखदौर्मनस्याङ्गमेजयत्वश्वासप्रश्वासा विक्षेपसहभुवः ॥ ३१ ॥

Duḥkhadaurmanasyāṅgamejayatvaśvāsapraśvāsā vikṣepasahabhuvaḥ

Duḥkha: pain; *daurmanasya*: depression; *aṅgamejayatva*: shaking of the body; *śvāsapraśvāsā*: inhalations and exhalations; *vikṣepa*: distraction; *sahabhuvaḥ*: accompanying symptom

Pain, depression, shaking of the body and unrhythmic breathing are the accompanying symptoms of mental distraction.

Everyone, whether a spiritual aspirant or not, is prone to the nine obstacles and their accompanying symptoms. With some persons these become very natural conditions. The distraction in the inward process of awareness must be carefully studied. One should be able to know whether an obstacle is happening as a natural process, or if it is due to meditation and other practices. For example, even a person practising meditation may be full of doubts, fabrications and apprehensions. Disease may occur as a natural process or when one is going inward in the process of meditation. The sutra tells us that if there is pain, or mental depression, or shaking of the body, or unrhythmic breathing during the sadhana, you may be sure that chitta is undergoing a distracted condition.

The symptoms that are presented in the form of distractions and those enumerated in the previous sutra are not mental processes; they are psychic manifestations. They are common both to the average person and to the aspirant whose mind is turned inward during meditation.

Sutra 32: Removal of obstacles by one-pointedness

तत्प्रतिषेधार्थमेकतत्त्वाभ्यासः ॥ ३२ ॥

Tatpratiṣedhārthamekatattvābhyāsaḥ

Tat: that; *pratiṣedhārtham*: for removal; *eka*: one; *tattva*: principle; *abhyāsaḥ*: practice

For removal of those (obstacles and accompanying symptoms) the practice of concentration on one principle (is to be done).

We have already noted that Patanjali has recommended the four qualifications such as shraddha, veerya, etc. for those aspirants who have indomitable will and courage. For the one who is weak and infirm he has recommended intense devotion and japa of Aum. In this sutra he shows a way of overcoming the obstacles and the accompanying symptoms. The way involves concentration of the mind on a single tattwa. We must understand the meaning of this. If you practise mantra, it should be on one mantra. If you practise dhyana, it should be on one symbol. Those who keep on changing the methods, techniques and symbols in meditation every now and then will suffer from the obstacles. Those who are serious about realization, about attaining the deeper stages of consciousness, should understand this sutra clearly. One should not change the symbol of meditation because the process of meditation is only a basis for the consciousness to go deeper and deeper. There will be confusion if the basis is changed time and again.

Therefore, Patanjali has emphasized one kind of sadhana in this sutra. If you change it, be sure that you will come to grief. We find this happening in the case of those sects where emphasis is placed on rather diversified symbols. For example, in the sadhana known as tantra, many symbols are used, ignoring the principle of ekatattvabhyasah, and we find that many practitioners are suffering as a result. The same is the case with some kinds of sadhana in ancient Buddhism which have never flourished, due to the defect that many symbols were used for concentration. This fact is borne in mind by real gurus who do not change the mantra once it is given to a disciple, even if it was given previously by another guru. If the mantra is changed, there may be confusion in the mind of the disciple. A wise guru will never allow this confusion to arise. He will give a sadhana not merely according to the disciple's liking, but according to the disciple's capacities.

There is no actual difference between the different symbols. One may be devoted to Lord Ganesha or Shiva, Kali and so on, but if one changes the object of devotion after taking up one of the symbols, then confusion is bound to arise. The best way to avoid this confusion is to keep to the one symbol, to ekatattvabhyasa. The obstacles can be removed from the way of an aspirant only when he does not allow his mind to run helter-skelter, but fixes it on one single tattwa, come what may.

Sutra 33: (ii) Or by cultivating opposite virtues

मैत्रीकरुणामुदितोपेक्षाणां सुखदुःखपुण्यापुण्यविषयाणां
भावनातश्चित्तप्रसादनम् ॥ ३३ ॥

Maitrīkaruṇāmuditopekṣāṇāṃ sukhaduḥkhapuṇyāpuṇyaviṣayāṇāṃ bhāvanātaśchittaprasādanam

Maitrī: friendliness; *karuṇā*: compassion; *muditā*; gladness; *upekṣāṇāṃ*: indifference; *sukha*: happiness; *duḥkha*: misery; *puṇya*: virtue; *apuṇya*: vice; *viṣayāṇāṃ*: of the objects; *bhāvanātaḥ*: attitude; *chitta*: mind; *prasādanam*: purification, making peaceful

In relation to happiness, misery, virtue and vice, by cultivating the attitudes of friendliness, compassion, gladness and indifference respectively, the mind becomes purified and peaceful.

It is impossible to practise concentration of the mind unless the mind is purified, that is, made peaceful in nature. The best way for this is shown in this sutra. It is the way of cultivating the attitude of friendliness, compassion, gladness and indifference in respect of people or events which are causing happiness, misery, virtue or vice. By maintaining this attitude, that is, friendliness to the happy, compassion for the unhappy, gladness about the virtuous and indifference to those who are full of vice, the mind of the aspirant becomes free from disturbing influences and as a result it becomes peaceful and undisturbed. The process of introversion follows easily. The mind by nature is full of unrest, like a pond that is disturbed by the falling of objects like boulders, stones, etc. The unsteady mind cannot become concentrated easily.

It is said in the *Kathopanishad* and elsewhere that the mind has a natural tendency to be attracted towards the outside world. It is not in the nature of the mind to look within. Therefore, when you are trying to turn the mind inside, the obstacles and impurities must be first removed. Jealousy, hate and the element of competition cause a lot of impurities in the mind. When we see a happy and prosperous person, we feel jealous. This causes a disturbance in the subconscious mind and obstructs the mind from being concentrated. This results in fearful visions. When we come across a person suffering, we enjoy it if he happens to be an enemy. This is also one of the impurities of the mind. Similarly, we often criticize virtuous persons and hail the deeds of vicious persons. All this causes disturbance in the mind and comes in the way of peace and meditation.

Patanjali has shown a way of overcoming these disturbances. The fourfold attitude which he asks us to develop gives rise to inner peace by the removal of the disturbing factors, not only from the conscious level, but also from the deepest parts of the subconscious.

Sutra 34: (iii) Or by controlling prana

प्रच्छर्दनविधारणाभ्यां वा प्राणस्य ॥ ३४ ॥

Prachchhardanavidhāraṇābhyāṃ vā prāṇasya

Prachchhardana: expiration or rechaka; *vidhāraṇābhyāṃ*: holding, kumbhaka; *vā*: or; *prāṇasya*: of breath

Or by expiration and retention of breath (one can control the mind).

Temperamentally, not all people can surrender to God. Even though one may believe in God, it may not be possible for one to do Ishwara pranidhana. For such people, Patanjali here gives a way by which the mind can be made pure, controlled and steady. Some of us are dynamic by temperament, others are emotional, yet others are mystic and some are rational. So the entire mental structure can be divided into these four kinds. For the dynamic person, karma yoga is best suited. Bhakti is better for those who are emotional, who can surrender to God; they form the majority of the population. The third group, mystic people, are prone to practise raja yoga and the allied practices of hatha yoga, swara yoga, kriya yoga, nada yoga and trataka, etc. The fourth type form the few jnana yogis. They like to read the Upanishads, the Gita, etc. wherein the deeper aspects of life, the universe and meditation are described. Many of us have a mixture of these four tendencies. Hence a mixture of practices is to be recommended and therefore Patanjali has described a variety of practices. We should select the sadhana which is most suitable for us.

Beginning from the videha and prakritilaya yogis, Patanjali has described various types of sadhana for various types of aspirants in the past few sutras. In this sutra he explains pranayama. We should understand the meaning of *prachchhardana* and *vidharana*. The former word means exhalation and the latter means holding the breath outside. This constitutes *maha bandha*, which includes performing the three bandhas together, namely, jalandhara, uddiyana and moola bandha, while doing kumbhaka. The beginner should not be taught maha bandha. He should only do rechaka, that is, exhalation – say 21 times, 51 times or 100 times. This may be called kapalbhati or agnisar.

Just by practising rechaka, kumbhaka and the three bandhas, the mind can be brought to a state of stillness. In one of the ancient books, it is said that consciousness has two supports: prana and vasana. These are the supports on which the mind rests and consciousness works. If one of them is removed, the other goes automatically. Prana is gross as well as subtle. The subtle prana is in the form of energy, and the gross prana has the form of breath.

There are five major pranas: prana, apana, udana, samana and vyana. Then there are the five minor pranas: devadatta, nada, kurma, krikara and dhananjaya. They are all responsible for different activities in the human body. Prana is responsible for inhalation and works in the mouth and nose, digests the food, separates the digested materials, converts water into sweat and urine, and controls the glandular secretions. Its sphere is from the nose to the heart. Apana brings about excretion and throws impurities away, outside the body. Its region is from the navel to the soles of the feet. It brings about the downward movement. Samana is formed in the limbs and nadis. It works between the heart and the navel. Udana maintains muscular strength and is responsible for the removal of the karmic body from the gross body at the time of death. By controlling udana the yogi can travel in the air. It acts from the throat to the head. Vyana causes the circulation of blood and moves through the nerves. It is situated in the anal region.

Among the minor pranas, nada brings about coughing and sneezing, kurma causes contraction, while krikara brings about hunger and thirst. The action of devadatta causes drowsiness and sleep. Dhananjaya maintains nourishment.

In addition to these, there are fifteen fine currents of prana. They are called nadis. *Nadi* means nerve or current of energy, or blood. They carry impulses to and from the brain. Their names are sushumna, ida, pingala, gandhari, hastijihwa, poosha, aswini, shoora, kuhoo, saraswati, varuni, alambusha, vishvodari, shankhini and chittra. In all, there are 72,000 nadis in the body which carry the finer sensations. Three of them are the most important, namely, ida, pingala and sushumna. These three nadis are very important in yoga because they carry the higher currents of higher knowledge. Sushumna is the most important of the three. It is a very fine passage situated in the centre of the spinal cord. Emerging from the root of the anus, it goes up to ajna chakra or the medulla oblongata. The three nadis emerge from mooladhara, which is called *muktatriveni*. The consciousness, the sensations, are liberated here and they become one. They meet at ajna chakra. Triveni is a place in India where the three rivers, Ganga, Yamuna and Saraswati, meet. In comparison, ajna chakra is called *yuktatriveni*. Within the framework of sushumna there are two more nadis: the outer one is called *vajra nadi*, while the inner one is named *chittra nadi*. Within the chittra is a finer canal known as *brahma nadi*.

The breathing process has a definite timetable; the movement of the moon influences the movement and control of swara or breath. Breath has a direct effect on the individual movements. Breath controls thinking as well as the past, present and future. In twenty-four hours one breathes predominantly through the right nostril for one hour, then the left nostril, alternating twelve times. The left nostril is called ida, or chandra; the right nostril pingala or surya. Similarly, ida is called Ganga and pingala is called Yamuna.

After every hour, the breath changes position in the nostrils. During the change from ida to pingala or from pingala to ida, sushumna flows momentarily. This we know from the science called shiva swara yoga. On the first three days of the bright fortnight of the moon, the left nostril flows at sunrise, and after every hour the nostrils change. On the next three days, the right nostrils flows for one hour after sunrise. During the dark fortnight of the moon, the right nostril flows at sunrise on the first three days. Thus the cycle changes every three days. During illness this order may change. Disease can be predicted with the help of swara yoga.

Heavy work can be done when the pingala or sun nadi is flowing and light work when the ida or moon nadi is flowing. Meditation should be practised when sushumna is flowing. The flow in the nostrils can be changed by certain practices. By closing the eyes and meditating on the left nostril, it can be made to flow, but this depends on the depth of concentration. The right nostril can be made to flow by lying on the left side and pressing the armpit with a pillow. Another method of making a nostril flow is by plugging the opposite one with cotton wool. There are many other ways available.

Breathing in pranayama should be done very slowly. Those who breathe slowly and deeply are found to live longer. The hare breathes eighty times per minute and lives for only eight years. The monkey breathes thirty-two times a minute and lives for ten years. The dog lives for twelve years and the horse for twenty-five years. They breathe twenty-nine times and nineteen times per minute respectively. Human beings breathe thirteen times per minute and should live for 120 years. The snake which lives for 1,000 years is found to breathe only eight times a minute, and the tortoise breathes five times a minute and lives for 3,000 years. This shows the importance of retention of breath.

The kumbhaka involved in this sutra is of the outer type, in which the breath is held outside after rechaka.

Sutra 35: (iv) Or by observing sense experience

विषयवती वा प्रवृत्तिरुत्पन्ना मनसः स्थितिनिबन्धनी ॥ ३५ ॥

Viṣayavatī vā pravṛttirutpannā manasaḥ sthitinibandhanī

Viṣayavatī: sensuous; *vā*: or; *pravṛttih*: functioning; *utpannā*: arisen; *manasaḥ*: of the mind; *sthiti*: steadiness; *nibandhanī*: which binds

Or else the mind can be made steady by bringing it into activity of sense experience.

This sutra describes an additional technique which may be followed by those who are not able to practise Ishwara pranidhana, or even maha bandha or pranayama. It is true that many aspirants find it difficult to practise pranayama on account of a lack of proper guidance, or due to inefficiency, or lack of proper nutrition. This sutra provides a simpler method of bringing the mind under control through arousing an activity of sense perception. Here the mind is made to observe itself in sense perception; that is, perception through the senses of seeing, hearing, smelling, tasting and touching. By merging the mental consciousness into these sense perceptions, the mind comes under control. That is to say, the mental consciousness can be merged into sound consciousness by repetition of mantras, bhajan, kirtan, etc. A sophisticated person may not find this interesting, but it is true that if one goes deep, one can control the mind by making it sound conscious. This is a principle of nada yoga.

The mind can also be controlled by making it form conscious through trataka, which is concentration on a particular form, and similarly, in the case of touch consciousness and taste consciousness. The former happens when the guru touches the disciple on the head, and the latter is brought about by khechari mudra. By concentrating the mind on the tip of the nose, a subtle or psychic smell is experienced, which can be utilized for controlling the mind. Taste consciousness is developed by concentrating on the front part of the tongue. Colour visions are developed by concentrating on the palate in khechari mudra. Psychic touch is experienced by concentrating on the central part of the tongue. Psychic sound is developed by concentrating on the root of the tongue. All these psychic processes become the basis of self-control. When these psychic processes are developed, the student starts concentrating on them. In due course his mind transcends them and goes deeper. That is a state of complete mental control. All this involves the action of the senses, the indriyas, in dharana and pratyahara.

In certain Buddhist schools of meditation, the priests beat drums and meditate on the sound. It is a very elementary sadhana but it is useful for many of us. Bhajan is one of the popular sadhanas in India. The singer may sing only one line or only one song for hours together, with the eyes and ears closed to everything else except the sound of the bhajan. This is one of the elementary sadhanas but it is important insofar as it can easily lead to dharana and dhyana. Kirtan is also one of the easy, yet effective sadhanas. It is done with one person leading and others following. There are different methods in different provinces. Sometimes it can continue for twenty-four hours or even longer and produces wonderful effects on the audience.

Sutra 36: (v) Or by inner illumination

विशोका वा ज्योतिष्मती ॥ ३६ ॥

Viśokā vā jyotiṣmatī

Viśokā: without sorrow; *vā*: or; *jyotiṣmatī*: luminous, full of light

Or the luminous state which is beyond sorrow (can control the mind).

The mind can be made steady and controlled by manifesting the serene luminosity within by concentrating on nada, or on *bhrumadhya*, the centre of the eyebrows. The inner illumination is very serene, calm, quiet and peaceful; it is not a sharp illumination. It can be experienced while doing deep meditation. It is of two types. In sleep, sometimes there is a sudden explosion of light which is very disturbing. Patanjali is not talking about it here; he means the inner light which is quiet. The mind can be brought under control by experiencing that serene light. There are many methods through which the light can be seen. One of them is concentration on the centre of the eyebrows; another one is concentration on nada (sound).

Sutra 37: (vi) Or by detachment from matter

वीतरागविषयं वा चित्तम् ॥ ३७ ॥

Vītarāgaviṣayaṃ vā chittam

Vītarāga: passionless person who has transcended raga; *viṣayaṃ*: object; *vā*: or, also; *chittam*: mind

Or else the mind can be brought under control by making passionless persons the object for concentrating the mind.

Vitaraga is a person who has renounced raga, that is, human passion. By concentrating the mind on such persons, it can be made steady and controlled. Therefore, in the ancient meditative traditions it has been advised to use symbols of ishta devata and guru, as they represent an idea of some power transcending the human passions or of someone who has achieved this state by force of sadhana. Passion or any emotion is pure, raw, uncontrolled energy which can alter the normal state of perception either negatively or positively. By transmuting this raw energy, it has been proved possible to bring together the dissipated energies of the mind, focus them on the object of attention and make the psyche as powerful as a laser beam.

Sutra 38: (vii) Or by knowledge of dream and sleep

स्वप्ननिद्राज्ञानालम्बनं वा ॥ ३८ ॥

Svapnanidrājñānālambanaṃ vā

Svapna: dream; *nidrā*: sleep; *jñāna*: knowledge; *ālambana*: support; *vā*: or, also

Or else (the mind can be made steady) by giving it the knowledge of dream and sleep for support.

The mind can be controlled by developing the method of conscious dreaming and conscious sleeping. Conscious sleeping is the last state in antar mouna. There is a method of seeing dreams consciously, but it is dangerous and only a few can practise it. This process may be beneficial, especially for those who are psychic. In conscious sleeping and dreaming, one develops consciousness of the states of dream and sleep.

Usually we have unconscious dreams; they are experienced but not witnessed. We have no control over that, but in this method recommended here, the aspirant is able to introduce them and control them consciously. We can control our thoughts by conscious thought control, subconscious thought control or unconscious thought control. In this process not only the conscious actions and the intellect are controlled, but even the subconscious actions. During conscious dreams one does not hear anything from outside. In conscious sleep one goes on reading the book of sleep. Awareness of these two states can be made the support on which the mind can be concentrated. It is meant only for people who are psychic.

Sutra 39: (viii) Or by meditation as desired

यथाभिमतध्यानाद्वा ॥ ३९ ॥

Yathābhimatadhyānādvā

Yathā: as; *abhimata*: desired; *dhyanāt*: by meditation; *vā*: or

Or else by meditation as desired (mind can be steadied).

Here complete freedom is given. This is because dhyana on an object that one likes, such as the object of devotion, is the surest way of making the mind steady, controlled and peaceful. It is immaterial what object one takes for dhyana. It may be the cross, or the swastika, or an idol, or simply Aum – whatever is agreeable (*abhimata*). An aspirant should choose for himself that object on which he can concentrate his mind.

Sutra 40: Fruits of meditation

परमाणुपरममहत्त्वान्तोऽस्य वशीकारः ॥ ४० ॥

Paramāṇuparamamahattvānto'sya vaśīkāraḥ

Paramāṇu: ultimate atom; *paramamahattva*: ultimate largeness; *antah*: ending; *asya*: of his; *vaśīkāraḥ*: mastery

So the yogi is given mastery over all objects for meditation ranging from the smallest atom to the infinitely large.

The question may be asked, namely, are these practices described in the previous sutras capable of giving rise to samadhi? The reply is: no. One cannot attain samadhi by these practices, but one can definitely attain the psychic or spiritual power necessary for the finer stages of samadhi. This is just like passing the higher secondary examination and becoming qualified for entrance into college. So, by practising the various sadhanas mentioned, the aspirant acquires mastery over the finest atom as well as the greatest infinity. He becomes a master of the finest as well as the largest forces. These sadhanas confer on him the power of omnipotence. These practices are very necessary for making progress towards the subtle perception of the finer states of samadhi. Just as the scientist arrives at the finer conception of matter and energy, likewise the yogi becomes capable of practising concentration even on subtle thought and also on infinity.

We find people who are unable to grasp the subtle meaning of things because they have no mastery over their mind. The above-mentioned concentration practices can make the consciousness very refined. The mind can be introverted at will. This is observed equally in the case of solving problems of mathematics or science or meditation. With training, the mind can be made to concentrate properly. The first psychic power in yoga is the achievement of this mastery. Then the mind can be fixed on any object, gross or subtle.

There is an interesting example. When Swami Vivekananda was in the USA, he used to borrow several books from a library every day and return them the next day. The librarian, wondering if so many books could be read in a single day, wanted to test the swami, but to his astonishment he noticed that the swami remembered every word and line he had read. This is how a yogi has control over the finest and largest.

A person can go into samadhi only when he is able to perceive even the ideas and thoughts. This is because in the finer states of samadhi one has to pick up the dynamic consciousness and hold on to it. There are states of samadhi wherein the aspirant has nothing but the awareness of the effort of control that he has been making. That effort has to be brought as an idea and then it has to be thrown out. It is very difficult to understand this. In that state one is able to annihilate all other thoughts except the thought of elimination. That can only be done if one has mastery over the four processes which are not the conscious thought processes.

In the finer states of samadhi, one has to have mastery of the name, the form, and the object meant by the name; for example, the name cow, the form cow and the object cow. The difference has to be known. This is not possible without training, because through habit we are usually prone to mixing up all these three things together in our understanding. A yogi who has control over his mind can understand factors separately. Unless this is achieved, it is impossible to get ahead in meditation. One has to be able to practise meditation on the object without the intervention of word or form.

Sutra 41: Oneness of chitta with object

क्षीणवृत्तेरभिजातस्येव मणेर्ग्रहीतृग्रहणग्राह्येषु
तत्स्थतदञ्जनता समापत्तिः ॥ ४१ ॥

Kṣīṇavṛtterabhijātasyeva maṇergrahītṛgrahaṇagrāhyeṣu
tatsthatadañjanatā samāpattiḥ

Kṣīṇavṛtteh: whom the vrittis have weakened; *abhijātasya*: well-polished, purified; *iva*: just like; *maṇeḥ*: of the crystal; *grahitṛ*: cognizer; *grahaṇa*: senses; *grāhyeṣu*: in the objects of cognition; *tatstha*: on which it stays or rests; *tadañjanatā*: taking the colour of that; *samāpattiḥ*: complete absorption

Samapatti is a state of complete absorption of the mind which is free from vrittis into (the three types of objects such as) cognizer, cognized and the senses, just as a polished crystal takes the colour of that on which it rests.

The word *samapatti* means complete acceptance, just like the ocean fully accepts all the water poured into it by rivers. It is the state of mind acquired by various practices like pranayama, penance, sadhana, etc. It is the immediate end in view before one practises samadhi. Until samapatti is attained, one cannot speak of higher practices, but what higher practice and lower practice means would depend on the capacities of an individual. For example, a person with higher consciousness does not need japa or kirtan; he just closes his eyes and goes into a deep mental state, but for those whose minds may be full of thoughts, this state may be considered very high. Instead of using the words higher and lower, we may call it simple and harder sadhana.

One cannot go into the state of meditation unless the mind is clear. If the mind is clear, the state of meditation can come as easily as sleep comes to an ordinary person. For this, the vrittis must diminish. It may be remembered that the vrittis are not to be annihilated completely; they are just to be diminished or weakened. It is like sleeping in a train. In that state one is aware of the coming and going of people, of the stoppages of the train, but there is no full awareness like that of the waking state. That is called diminished awareness. It can be achieved through various techniques of steadying the mind mentioned in the previous sutras.

When the fragmentary consciousness also fades away, the mind becomes as pure and clear as a crystal. It can be applied in toto to any object. It is samapatti. A piece of white chalk placed on a piece of coloured paper does not take the colour of that paper, but if you place a crystal there it will show in itself the colour of the piece of paper. This is because the crystal is absolutely pure. Similarly, there is a difference between a mind in samapatti and an ordinary mind. The moment the vrittis are removed from the mind, it starts to function like a crystal. This gives rise to purely objective consciousness of the object upon which the mind is cast.

When you practise trataka or meditation on an object like a shivalinga, the vrittis diminish slowly, and ultimately there is a sudden flash of consciousness when the mind fuses completely with the object. The three facets of the object such as name, form and meaning can be experienced separately. There are six types of fusion, called respectively savitarka, nirvitarka, savichara, nirvichara, ananda and asmita. They are the stages of fusion of your consciousness in relation to the object on which you are meditating and, finally, a time comes when the object vanishes. It should be remembered that it is only when the object disappears from consciousness that you have achieved something.

When there is fusion, the modifications of consciousness are almost annihilated from consciousness. This is ekagrata or one-pointedness. During that state, all the three things:

meditation, its object and its consciousness, become one. So long as one does not attain the state of samapatti, one is aware of these three things. There is simultaneous awareness of the three vrittis. In samapatti these three sorts of awareness fuse into one single consciousness, so that you do not see anything except the form. Only the form of meditation shines in that state.

Sutra 42: Savitarka samadhi

तत्र शब्दार्थज्ञानविकल्पैः संकीर्णा सवितर्का समापत्तिः ॥ ४२ ॥

Tatra śabdārthajñānavikalpaiḥ saṅkīrṇā
savitarkā samāpattiḥ

Tatra: there, in that state; *śabda*: word, sound: *artha*: true knowledge; *jñana*: reasoning; *vikalpaiḥ*: by alternation; *saṅkīrṇa*: mixed up, confused; *savitarkā*: with worded thinking; *samāpattiḥ*: complete absorption

In that state (of samadhi) on account of alternating consciousness between word, true knowledge and sense perception, the mixed state of mind is known as savitarka samapatti.

It should be remembered that samapatti, or samadhi, is not a particular state; it covers a whole range of awareness comprising a field of superconsciousness. The waking state can also be described as a field of consciousness, for in it are included several activities such as talking, walking, laughing, etc. In the same way, samapatti includes various states. As the samadhi becomes deeper and deeper, the aspirant goes into finer and finer realms of consciousness. The first state of the superconscious mind is called *savitarka*. In it the mind keeps moving between three things, namely: word, knowledge and sense perception. Thus our knowledge about an object is confused or mixed up.

When we think of a rose, we think of so many qualities: its colour, weight, smell, structure, and so on. Knowledge of these qualities is mixed up in our conception of the rose. This is the *savikalpa* state which is to be transcended in meditation. When the mind goes beyond these qualities and becomes one with the object without reference to particular qualities, it is the state of samadhi. In the first state, called savikalpa, there is a mixture of three elements, called shabda, artha and jnana. *Shabda* is the word – *vachaka*, that which indicates the object. The object proper is called *artha*. We know that the word shivalinga is one thing, while the object shivalinga is quite a different thing. Furthermore, the knowledge that arises in our mind while meditating upon the shivalinga is quite a different thing altogether; it is the pratyaya arising in our mind and is called *jnana*. All these three elements are necessary aspects of the process of concentration. In savitarka they are mixed up.

Sometimes there is simultaneous awareness of shabda, artha and jnana, and sometimes there is only awareness of them at one time. These two states keep on changing. If you are concentrating on a particular form, the form remains but the continuity of that awareness goes on changing. For example, sometimes you are aware of shivalinga, sometimes of mantra, sometimes of linga, etc. There should be a continuous awareness of a single factor but this does not happen and the elements get mixed up. This is because of *beeja* (seed). This seed has different layers; the outermost layer is just the husk, the innermost layer is really the essential part. Due to this seed, that is, impurities caused by past experience, the elements of knowledge become mixed.

Seed means a basis for the mind. It is the awareness of the support which the mind takes. When we meditate we first visualize the form; it is like taking off the outer layer. Then the deeper qualities can be visualized and, finally, the innermost layer can be visualized. Savitarka is the outermost layer of the seed and below it are the layers called nirvitarka, savichara and nirvichara. The sense consciousness is the outer layer of the seed. When it transcends pratyahara, dharana and dhyana, it transcends also savitarka samadhi and the other finer states. Ultimately it sees the finest entity, called drashta, or atman.

Without a seed, the consciousness cannot function. In yoga it is called pratyaya, basis. Then we need a symbol also, which is called linga. In savitarka they cannot be separated; they are mixed.

Those who are practising japa and meditation with mantra and form should remember that after having seen the form in meditation, the consciousness should alternate between shabda, artha and jnana. Shabda is a thought process in the form of words. It is mental argumentation. Jnana is inner sense perception and artha is the object such as shivalinga. Artha means the ultimate purpose, and that is very difficult. It is the real knowledge of the object.

By attaining samadhi through a particular symbol, you have complete control of the awareness of the object on which you are meditating. This is what happens in samyama, which includes the threefold processes called dharana, dhyana and samadhi. *Samyama* means holding the object completely in awareness and keeping the awareness of the object under full control.

The result of complete conception, absorption or fusion in different objects is different. It is absolutely meaningless to say that you get only one thing from meditating over different objects; for example, if you hold completely to the awareness of cotton, the result will be altogether different from that which you obtain when you do samyama on other objects such as physical strength, etc. During the process of samyama, the ultimate result which we obtain is artha but the purpose is there, although you may not know it in the beginning. The purpose has to be arrived at by separating it, and the separation takes place spontaneously.

In savitarka samadhi the awareness is free from imperfections. There is absolute peace and tranquillity. There are no alternating oscillations and waverings of the mind. There is another kind of samadhi which is called nirvitarka. It is important to note that there is already in us a fragment of achievement of the superconscious state, but that lasts only for one or two moments.

When you have an object for meditation, you must try to see the three aspects of the object separately. You should try to visualize them, alternating name, form and meaning. You should try to see your own awareness on the basis of those elements. Then you should try to see them as one. You should be aware of the name, form and meaning together. Ultimately you try to see them separately. It is one of the most important methods of dhyana.

This is a wonderful method of concentration. If you find it difficult to keep your consciousness alternating between the three states, you should practise only japa in which the word is inaudible. You first think about the word and also you produce the word; then you may add the form of the object. Then you should think of its various qualities. It is difficult to give a correct explanation of this state of mind but it is a wonderful method of mental control when you separate the three elements of consciousness and make them fuse into one again.

Sutra 43: Nirvitarka samadhi

स्मृतिपरिशुद्धौ स्वरूपशून्येवार्थमात्रनिर्भासा निर्वितर्का ॥ ४३ ॥

Smṛtipariśuddhau svarūpaśūnyevārthamātranirbhāsā nirvitarkā

Smṛti: memory; *pari*: complete; *śuddhau*: purification; *svarūpa*: one's own form; *śūnya*: devoid of; I: as if; *artha*: object, purpose; *mātra*: only; *nirbhāsā*: shining; *nirvitarkā*: without vitarka

After the clarification of memory, when the mind is as if devoid of self-awareness and the true knowledge of the object is alone shining within, that is nirvitarka.

Nirvitarka is the samadhi without argumentation, without a confusion of the three aspects of an object, namely name, form and meaning. In it there is neither the subjective awareness of the object, nor that of the word. Memory becomes absolutely free of past impressions and associations. Usually our memory is not clear; for us, memory constitutes the collection of past impressions. *Smriti* is an independent awareness on which the impressions are imbedded, and even if everything of the past is cleared up, the smriti remains. On the tablet of smriti there are past impressions which present themselves in deeper states. In the waking state, the reproduction is brought about by conscious thinking but in samadhi they come up on their own. Sometimes in this deeper state of consciousness, impressions of early childhood are seen but if all these impressions are cleared up, then memory does not disappear, because memory is different from the impressions.

It is as if the brain is different from the mind or thought. Similarly, the vritti called memory is different from past impressions. Smriti is awareness of one's own self. Smriti can be purified by different sadhanas and then it becomes swaroopashoonya-eva. It is a state of self-awareness and it appears as if everything has become void, but actually it is not void. The word eva is used to show that although you are not aware of the object, yet the object is there. That is, when the past impressions of the object, such as shivalinga are gone, you are not aware of the shivalinga and it appears as if your mind becomes absolutely devoid of the impressions of the shivalinga, but it is not so. The smriti does not become free of the impressions of the shivalinga, but the impressions permeate the entire structure of your awareness. Every part of it becomes filled up with the impressions of the shivalinga. In this state, the mind loses its subjective awareness.

Here the mind loses the knowledge of the object although the awareness and the knowledge are present in the mind. That is the peculiarity. You remember that you are concentrating on the shivalinga, then next there is only the shivalinga and you do not remember that you are concentrating on it. Again, there comes a time when the shivalinga is also seen, although the awareness that you are meditating is gone. The whole mind appears to have become completely void, but it is not actually so. Just as salt mixes completely and inseparably with water, in the same way, the form or awareness of the shivalinga fills the whole mind, although it cannot be known separately. It is because the mind is completely permeated with the memory of the object. This is known as *parishuddhi*, purification of memory. Thus purification of memory is the cause of *swaroopashoonya-eva*.

It is necessary to remember the subtle point that if the smriti is not pure, the mind will slip into blankness. If the smriti is purified, then the object such as the shivalinga will permeate the whole of the consciousness and become one with the state of mind. Mind and object will become one. The mind and the memory of the form become inseparable; memory does not exist separately. At that time there comes a momentary experience of void (shoonya). It is the state of laya in which the consciousness of memory of the object merges completely in the mind. For a moment the mind blinks and sleeps. In that sleeping state, the presentation of memory is not there.

In that state, true knowledge of the object shines within. This is the difference between nirvitarka samadhi and laya. In the former there is true knowledge; for example, the shivalinga has vanished and behind that you may see bright light. The true knowledge will appear: it is revealed to the aspirant. The difference between the inner and outer state is completely lost. In dream the experience is very intense, but in nirvitarka samadhi it is far more intense. You should be aware of the real knowledge or real form of the object of concentration, for otherwise you may be misled by your own mind. When you come to the nirvitarka state, you will have to know the real form of the symbol, whether it is a rose, or shivalinga. When true knowledge is to emerge in the nirvitarka state, the form is to be brought about once again and that form is not of Shiva, but of Shakti, because the subjectivity of the mind is lost. It is not the mind which thinks or dreams or sleeps. This state of mind is very definite because of the absence of memory and so you never remember the experiences of meditation because the normal consciousness is not functioning. For example, an ant is unable to see the elephant; to see it, the ant must grow in size. In the same way, the conscious mind is not allowed to penetrate the state of meditation. Thereafter a different state of mind takes charge of your awareness. The conscious purusha stops working and another purusha takes its place. This state continues up to a certain point, and there it stops. Then the third purusha comes and takes you further. Likewise you may progress through different planes of consciousness.

It is not even the mind which dreams, which remains aware of the dreams and remembers in the morning. This state of mind is a different state. If at all you have achieved this blessed state, it may not even be possible for you to remember it because of the absence of the same memory, because of the absence of the mind. That state of mind is different and this state of mind is different and unless you are able to bring that mind into operation here in this instance, you may not be able to remember what you have seen. If you remember the experience of meditation, samadhi, either you have not achieved meditation, or if at all you have achieved meditation, then your normal consciousness is of a very high order.

In this context we may quote one of the most misunderstood clauses of the *Garuda Purana*. It is usually recited when a family member dies. It talks about the hell and the heavens and the tortures in the kingdom of the Lord of Death. It says that after death the jiva is taken to various planes by various devatas, gods, but actually it is not about death at all. We should understand the Purana as talking about the transcending position of consciousness. Thus it should be understood that various purushas conduct the mind to deeper and deeper states of superconsciousness. This is because the conscious mind does not function in the nirvitarka state. So, to sum up, the nirvitarka state involves purification of smriti, which gives rise to true knowledge of the object of concentration.

Sutra 44: Other forms of samadhi

एतयैव सविचारा निर्विचारा च सूक्ष्मविषया व्याख्याता ॥ ४४ ॥

Etayaiva savichārā nirvichārā cha
sūkṣmaviṣayā vyākhyātā

Etaya: by this; *eva*: itself, alone; *savichāra*: samadhi with reflection; *nirvichāra*: samadhi without reflection; *cha*: and; *sūkṣmaviṣayā*: subtle objects; *vyākhyātā*: explained

By this explanation alone savichara samadhi, nirvichara samadhi and subtler stages of samadhi have been explained.

After nirvitarka there are four more stages, namely savichara, nirvichara, ananda and asmita. The words *sukshma vishaya* mean the subtle stages of samadhi: ananda and asmita samadhi, in which the object of fusion is bliss and awareness respectively. In the samadhi before savichara, the student is aware of an object, its name, form and qualities. These three either alternate with each other or the essential nature is perceived. In savichara the whole process is through reflection; there is no form present. This is difficult to explain. You must sit down quietly and meditate on Shiva or any object. The concentration is in the form of reflection, there is no word-thinking.

The process of reflection has no language but ordinary thinking always involves language; for example, when we think about geography, science, religion, history, or the present or future, we use language. Language is present during the states of savitarka and nirvitarka. When thought is devoid of language it is called vichara. In savichara there are three things: time, space and idea. There is a difference between Samkhya and yoga regarding meditation; that is to say, there are no states of dharana, dhyana and samadhi in Samkhya. In Samkhya the aspirant becomes aware of nirahara; he does not think of any object in terms of normal understanding, as in a language. He is only aware in the form of vision. It is a higher sadhana. In savichara the mind alternates in time, space and idea. There is no fusion. There is absolutely pure awareness of each separately. The time, space and idea are called vichara. It is not thinking. The definition of vichara is when the consciousness is flowing without the basis of language. It should be noted that meditation on form involves language; even one-pointedness is based on language. A student can transcend the basis of language only through having a sudden flash of vision.

In ananda samadhi there is the feeling of absolute peace and absolute bliss, but that bliss is not the state of your sense experience. When the particular argumentation of mind in the form of a particular language has been taken out, that becomes savichara. It is a deeper plane of consciousness. The consciousness in savichara is called *pratyabhijna*, which means illumined knowledge. It guides all our processes in the deeper states of consciousness. In nirvichara the space, time and idea are taken out but behind that something else remains, and that is called the essential nature of thought.

In asmita, the awareness is absolutely pure, there is no thought, there is no awareness of time or space, and there is complete understanding or realization of that awareness.

Sutra 45: Extent of samadhi

सूक्ष्मविषयत्वं चालिङ्गपर्यवसानम् ॥ ४५ ॥

Sūkṣmaviṣayatvaṃ chāliṅgaparyavasānam

Sūkṣmaviṣayatvaṃ: the subtle stages of samadhi; *cha*: and; *aliṅga*: prakriti; *paryavasānam*: extension

The stages of samadhi in respect to subtle objects extend up to prakriti.

The field of experience of ananda and asmita samadhi extends up to alinga. *Alinga* means the last state in which the three gunas are equally and completely mixed with each other. There are four stages of the gunas and the last one is called alinga. It is without a mark or any characteristic which differentiates it.

The first stage of the gunas is a particular stage called specific. The second stage is archetype, or non-specific. The third one is with mark and the fourth one is without mark. After meditation in savitarka, nirvitarka and asamprajnata, savichara, nirvichara and asamprajnata, ananda, asamprajnata and asmita asamprajnata, nirbeeja samadhi starts. Up to this point we have been discussing samadhi with seed. Sometimes it has a specific seed, a specific basis, such as Rama, Krishna or Shiva. The further you go, the archetype is present which is universal, beyond which there is a certain mark. A symbol might come to you, perhaps in the form of Christ, a cross, Shiva, or Aum, but that will be different from what you have already seen. It is merely with mark. Your consciousness is seen by you as a mark. In the fourth stage there is no mark; you cannot say where the consciousness is. There is first the awareness, therefore alinga is the fourth stage of the three gunas: sattwa, rajas and tamas.

In the first stage there is the combination of sattwa, rajas and tamas. In the second stage sattwa grows and rajas and tamas become subservient. In the third stage sattwa alone remains, and in the fourth stage sattwa, rajas and tamas are in equilibrium. When the three gunas are in equilibrium, then the alinga state is reached.

Sutra 46: Samadhi with seed

ता एव सबीजः समाधिः ॥ ४६ ॥

Tā eva sabījaḥ samādhiḥ

Tāh: those; *eva*: only; *sabījaḥ*: with seed; *samādhiḥ*: samadhi

Those (stages which have been explained before) are only samadhi with seed.

The object on which you are meditating is beeja, or seed. It forms the basis of support for the consciousness. Finally, when the consciousness becomes concentrated in the form of that beeja they become one, like salt and water, and the subjectivity of the mind is lost. The mind loses itself in the seed and vice versa but then there is a stage where even this consciousness should be eliminated. Asmita consciousness is the last, the highest stage of consciousness. In that state neither the consciousness nor the object of consciousness is lost, but they are in dependent existence with each other. There is no differentiation. After this, the awareness of asmita is to be eliminated. Thus, the consciousness as well as the seed is to be removed. It is just like evaporating the water from a mixture of salt and water. The very process of awareness is eliminated and this is difficult indeed.

The whole process from vitarka to asmita is sabeeja asamprajnata. There, the superconsciousness has a basis to rest upon. After this it is nirbeeja. The arrow is your personal consciousness going through the planes or lokas. In each loka you have savitarka and nirvitarka; that is, first there is development of the positive and then of the negative. First there is language for the basis of awareness, then it is in the form of reflection, and after that it is simple experience. There is no word, no idea, nothing. You do not know what it is; it is just awareness. It should be noted that there is a difference between samprajnata and sabeeja samadhi. Asamprajnata, nirbeeja and nirvikalpa are different stages of samadhi. They should no be confused or equated with one another.

Sutra 47: Then spiritual light dawns

निर्विचारवैशारद्येऽध्यात्मप्रसादः ॥ ४७ ॥

Nirvichāravaiśāradye'dhyātmaprasādaḥ

Nirvichāra: nirvichara samadhi; *vaiśāradye*: after becoming absolutely expert; *adhyātma*: spiritual; *prasādaḥ*: illumination, or purity

After becoming absolutely perfect in nirvichara samadhi the spiritual light dawns.

Nirvichara samadhi is the highest form of superconsciousness. This spiritual illumination comes to the mind in the last stage of nirvichara samadhi. After that there is an end of consciousness where intellectual functioning ceases completely. Hereafter a different consciousness overtakes the aspirant. It has been said in the form of stories in many puranas that after the death of the jiva he is conducted by different purushas to different planes, lokas or worlds. The concept of death here means the death of the intellect and not the death of the body.

There is a stage in spiritual meditation when the consciousness which is pervaded and permeated by intellectual consciousness completely dies out. In the same way, the intellectual consciousness gives rise to different kinds of consciousness. That stage is achieved by self-realized persons, perceivers of the self. That is a special instrument, a special form of consciousness, which is called *atmadrashta*. When the nirvichara stage is perfected, a different aspect of awareness is born. Those people who practise dhyana develop a different stage of awareness, about which it is said that it is the shadow that you see in trataka, when there is no consciousness about the world or about yourself.

That shadow, called *chhaya purusha*, is the last trace of your intellect, which is again replaced by something else. Black magicians can go as far as that. Through it, they play many wonders. Likewise siddhas who are endowed with psychic powers can play wonders, but they are ignorant of the higher fruits of existence. Their state of consciousness is the materialization of consciousness in the form of a shadow, where the principle of buddhi is eliminated.

Sutra 48: Cosmic experience

ऋतम्भरा तत्र प्रज्ञा ॥ ४८ ॥

Ṛtambharā tatra prajñā

Ṛtambharā: full of experience; *tatra*: there; *prajñā*: superconsciousness

There (at the borderline of nirvichara samadhi) the superconsciousness becomes full with cosmic experience.

Ritam and satyam are two words upon which the entire structure of Indian belief is laid. Faith and superstition are not the basis of Indian philosophy and religion, ritam and satyam are. Indian philosophers consider that this world and creation are a process of evolution, but they do not believe that this universe is only a manifestation of nature or matter. They consider that energy is the root cause of the universe.

Sat is subtler than energy; *sat* means existence. It has two aspects called ritam and satyam. *Satyam* is the relative aspect of creation and *ritam* is the absolute or cosmic aspect. Satyam is perceptible by the senses and understandable by the mind; in it there can be a change. It is interdependent, but ritam is not so; it is changeless. These are the two aspects of the entire universe. The world of planets and stars is satyam because it is relative, but the absolute, ritam, is beyond energy and change. Ritam is the ultimate truth beyond matter and energy. After nirvichara, the superconsciousness of the spiritual aspirant becomes full of ritam, absolute knowledge, where the senses do not work. It is like sound becoming silent when it attains the highest vibrations; when light attains the highest vibrations it becomes darkness. Likewise, when the inner experience attains the highest vibrations, it appears to be void.

This particular state of void, shoonya is vibrating at a very high rate and so it becomes still. It is not seen and so it is said to be cosmic – ritam. The creation of the universe began with ritam and satyam. Satyam ultimately becomes part of ritam. It is believed in Indian philosophy that creation is eternal; there is no creator, no destroyer. The universe was never created. Energy and matter were there in a different form a few million years ago. There can be no creator, nor a day of creation, because the universe cannot arise from nothing, and how can there be nothing? How can it give rise to anything? So Indian philosophy believes in no creator. As it is beginningless, the universe must be endless also. Matter and energy will be undergoing change in name and form, but this cosmic law can be understood only through spiritual consciousness.

Sutra 49: Characteristics of this experience

श्रुतानुमानप्रज्ञाभ्यामन्यविषया विशेषार्थत्वात् ॥ ४९ ॥

Śrutānumānaprajñābhyāmanyaviṣayā viśeṣārthatvāt

Śruta: heard; *anumāna*: inference; *prajñābhyām*: from the two types of consciousness; *anyaviṣaya*: another object; *viśeṣārthatvāt*: because of having a particular object

This knowledge is different from the knowledge acquired through testimony and inference because it has a special object.

Consciousness is of two types, lower and higher. The lower depends upon the senses for knowledge; that is, we cannot see or hear without eyes and ears. This is the shruta and anumana kind of knowledge. There are two ways of knowing higher consciousness; one is direct, as in Vedanta; the other is indirect. You hear about atman from the guru or from the scriptures. *Shruta* means the Vedas, because they were revealed. Through them, we know the supreme being and atman.

Anumana is inference. We can have knowledge about unperceivable things through inference. Through inference we know that there should be a creator of this world. The inference is based on theology, ontology and cosmology. Knowledge from inference and testimony differs from individual to individual. That is why there are clashes between individuals and nations, but realized people do not differ in the supreme knowledge. The sensations carried through the indriyas are different, but supreme knowledge is one.

The difference between the higher and lower consciousness is that the former sees things directly as they are, whereas the latter depends upon the senses, testimony and inference. Knowledge based on information, whether it is from a person or from a book, is not enough. This is indirect knowledge, a lower kind of knowledge. The second type is direct knowledge. It is not classical but actual. He who has seen the self cannot speak about it although he has direct knowledge of atman, because it is not a subject of speech and mind. The spiritual nature of consciousness can be known through self-experience. Lower consciousness has two phases, the indriyas or senses, and buddhi.

Sutra 50: Dynamic form of consciousness in samadhi

तज्जः संस्कारोऽन्यसंस्कारप्रतिबन्धी ॥ ५० ॥

Tajjaḥ saṃskāro'nyasaṃkārapratibandhī

Tajjaḥ: born of that; *saṃskārah*: dynamic consciousness; *anya*: of other; *saṃskāra*: dynamic consciousness; *pratibandhī*: that which prevents

Dynamic consciousness born of that (sabeeja samadhi) prevents other states of consciousness.

A samskara is a dynamic state of superconsciousness in the deeper layers of the seed (beeja) which can be awakened within the consciousness, for example, shivalinga is the seed or a symbol is the seed. Samskara is not a state of dormant consciousness, but a state of dynamic consciousness. In the highest stages of sabeeja samadhi the consciousness of beeja remains but the consciousness of other objects is eliminated. Even in ordinary life it is found that when one thought predominates in the mind, the others are subdued. Likewise, one samskara can prevent other samskaras. When the chitta is full of external awareness, such as seeing, hearing, feeling and so on, that is also a dynamic consciousness, and that is to be prevented. This can be done through pratyahara and dharana as well as dhyana. When the mind is not engaged or concentrated, various thoughts arise. This happens in the lower stages of sabeeja samadhi also, where there are visions as well as chitta vrittis. When ritambhara prajna arises, the highest state of sabeeja samadhi is attained. Then the other samskaras are not only prevented from arising but they are finished.

The three states, namely concentration, meditation and samadhi, together constitute samyama, which is complete mental control over the awareness of the object. Through samyama, other states of consciousness vanish but the seed remains. The seed, such as the shivalinga, is also called pratyaya. It is the basis for consciousness. This happens in asamprajnata in asmita. From asmita, the aspirant takes a plunge into nirbeeja samadhi.

Until now the consciousness was descending deeper and deeper, but it was not one with the drashta. After sabeeja samadhi, there is the ocean called oneness with the drashta. Two things should be remembered here. First, we must remove the misunderstanding that the spiritual path is a very short path. This is a mistake of enthusiastic students and teachers; it must be corrected. Secondly, there should be clear understanding through meditation on the concrete form of consciousness. The moment that an aspirant has transcended sagunopasana he can go in for nirgunopasana after ritambhara prajna, for example, in the case of Ramana Maharshi, who became a mukta from birth. He did not practise sadhana.

Certainly those who are not spiritually developed, who have no voluntary control over their mental functions, should first practise sagunopasana. According to yoga, this whole range of upasana is divided into two categories, namely, means and ends. Meditation is the means to samadhi, dharana a means to dhyana, pratyahara a means to dharana; in the various states of samadhi every lower state is a means to a higher state. Therefore, all these practices first break different patterns of consciousness and ultimately reach outside the range of prakriti.

Sutra 51: Then one attains samadhi without seed

तस्यापि निरोधे सर्वनिरोधान्निर्बीजः समाधिः ॥ ५१ ॥

Tasyāpi nirodhe sarvanirodhānnirbījaḥ samādhiḥ

Tasya: of that; *api*: also; *nirodha*: by blocking; *sarva*: all; *nirodhān*: by blocking; *nirbījaḥ*: seedless; *samādhiḥ*: samadhi

After blocking of even that due to blocking of all chitta vrittis, seedless samadhi is attained.

The seed has the quality of becoming many. It is to be burnt so that it does not divide and produce. Even this samskara of the seed in the form of purusha, Shiva, Aum, etc. will have to be eliminated. For that you need a different consciousness called ritambhara prajna and that does all the work. There is a different consciousness when the seed that is the basis of upasana is destroyed and unless it is eliminated, samadhi without seed cannot arise.

Whereas other samskaras multiply their effects, the ritambhara prajna gives rise to the seedless state. To see, to hear, to feel, etc. are all seeds of consciousness. Even the study of the *Yoga Sutras* is a samskara. It has multiplied like a seed and you will feel like reading the Upanishads, etc. However, in the final stage all samskaras are eliminated through ritambhara prajna such as the shivalinga, or Aum, etc. This is because the limits of the intellectual boundary are crossed and the aspirant attains a state of bliss. The form is finished.

That state of shoonya is not static, it is dynamic; it is a transcendental stillness. It appears void in the dynamic aspect only. The ultimate state is peaceful, yet dynamic. There is the light of purusha which illumines the whole consciousness. That particular light which was illuminating the objects is withdrawn; that is the only process. It is withdrawn from the outer world and goes inside, and while it goes inside, it keeps on illuminating the inner passages, the inner chambers of vitarka, vichara, ananda and asmita. It is very difficult to explain this. It is not possible to explain the exact nature of nirbeeja samadhi because one who knows it cannot express or convey it.

Chapter Two

Sadhana Pada

(55 sutras)

Sutra 1: Discipline for sadhana

तपःस्वाध्यायेश्वरप्रणिधानानि क्रियायोगः ॥ १ ॥

Tapaḥsvādhyāyeśvarapraṇidhānāni kriyāyogaḥ

Tapaḥ: austerity; *svādhyāya*: self-study of scriptures; *īshvara praṇidhāna*: surrender to God; *kriyā yoga*: practical yoga

Tapas, swadhyaya and Ishwara pranidhana constitute kriya yoga.

The word *tapas* literally means to burn, to create heat or to produce energy. Usually tapas is translated as asceticism, austerity or penance, but really it means a process which completely illuminates the imperfections, the dross of the inner personality. It is said in the *Bhagavad Gita* that the fire of jnana burns the entire stock of karma, which means it burns the accumulated karmas, the current karmas and the karmas that are already sacrificed. It is said by Nagarjuna that a seed when not burnt is capable of giving rise to many seeds and plants. In the same way, when the chitta is not freed from the samskaras, it is capable of producing many more samskaras, bodies and reincarnations. A roasted or burnt seed becomes incapable of reproducing. This process is tapas, which involves self-purification.

Sometimes the impurity is small and needs very little washing, but when avidya is too much, it becomes necessary to put the material impressions into a fire. Tapas is a sadhana which cleans an extremely dirty mind full of avidya. Tapas also means conservation of heat and energy. It even creates physical heat, as in pranayama. The word tapas is used here in a very high context. In sutra 32 of this chapter, the word tapas will occur. There it will be an elementary sadhana. In this sutra, tapas is not used in the sense of austerity or penance, but in the sense of generating a kind of heat. That heat can be generated by pranayama, hatha yoga, mudras and bandhas, by concentration of mind, by brahmacharya, or ahimsa. It is not only physical heat, it is also pranic heat, mental heat, or spiritual heat. It has a psychic nature.

When you want to eliminate a bad habit, the more you want to get rid of it, the more powerful it becomes. When you abandon it in the waking state, it comes in dreams. If it is stopped in dreams, it will express itself in your behaviour, otherwise it will give rise to disease. This particular habit has got to be destroyed at its psychic root, not at the conscious level only. The samskara or complex must also be eliminated. For that, a kind of psychic activity such as pranayama or ahimsa, which will uproot it even from the layers of the subconscious, is required. The word tapas should be understood in this sense.

In the same way, the word swadhyaya needs an explanation. Etymologically it means one's own analysis, or study, but it is used for studying scriptures such as the *Bhagavad Gita*, or the Bible. That is not the meaning of swadhyaya in this sutra, it is the meaning in sutra 32. Here it means trying to perceive your own self in different perspectives. When you look at your nose or teeth in the mirror, it is called adhyaya of your own face; that is, detailed study. Likewise, *swadhyaya* means the detailed study of your own self, which includes study of the entire structure of your personality, which includes the physical, mental, emotional and spiritual aspects. In kriya yoga, the different practices lead to perception of the self. It is the process of seeing your own consciousness. If you are trying to visualize a psychic smell, you perceive yourself in the form of smell. This is swadhyaya, wherein you are looking at your own consciousness.

Thus, in this sutra the word swadhyaya does not mean the study of scriptures or doing japa. Rishi Patanjali uses the same word in different places but with different meanings.

It is the same with *Ishwara pranidhana*. Usually it means surrender to God, but here it means placing completely in innermost awareness, which means placing your consciousness completely or fusing it completely in inner awareness. Ishwara is inner awareness. It is not a personal self anywhere outside. It is within us, and in kriya yoga you have the kriya in which the mind is placed completely at the disposal of the inner self.

Kriya yoga means practical yoga, yoga with practical techniques. It involves acts of self-purification, self-observation and evolving self-awareness. These three acts constitute kriya yoga. It may also be explained as certain kriyas producing heat and conserving heat, which involves awareness of the self, and kriyas by which your mind is placed at the disposal of your inner awareness. Kriya yoga is one of the methods of raja yoga. Since it is not customary to write anything about kriya yoga, the rishi has given just one sutra to it.

Sutra 2: Why discipline?

समाधिभावनार्थः क्लेशतनूकरणार्थश्च ॥ २ ॥

Samādhibhāvanārthaḥ kleśatanūkaraṇārthaścha

Samādhi: samadhi; *bhavānārthaḥ*: for developing the state of; *kleśa*: cause of afflictions; *tanu*: thin; *karaṇārtha*: for making; *cha*: and

For developing the consciousness of samadhi and for the purpose of thinning out the cause of afflictions (kriya yoga is practised).

Kriya yoga is to be practised with the purpose of developing samadhi and for thinning out the kleshas. Samadhi need not be discussed now. It is one purpose of kriya yoga. The second purpose is to overcome the kleshas.

The causes of afflictions are gradually diminished and for this purpose kriya yoga is to be practised. These are the twofold purposes of kriya yoga. It appears that by the practice of kriya yoga an emotional state of samadhi, called trance, is attained. This samadhi is completely different in that the bhakta develops an emotional trance-like state by intense bhakti or singing devotional songs. It is also a state of fusion, but the fusion is sublimation on an emotional level.

Maybe by kriya yoga the physical, psychic and emotional bodies are largely modified. As a result of that, the entire structure of samadhi is on a different level. By kriya yoga the kleshas are removed and thereby the higher state of samadhi becomes easier.

Sutra 3: Causes of pain

अविद्यास्मितारागद्वेषाभिनिवेशाः क्लेशाः ॥ ३ ॥

Avidyāsmitārāgadveṣābhiniveśāḥ kleśāḥ

Avidyā: ignorance; *asmitā*: I-feeling; *rāga*: liking; *dveṣa*: repulsion, dislike; *abhiniveśāḥ*: fear of death; *kleśāḥ*: afflictions

Ignorance, I-feeling, liking, disliking and fear of death are the pains.

In the first chapter, the chitta vrittis were divided into painful and painless types. The word klesha was used there and it was said that klesha is removed by samadhi. Now the rishi gives the details of the kleshas. Because of materialistic tendencies, man thinks that selfish miseries are the only miseries. Philosophers and psychologists have tried to discover the basis of pain and they have found that pain is not rooted in the present mind but far back in the past.

Klesha is a kind of agony which is inside our very being. Everyone feels subconscious pain, but our superficial daily activities do not allow us to be aware of it, otherwise we would see pain in all its vividness. It is difficult to understand that the outer man is different from the inner man. In depth psychology it is said that there are different phases of human life, and that the inner self behaves in a different way altogether. While man speaks truth outwardly, he lies inwardly. The movements of the outer man and the inner man are opposite. The student of yoga should know about depth psychology, which tells us that real happiness is not skin-deep. The inner life may be very different from the outer life, so we cannot judge from the outer life. Thus we see that even a rich and educated person can be extremely unhappy within, whereas a poor person having no wealth may have happiness inside. He may be in bliss. Patanjali's explanation of the kleshas must be viewed from the point of view of depth psychology.

We are usually not aware of the fear of death but it is there in the subconscious. There is fear when one has to undergo an operation. This fear is *abhinivesha*, fear of death. It is a reflex action, like a person moving away automatically when a car suddenly comes. He is not aware of death but he gets out of the way. The fear of death is there at the root. Even animals have kleshas.

Sutra 4: Avidya is the root cause

अविद्याक्षेत्रमुत्तरेषां प्रसुप्ततनुविच्छिन्नोदाराणाम् ॥ ४ ॥

Avidyākṣetramuttareṣāṃ prasuptatanuvichchhinnodārāṇām

Avidyā: avidya; *kṣetram*: field; *uttareṣāṃ*: of the following; *prasupta*: dormant; *tanu*: thin; *vichchhinna*: scattered; *udārāṇām*: fully operated, expanded

Avidya is the field of the following ones (kleshas) in the states of dormant, thin, scattered or expanded.

The expression of the kleshas is not only pain, it is in the behaviour of man. Ambition and effort for success means klesha. In this context the word klesha is not individualistic; it is collective. It is due to the compulsion of klesha that an individual or a whole nation may set itself to work for achieving new goals. To avoid the unpleasant conditions of life is one of the compulsions of klesha. Animals do not know this but they also behave instinctively and naturally. If you analyze the psychology of change of behaviour during different seasons under different conditions, you will know that those changes have the kleshas for their basis. When it is hot summer we want fans and air-conditioning and we bathe many times a day; when it is winter we do not bathe properly and we do not think of throwing off our clothes. This looks completely natural, but if only you could analyze the psychology of your changed behaviour you would know it is not due to winter; behind it is the philosophy of klesha. We do not like to be tortured on account of the biting winter, we do not want to suffer pain. This is not on the surface, but it is in the background.

Avidya is the source of asmita, raga, dwesha and abhinivesha. Just as the seed is the cause of the whole tree, so avidya is the source of the other four kleshas. The kleshas have four states of expression. They may be dormant, when you cannot perceive them; sometimes they become thin and they are experienced in mild fashion. In the scattered condition they give rise to an oscillating state; otherwise they may be fully expressed. These various stages of the kleshas are observed in various people at different times. Usually we are never free from them. Except in the case of a great yogi who overcomes them, the kleshas are found in other persons. So long as they are there, it is impossible to realize the self.

Avidya is the parent of all. The whole scene is in a series: from avidya, asmita is born; from asmita, raga; from raga, dwesha; and from dwesha, abhinivesha. The root cause of all these is avidya, hence it must be properly understood. If one is able to control avidya, one will easily control all the other kleshas.

The whole process of uprooting avidya must start from the upper end. It is a process of involution. The process of evolution is from abhinivesha to dwesha, then to asmita, then to avidya and then to vidya or enlightenment.

Sutra 5: (i) Avidya – ignorance

अनित्याशुचिदुःखानात्मसु नित्यशुचिसुखात्मख्यातिरविद्या ॥ ५ ॥

Anityāśuchiduḥkhānātmasu
nityaśuchisukhātmakhyātiravidyā

Anitya: not eternal; *aśuchi*: impure; *duḥkha*: pain; *anātmasu*: non-atman; *nitya*: eternal; *śuchi*: pure; *sukha*: happiness; *ātma*: self; *khyāti*: knowledge; *avidyā*: avidya

Avidya is to mistake the non-eternal, impure, evil and noumenon for the eternal, pure, good and atman (respectively).

This sutra gives the most classical definition of avidya. Ordinarily, *avidya* means ignorance but in this sutra it means something different. It is mistaking the above-named things for altogether different things. It is an error in spiritual perception. When a rope is mistaken for a snake, the form of your consciousness at that time is avidya. Avidya is a kind of psychosis, not a neurosis. It causes duality through which name and form are fabricated. In the *Bhagavad Gita* it is said that under the influence of avidya, dharma is mistaken for adharma, and vice versa. In Vedanta it is said that the body, the senses and buddhi have their limitations; beyond them there is one consciousness. Consciousness is pure, while the base is impure. Consciousness is eternal, ananda, while the base is non-eternal and unhappy. Therefore, avidya should be indifferent to the inner atman, for avidya is to identify with the body.

Avidya is the divine illusion, a kind of veil, a morphic dose, a defect of psychic vision. We misunderstand our relations with people due to avidya, just as we mistake a rope for a snake. The error conditions our brain and thoughts.

Avidya is a mistaken idea which has come with the jivatman from the very beginning. Its end marks the beginning of enlightenment. This is possible only with a complete distinction between body and consciousness, but this is very difficult. We cannot separate our consciousness from buddhi even in meditation. Even intellectually it is impossible, but actually the body is different from atman, from mind, from consciousness. Only in deep meditation can we see them as two. At present, matter and energy appear to be one in us. Intellectually we may consider them as two, but we cannot experience them as two because of avidya. We do not understand the essence of things for we know things only superficially; for example, a coconut. We can properly understand the essence only through viveka.

In Indian mythology there is a bird called hamsa which can separate milk from water. This is a process of viveka which leads you away from avidya towards vidya. The village women throw away the husk and keep the grain but before that they have to separate the two; that is, the grain from the husk. This is viveka. Avidya is a negative aspect; it is an absence of a positive state. Just as we do not have to fight with darkness in order to remove it – darkness can be removed by light. In the same way, avidya is removed by viveka; that is enlightenment. Enlightenment is of two types – temporary and permanent. Viveka is the former type of enlightenment through which we can distinguish between the body and atman. Avidya is called maya in Vedanta. In a cosmic context it is maya; in an individual context it is avidya. The mistaken notion of avidya can arise only on a positive basis, and that basis is Brahman.

Sutra 6: (ii) Asmita – 'I-feeling'

दृग्दर्शनशक्त्योरेकात्मतेवास्मिता ॥ ६ ॥

Dṛgdarśanaśaktyorekātmatevāsmitā

Dṛg: purusha, power of consciousness, power to see; *darśana*: that which is seen, cognition; *śaktyoh*: of the two powers; *ekātmatā*: identity; *iva*: as if; *asmitā*: I-feeling

Asmita is the identity as it were of the purusha with the buddhi.

The awareness of 'I am' is mixed with existence, with the body, actions and mind. It is as if a prince in the garb of a beggar is identifying with the role he is playing. This is asmita. When the inner consciousness, representing the highest truth in man, asserts itself through the medium of the body, buddhi and the senses, it is asmita. It has different stages. In the case of a primitive person with an underdeveloped intellect, asmita is rooted in identification with the body. An intellectually developed person identifies with the higher functions of the mind.

So, asmita is a consciousness which identifies the purusha with its vehicle; for example, when we say the bus is coming, we really mean the bus is being driven by a driver. Buddhi is the vehicle and so are the senses. The atman or purusha does the work of cognition. The power of seeing, thinking and hearing belongs to purusha, but this power is transmitted to the buddhi and senses. This conception of blending together is called asmita. It is the shakti, the power of purusha, which does the thinking, the seeing, etc., but this is shifted to the vehicle and it appears as if the eyes are seeing, etc.

When the purusha is realized, then there is no identification of the purusha with the body or with the intellect, but we are not aware of this fact, and this very non-awareness is called asmita.

It is said very clearly in the *Kenopanishad* that it is the power of the self (atma) by which the ears hear, the eyes see, the pranas move and the mind thinks. The mind does not know the atman but it knows everything only through the atman. These mantras of the *Kenopanishad* clearly indicate the distinction between the power of cognition (*drigshakti*) and its vehicle (*darshanashakti*).

The power of seeing cannot be realized even through reading philosophy or through hearing great scholars, etc. Even the philosophers and thinkers identify the purusha with the body and buddhi in actual experience, so it is not possible to overcome asmita through the intellect. It can only be done through meditation. It happens in meditation that something comes out of you and you see it. Ramana Maharshi had this kind of experience at a very young age. He saw his own dead body in meditation, and he also saw that he was observing his own dead body. So there were three persons – the dead body, the seer of the dead body, and the seer of the seer. So asmita is the blending together of this twofold or threefold principle. Most of us are in asmita and therefore it is said in this sutra that this particular aspect of asmita is nothing but 'I am'. This 'I am' is the identification of atman with the lower principles.

There is a story about Indra and Virochana, who were respectively the kings of the gods and the rakshasas (demons). Both of them went to Prajapati to receive instruction. He told them the two great instructions, namely, *aham Brahmasmi* (I am Brahman) and *tatvamasi* (thou art that). Virochana mistook aham for his body and was ultimately destroyed because of asmita. Indra meditated upon the real meaning and became happy. Thus, if you are able to go higher in meditation, crossing avidya, you can realize the real nature of purusha. Then asmita is transcended.

This is possible by two methods: one is the powerful but difficult method of dhyana, the other is the analytical method of the jnana yogis, which was employed by Indra but that method requires a purification of the heart and the intellect. Thus asmita, which is an offshoot of avidya, can be overcome.

Sutra 7: (iii) Raga

सुखानुशयी रागः ॥ ७ ॥

Sukhānuśayī rāgaḥ

Sukha: pleasure; *anuśayī*: accompanying; *rāgaḥ*: liking

Raga is the liking accompanying pleasure.

Sutra 8: (iv) Dwesha

दुःखानुशयी द्वेषः ॥ ८ ॥

Duḥkhānuśayī dveṣaḥ

Duḥkha: pain; *anuśayī*: accompanying; *dveṣaḥ*: repulsion

Dwesha is the repulsion accompanying pain.

Whenever there is an object of pleasure and the mind runs after it, wishing to have the pleasurable experience again and again, this is called *raga*. This is not very difficult to eliminate; one can eliminate it from one's personality with a little jerk, given either by nature or created by one's own self. *Dwesha* is the opposite of raga. Both of them bind innumerable persons and things, either positively or negatively. They are definite conditions of our mind and that conditioning is done on the basis of a sense of happiness or repulsion.

Raga and dwesha bind us down to the lower levels of consciousness. So long as they are there the mind cannot be raised to spiritual heights. It should be remembered that they are the two sides of the same coin. They are the twofold expression of an inner raga. Liking for one thing involves repulsion for something else, so they are not the opposite of each other, but are the two sides of the mind. Dwesha should be removed first and then raga will also go. It is found that even the spiritual aspirant has raga and dwesha. It is dwesha which is a more powerful binding force. It is a great hindrance. When dwesha is removed, meditation becomes deeper and then raga can be given up. It is said that man is affected more by dwesha than by raga, therefore, one should get rid of hate.

Sutra 9: (v) Abhinivesha – clinging to life

स्वरसवाही विदुषोऽपि तथारूढोऽभिनिवेशः ॥ ९ ॥

Svarasavāhī viduṣo'pi tathārūḍho'bhiniveśaḥ

Svarasavāhī: substained by its own force; *viduṣah*: of the learned; *api*: even; *thatā*: like that; *rūḍhah*: dominating; *abhiniveśaḥ*: fear of death, clinging to life

Abhinivesha is the desire for life sustained by its own force which dominates even the learned.

Even learned people fear death. They have an equally strong desire for life. This is true of the philosopher, the thinker and the layman. It can be seen in everybody, therefore, it is called *svarasavahi*; it is a natural force inherent in everyone. It is associated with each incarnation. *Vidushah* means learned or wise, and they also are not free from it. In childhood it is dormant. When we grow older and see others dying, it becomes an alternating factor. It may crop up some time or other. This happens between the ages of thirty-five and forty-five and becomes strong during the later part of life. The fear of death increases. It should be remembered that this is one of the most dominant kleshas.

The process of involution is exactly the opposite of the process of evolution. It starts with abhinivesha, then dwesha, then raga, then asmita, then avidya and lastly vidya. This is the way to go back. While overcoming the kleshas, one should start with abhinivesha and go up to avidya.

Abhinivesha is a universal truth. You will find it in an ordinary creature, an insect, a monkey or a bird, among people rich and poor, literate and illiterate. You will find this klesha in latent, dormant or active condition. It is latent in sannyasins. This klesha is on the verge of extinction in those who have attained viveka, but in most people you will find it in a most active condition, so much so that if anyone is suffering from disease, everyone will be in a panic. This panic is due to abhinivesha.

In the Indian scriptures it is said that this abhinivesha is due to attachment to the body. If attachment is reduced from an active state to a potential state, then fear of death can be reduced to a minimum.

Sutra 10: Kleshas can be reduced

ते प्रतिप्रसवहेयाः सूक्ष्माः ॥ १० ॥

Te pratiprasavaheyāḥ sūkṣmāḥ

Te: they (kleshas); *pratiprasavaḥ*: involution; *heyāḥ*: reducible; *sūkṣmāḥ*: subtle

Those kleshas are reducible by involution when they are subtle.

Sutra 11: By meditation

ध्यानहेयास्तद्वृत्तयः ॥ ११ ॥

Dhyānaheyāstadvṛttayaḥ

Dhyāna: meditation; *heyāh*: reducible; *tadvṛttayaḥ*: their modification

The modifications of the kleshas are reducible through meditation.

This eleventh sutra should have come before the tenth one. The five kleshas have four stages each, namely latent, attenuated, alternating and active. This happens like a stream coming out of a mountain and gradually becoming larger and larger. When a river merges in the ocean, it is very big. The kleshas also grow in their force, like a river. Thus in the beginning the kleshas are latent but slowly they become more and more active.

One can understand these kleshas by just watching one's mind. They are not only in the subconscious but are also found in the conscious mind. From their active state they should be brought down to the alternating state, from there to the attenuated state and, ultimately, to the latent state. First the attenuated form is to be reduced to the inactive condition. This is very important and therefore it should be done first.

We cannot see the stages of the different kleshas in the conscious and subconscious levels of the mind. All of them can be brought to the latent form from the attenuated form. Thus, by meditating upon the various stages of the kleshas, they can ultimately be annihilated. This includes the evolutionary process as well as the involutionary process. From avidya to abhinivesha is the evolutionary process, while from abhinivesha to avidya is the involutionary process. There are various stages in both the processes, such as subtle, active and so on.

We cannot see the kleshas unless we are very careful. For example, you may say that you have no fear of death, but that is not true because it is said that only after attaining dharmamegha samadhi are the seeds completely burned, not before. So, until kaivalya there is every possibility that the seeds of the kleshas may again become active. A spiritual aspirant will find that for many years the vrittis do not trouble him and he finds himself at ease for a long time. Sometimes he thinks that he has finished with every samskara and klesha, but suddenly one day he finds that he is failing unexpectedly. That unexpected failure is due to the presence of the seed of the kleshas in his mind.

As you know, everything has three states; it is capable of production but not producing, which is called the latent state; when it produces, it is called the active state; when the seed becomes incapable of producing anything, it is called scorched, finished. In order to scorch the seed of the kleshas, one must understand the whole involutionary process in action, not merely intellectually, because here the abhinivesha is to be resolved back to dwesha. These two are to be resolved back to raga, these three to asmita, and ultimately these four are to be resolved back to avidya.

Thus the aspirant has to cut the entire tree of the kleshas from top to bottom, but the strange thing about this tree is that its bottom is at the top and its top is at the bottom. This process is not of the intellect. For this, the entire yoga discipline, including yama, niyama and kriya, will have to be used. Dhyana for reducing the manifestations of the kleshas includes observation. You should be able to observe the kleshas by a process of dhyana in which you not only meditate on the ishta, but are able to see the different phases of mental phenomena taking place within yourself. In the practice of antar mouna, you will find these active vrittis coming; you have to suppress them. When you practise observation in this way, then you should observe all the thoughts, good and bad. When the kleshas are brought down to a latent condition, the aspirant should start the process of viveka, the rational method of raja yoga, or the method of kriya yoga. If you apply viveka when the kleshas are active, viveka may fail, because viveka needs certain mental preparation.

This dhyana is not one-pointedness but it is antar mouna, or observation of the active modification of the kleshas. By close observation, the active vrittis go back to the attenuated state, and then to the subtle state; therefore, you will find spiritual aspirants who practise meditation become calmer.

Thus the mischievous, restless mind can be made peaceful through meditation and kriya yoga. This is not because the person has become free of vasanas, but because the kleshas are subdued. Therefore, the aspirant is peaceful and tranquil. Through meditation one overcomes the tensions created by the kleshas.

Viveka should be introduced when this has taken place. By a rational approach, the cause of the kleshas should be found out and removed. One may find that one has attachment to one's mother, or son; perhaps one wants to achieve great success in some field. Finding the cause in this way, one should try to remove it by dwelling upon it, but this is very difficult. Kriya yoga can be used with advantage here.

If the process of finding out the cause is started in the very beginning through jnana yoga, then it is a good intellectual process. You will have complete knowledge, but it is very rare. So, a way is shown in the tenth sutra. The earnest aspirant should retire into seclusion for some time in order to see the seeds of the kleshas in their manifested form. Thus he can overcome or eliminate the kleshas. Through going into seclusion and coming back to society once again, the kleshas can be eliminated. Then one should apply viveka so that the seeds are completely scorched.

The kleshas in their subtle form are absolutely psychic. They are embedded in our life. The process of eliminating them is twofold, namely, dhyana and viveka. The former is a method of raja yoga, the latter of jnana yoga. Side by side, karma and bhakti yoga will also have to be practised because sometimes the explosion of the pressure is so great that it will catch you unaware. You may not be able to go back to seclusion once more, so karma and bhakti yoga will be of tremendous help. They are the lifebelts for one who wants to plunge into the sea of self-realization. It is very difficult to observe the subtle kleshas and to find out whether you have them, because they are in your inner nature. It will be said in a later sutra that these obstructions or hindrances must be removed.

Sutra 12: Karmashaya and reincarnation

क्लेशमूलः कर्माशयो दृष्टादृष्टजन्मवेदनीयः ॥ १२ ॥

Kleśamūlaḥ karmāśayo dṛṣṭādṛṣṭajanmavedanīyaḥ

Kleśa: affliction; *mūlaḥ*: root; *karma*: action; *āśayo*: reservoir; *dṛṣṭa*: seen, present; *adṛṣṭa*: not seen, future; *janma*: birth; *vedanīyaḥ*: to be experienced

This storehouse of karmas which is the root cause of afflictions is to be experienced in the present and future births.

In this sutra there is a reference to the laws of karma and reincarnation. It is said that in the past, present and future births you can see the afflictions. It means that one's karmas are caused by the afflictions and with cessation of the karmas the possibility is finished, but so long as the afflictions are there, they keep on giving experiences in the present and in future births. This is because every individual has to undergo the effects of past karmas. If the karmas are to be annihilated, it becomes essential for one to go back to their source, namely, the fivefold afflictions. It is a two-way process; the karmas cause kleshas and the kleshas give rise to fresh karmas. With the fresh karmas, one accumulates fresh samskaras and then those samskaras once again strengthen the cause of afflictions.

Sutra 13: Fruits of karmashaya

सति मूले तद्विपाको जात्यायुर्भोगाः ॥ १३ ॥

Sati mūle tadvipāko jātyāyurbhogāḥ

Sati mūle: so long as the root is there; *tat*: it; *vipākah*: ripening; *jāti*: birth, class; *āyuh*: span of life; *bhogāḥ*: experience

So long as the root of karmashaya is there, it ripens and gives birth and class, span of life and experience.

So long as the root is there, the tree should flourish and if the tree is not disturbed, then it must also ripen. This life is the tree and the afflictions are its roots. If the root is cut, that is, the fivefold afflictions are won over, naturally this great tree of life would become lifeless. It would not produce any fruit, and life is nothing but birth, span of life and different experiences. The experiences are of three kinds, namely enjoyable, painful and mixed. The span of life may be long or short. Birth in a particular country, society or family is called *jati*. All these three things are the fruits of the karmashaya.

As every fruit is connected with the tree and every tree with the roots, so birth, etc. are connected with life, which is the result of the past karmas. Similarly, karmashaya is dependent on the roots of afflictions. If the fruiting is to be stopped, then the tree must be destroyed and for this the roots, that is, the afflictions, must be cut out. Those who know the theory of reincarnation have said that whatever work we do leaves behind an impression. The stock of these impressions is called karmashaya.

Students of physiology understand the different actions of the brain very well and they tell us that we are able to remember our past because of the past impressions stored in the brain. The impressions are not lost and they give rise to memory. Thus, any activity done by the body is recorded. This karmashaya may be called a microcosmic film of past actions; sometimes it comes onto the screen and sometimes it remains underground.

Karmashaya has three divisions. The first is the accumulated impressions and samskaras, called impressions in stock. The second is the storehouse from which a regular supply is made to give rise to new karmas. This is the present karma; in the course of time it is transferred to the first division. The third division includes the impressions which are expressed in life and go out from the stock of impressions. All these are known as *prarabdha*, destiny. Its fruits are experienced in the present and future births. Whatever acts we do now are called current karmas. The impressions are added to the store of karmashaya and from it new karmas arise.

These three divisions of karmashaya are part of the causal body, known in Vedanta as karana sharira. This is one of the subtle vehicles of consciousness which is beyond the manomaya kosha. This karana sharira finds manifestation in the present and future life. For example, a farmer goes to his seed house and takes out a bag of seeds that is required. This is the first division of karmashaya. Then he goes out to the field and sows the seeds. That sowing is the present karma. After a few months he harvests his crop; that is called *vipaka*, fructification or ripening. After reaping the harvest, a part of it is again stored in the seed house; it is the same with karma. Thus karmashaya is the sleeping place of karmas. Here the karmas remain waiting to produce their effects, but they are in a latent condition.

From this theory, we can logically understand the process of reincarnation. It would be illogical to believe that the impressions of the karmas are destroyed with the death of the body. It is absurd and impossible to postulate a cause without an effect, or an effect without a cause. According to the theory of transmigration, it is not the body which transmigrates, it is not even the mind; it is only the impressions of our past acts that transmigrate. It is the sleeping place of karmas which moves from one body to another, and this is called *karana sharira* in Vedanta. It is not a physical thing. We must assume something continues even after the dead body is burned or buried, and it is nothing but the karana sharira. It is rooted in the afflictions. You cannot merely cut down a tree and destroy it; its roots must be destroyed. So, not the body but the karana sharira and especially its roots, that is, the afflictions, should be removed.

So long as there are afflictions, there will be karmashaya, which will certainly produce effects. In order to know that there is reincarnation, there are only two methods. One is to know about the practices of yoga, especially the psychic powers. The other method is logical epistemology and the impartial analysis of the natural laws of cause and effect.

Sutra 14: Fruits depend on past merits

ते ह्लादपरितापफलाः पुण्यापुण्यहेतुत्वात् ॥ १४ ॥

Te hlādaparitāpaphalāḥ puṇyāpuṇyahetutvāt

Te: they; *hlāda*: joy; *paritāpa*: sorrow; *phalāḥ*: fruits; *puṇya*: merit; *apuṇya*: demerit; *hetutvāt*: on account of

They (birth, etc.) have happiness or sorrow as their fruits depending upon merit or demerit.

We enjoy two kinds of fruits of the past karma according to whether it involved merit or demerit. Merit gives rise to joy and happiness; demerit gives rise to suffering. It may be expressed in birth, or span of life, or the various experiences. Happiness and suffering are not only dependent upon financial and social conditions. Happiness and suffering depend upon the kind of acts which were done in the past. If it was an act of merit, it will give rise to happiness, otherwise it will cause misery.

It is not necessary to decide what is merit, *punya* or virtue, and what is demerit, *apunya* or vice. Orthodox religion views it as understood and does not tell you the right and wrong side of virtue and vice. We should understand them in a scientific way, in conformity with the universal moral law. This law is universal in action and in application. The effects of karma are mathematically obtained, and thus from the past actions we get various fruits in the form of birth, span of life and experiences, which may be enjoyable or distressing.

Just as the quality of a photograph depends upon the type of paper it is printed on, the kind of exposure, etc., similarly, our experiences depend upon our past actions, good or bad.

Sutra 15: Pleasure and pain are both painful

परिणामतापसंस्कारदुःखैर्गुणवृत्तिविरोधाच्च दुःखमेव सर्वं विवेकिनः ॥ १५ ॥

Pariṇāmatāpasaṃskāraduḥkhairguṇavṛttivirodhāchcha duḥkhameva sarvaṃ vivekinaḥ

Pariṇāma: result, consequence; *tāpa*: acute suffering; *saṃskāra*: impression; *duḥkhaih*: by these three pains; *guṇa*: (three) gunas; *vṛtti*: modification of mind; *virodhāt*: on account of, opposing; *cha*: and; *duḥkham*: pain; *eva*: only; *sarvaṃ*: all; *vivekinaḥ*: those who have discrimination

In the case of one who has discrimination (viveka), all is painful because of pains due to change, acute suffering, samskaras, and also due to gunas and vrittis in opposition.

For one who has developed discrimination, who has analyzed life thoroughly, who is able to know truth and untruth and the complete difference between light and darkness, everything in life is painful, even so-called happiness, such as success, position, power and so on. The logic behind this is that every action is always accompanied by three things: change, misery and impression. For example, a person may acquire a large property. He may look happy, but in the deep layers of his mind there will be acute anxiety. Thus anything that is enjoyable, according to us, is painful in the ultimate analysis. Pain is at the bottom, psychic pain.

The first pain is change (*parinama*). For example, milk becomes curd, life changes into death, and so on. The second is acute anxiety (*tapa*). An achievement, success, love, etc. are all found to give rise to anxiety at some time or another. Unfair dealings, illegal business, etc. cause anxiety. The third factor is *samskara*, or habit. We become so used to happiness and luxury that we are afraid of losing it. One becomes a slave to circumstances and habits, and that gives rise to pain.

Property and wealth can become the cause of anxiety because one is afraid of losing the property and wealth. Psychiatrists do not usually understand this and they go on enquiring about petty matters which may not be the real cause of anxiety. One should go to the very root of the anxiety and only then can it be removed. It should be understood that everything is painful at the bottom, if not on the surface. The second point is that there is always a conflict between the three gunas and the mental tendency. This must be properly understood.

For example, I want to relax; I do not want to work. This is the demand of tamo guna, but if I have to feed my wife and children, I have to work. This gives rise to conflict. The gunas compel me to do one thing when I would like to do an altogether different thing. Thus there is conflict between the gunas and our mental tendencies: they never agree. So long as there is this disagreement, there will be pain. This is true of intelligent, sensitive people. There is always a conflict at the conscious or subconscious level. Thus everything in life is painful in essence. You may not like your job but you have to do it. You may desire a change, which may not come; this gives rise to pain. Even great and learned people have mental conflicts. They may read and learn the scriptures, philosophy, religion or science, but their minds are not out of conflict.

Even a spiritual aspirant is not free from conflict. His mind may wish to have a deeper sadhana or a different sadhana; it feels dull. He wants to follow different people, so there is conflict. Conflict in our personality proves that everything in the world that we experience is full of pain, as described in the next sutra.

Sutra 16: Future pain avoidable

हेयं दुःखमनागतम् ॥ १६ ॥

Heyaṃ duḥkhamanāgatam

Heyaṃ: to be avoided; *duḥkham*: misery; *anāgatam*: future

Suffering which has not yet come should be avoided.

Suffering should be avoided, and we can avoid what has yet to come. The present suffering has to be undergone and finished with. According to the law of karma, the present suffering which has become ripe cannot be set aside. It must be finished with through experiencing it, but future pain and misery must be avoided. So long as one has a body, one has to suffer but so far as the future is concerned, it can be changed. For example, the harvest you are reaping cannot be changed, but you can modify the next harvest by changing the seeds and other conditions. The bullet which has been fired cannot be brought back, but the one which has yet to be triggered off can be held up. Similarly, the future fruits of karma can be modified if you do your present karma accordingly.

In human life there are certain karmas which have become ripe and their effects must be enjoyed in the form of destiny, in the form of happiness and misery. One should do tapasya, discrimination, sadhana, and undergo them, but the karmas which ripen in the future may be disposed of by right action now. According to the law of karma, there is one department which is beyond your control but there is another department of karma which you can amend or modify. Thus the sutra declares that the suffering which is yet to come can be avoided.

Sutra 17: Cause of heya

द्रष्टृदृश्ययोः संयोगो हेयहेतुः ॥ १७ ॥

Draṣṭṛdṛśyayoḥ saṃyogo heyahetuḥ

Draṣṭṛ: seer; *dṛśyayoḥ*: seen; *saṃyogo*: union; *heyahetuḥ*: cause of heya, cause of what is to be avoided

The union between seer and seen is the cause of heya (which is to be avoided).

It is very important to know how to avoid the suffering which is yet to come. Every karma is capable of producing an effect, a fruit. This is a universal law. Our karmas of the past and present are in an accumulated condition. You cannot counteract the fruits of bad karmas through good ones and vice versa. You have to undergo both the good and bad effects together but there is a method by which the stock of ancient karmas which are the karmashaya should be finished. This sutra tells us that there is one cause of karmas, of suffering, which must be avoided if you want to avoid suffering, that is, the effect. That cause is the union or association of the seer, purusha, and the seer, buddhi.

There seems to be a kind of identification, a kind of oneness or association of them. Suffering begins due to this association. Thus, in order to avoid the cause of suffering, we will have to understand the process of union between the seer and the seen, between subject and object. The *drashta* is the seer and the *drishya* is the seen. This will be discussed in the next sutra.

Sutra 18: Properties of nature

प्रकाशक्रियास्थितिशीलं भूतेन्द्रियात्मकं भोगापवर्गार्थं दृश्यम् ॥ १८ ॥

Prakāśakriyāsthitiśīlaṃ bhūtendriyātmakaṃ
bhogāpavargārthaṃ dṛśyam

Prakāśa: light, illumination; *kriyā*: activity; *sthiti*: steadiness; *śīlaṃ*: qualities; *bhūta*: elements; indriya: sense organs; *ātmakaṃ*: being of the nature; *bhoga*: experience; *apavarga*: liberation; *arthaṃ*: for the sake of; *dṛśyam*: seen

The seen (drishya) has the properties of light, activity and stability; it is of the nature of the elements and sense organs and has experience and liberation as its objectives.

The seen has three qualities, namely, prakasha, kriya and sthiti. These are the three gunas and it is said that the seen is made up of the three gunas. The elements and organs together make the drishya. It has two purposes, namely, experience and liberation.

Drishya is anything that is seen. It does not only mean seen with the eyes but with all the senses, such as touch, hearing and so on. Seeing, hearing, means cognizing through any of the senses. It means experiencing. It also includes thinking. Thinking is divided into four varieties; for example, cognition through thinking, through reasoning, through memory and, fourthly, just by feeling. These are respectively the workings of manas, buddhi, chitta and ahamkara. So drishya means whatever is cognized through these various means, and drashta means the subject who cognizes. Cognition is not limited to the waking state. It may go on even in dream, or meditation. You may cognize consciously or subconsciously. So, drishya includes all the objective manifestations, the entire world. It means prakriti and all the cognizable objects, and drashta is the seer, the subjective manifestation.

Prakriti has three properties, namely, sattwa, prakasha: rajas, activity; and tamas, stability. Prakriti is composed of these three qualities. In science they mean vibration, motion and inertia. We must understand the three gunas if we want to know the properties of universal nature. Vibration is prakasha or sattwa, which has a kind of rhythm. Motion is rajas, and inertia is tamas. Rhythm can be illustrated by soldiers marching in rhythm on a parade ground. Motion, rajas, can be illustrated by a crowd moving in various directions. Tamas is a stagnant crowd which is practically not moving. Thus rhythm, motion and inertia are the physical properties of nature. In Samkhya philosophy they are known as sattwa, rajas and tamas. When there is harmony between rajas and tamas, sattwa develops. Therefore, sattwa is not something, but an effect of harmonizing these two principles of motion and inertia in their own nature. Thus harmony of rajas and tamas gives rise to sattwa.

Prakriti has for its nature the elements and sense organs. The elements are of five kinds: earth, water, air, fire and ether. The senses are ten, out of which five are the senses of action and five are the senses of cognition. In addition there are four internal organs called manas, buddhi, chitta and ahamkara. All these together are the manifestations of prakriti or drishya. For prakriti there are ultimately two purposes: the experience and the liberation of the purusha. In the world the drashta sees the drishya and thus undergoes various experiences in life. Ultimately, when the supreme consciousness develops, there is liberation.

Sutra 19: Four stages of the gunas

विशेषाविशेषलिङ्गमात्रालिङ्गानि गुणपर्वाणि ॥ १९ ॥

Viśeṣāviśeṣaliṅgamātrāliṅgāni guṇaparvāṇi

Viśeṣa: with difference; *aviśeṣa*: no difference; *liṅgamātra*: with a mere mark; *aliṅgāni*: without any mark; *guṇaparvāṇi*: state of the gunas

Vishesha, avishesha, lingamatra and alinga are the stages of the gunas.

There are four stages of the gunas in relation to the involutionary process of the superconsciousness. They bear correspondence to the four states of samprajnata samadhi. The first, vishesha, is the mental state of vitarka. It is a state of particular experiences. The second state, without any particular, is the astral state called vichara samadhi; in it the avishesha is the support of the mind. The third state, called ananda, is connected with the causal consciousness of lingamatra, and the fourth, called asmita samadhi, is the atmic state connected with alinga. It is without any mark.

Vitarka is the first state of the gunas. There is a difference in it and you are aware of the difference. It is the first state of the gunas. The second state involves no differentiation and there is complete fusion with the object. That is called avishesha, and the samadhi is vichara. In the third state there is only a single mark seen through samyama, through complete control of the object through the mind. Here you see the archetype of the object, that is, the essence. The essential nature of that object is seen with a mark. When you see a mark in that deeper state of consciousness, you should know that you are in ananda samadhi and the marks are different for different objects. In the final state of the gunas, when you are completely established in the highest state of superconsciousness (asmita), there is no mark at all. Here the consciousness enters another field altogether. Beyond that there is the area of nirbeeja samadhi.

These are the four stages of the gunas, which are finer and subtler according to the position of your consciousness. It should be remembered that the consciousness also has three gunas, and these three gunas change as the involutionary process goes on.

Sutra 20: The seer defined

द्रष्टा दृशिमात्रः शुद्धोऽपि प्रत्ययानुपश्यः ॥ २० ॥

Draṣṭā dṛśimātraḥ śuddho'pi pratyayānupaśyaḥ

Draṣṭā: seer, purusha; *dṛśimātraḥ*: only pure consciousness; *śuddho*: pure; *api*: also, though; *pratyaya*: concept; *anupaśyaḥ*: appears to see

The seer is pure consciousness only, but in spite of its purity it appears to see through the mental concept.

This sutra and the next one are important because they contain Samkhya philosophy. Everything that is subject to experience, cognition, is drishya. It may be a form, or a sound, or a thought, or a dream, or sleep. The scream of a baby, the talk and laughter of a young man and the thoughts of an old man are all drishya. It is ever changing and so cognitions are also changing. A civilized person has a higher manifestation of cognition than a tiger or a young baby or anybody else. Cognition is the same so far as a snake, a tiger or a civilized person are concerned but there is a difference in the expression of cognition; that is drishya.

The drashta is the seer who cognizes the drishya. Cognition will not take place if there in no subject but only an object. In the *Brihadaranyak Upanishad* we have a dialogue between the sage Yajnavalkya and Maitreyi. He says that if there is no subject in the higher state of samadhi, who will smell and see whom? Knowledge arises when there are both subject and object; if there is only one of the two there cannot be knowledge. The seer in yoga is pure consciousness. It cannot be seen or experienced. He is very pure but he sees through mental concepts. If there is a coloured covering around a lamp, we may know from the outside that there is light, but we would not know the light as it is. Similarly, the purusha is pure but looks impure due to pratyaya.

The purusha appears to peep into the world through mental concepts such as raga, dwesha, hatred and so on. When you remove them carefully, the light can manifest itself more clearly, and finally, when the last covering is removed, the light shines in its original splendour. The light has not changed but its covering obstacle has been removed, so there is a difference insofar as cognition is concerned. The light was not affected, it only looked different due to the pratyaya. Thus, in order to purify the facts of cognition, it is always necessary to remove the mental concepts, that is, the pratyayas.

Just as water kept in different coloured jars looks coloured, similarly, the purusha, although pure, appears to have consciousness due to the different pratyayas. Just as water, although pure, looks coloured due to the colour of the glass, in exactly the same way the purusha, although without any quality, appears to have knowledge. Purusha is pure consciousness without anything else, but it appears to be affected by pratyayas of happiness, avidya, death and birth.

Sutra 21: Prakriti is only for purusha

तदर्थ एव दृश्यस्यात्मा ॥ २१ ॥

Tadartha eva dṛśyasyātmā

Tadartha: for the sake of that (purusha); *eva*: alone; *dṛśyasya*: of the seen; *ātmā*: nature

For the sake of that (purusha) alone does prakriti exist.

Prakriti exists only for the sake of purusha. The entire process of evolution right from the very beginning is meant for serving the purpose of the purusha alone. Prakriti is only a vehicle. Purusha is the cognizer and prakriti is the medium of cognition. It is said in the scriptures that the entire structure of the universe is a manifestation of conjunction between purusha and prakriti. Prakriti gives rise to the universe only for the experience of the purusha and ultimately for its liberation.

It is something like a horse and rider going on a pilgrimage. The horse helps the rider and they go on and on. Every now and then the rider dismounts and takes care of the horse. The horse is for the purpose of the journey and for the purpose of completion of the journey; it is only a medium for the rider to arrive at his goal. Similarly, prakriti is only meant for the purusha; that is, for his experience, as well as for his liberation. Prakriti always works to complete the whole plan of evolution and when the purusha attains final liberation, the purpose of prakriti having been served, it retires completely with regard to that purusha.

Sutra 22: Prakriti after liberation

कृतार्थं प्रति नष्टमप्यनष्टं तदन्यसाधारणत्वात् ॥ २२ ॥

Kṛtārthaṃ prati naṣṭamapyanaṣṭaṃ tadanyasādhāraṇatvāt

Kṛtārthaṃ: a person whose purpose is fulfilled; *prati*: towards; *naṣṭam*: destroyed; *api*: although; *anaṣṭaṃ*: not destroyed; *tat*: that; *anya*: other; *sādhāraṇatvāt*: on account of being common

To one whose purpose is fulfilled the seen becomes non-existent but for others it is not destroyed because cognition is common to all.

When the purusha on a pilgrimage reaches the final point, the horse is left behind because it is of no further use. But the horse does not see this – it serves other persons. Similarly, when one purusha is liberated and its experiences are finished, it has nothing further to do with prakriti.

The pure consciousness which passed through different phases of evolution can be said to go through experiences of various kinds, and when it reaches the state of liberation, then prakriti becomes non-existent for that purusha. However, when a purusha is liberated, when its purpose is fulfilled, cognition might become non-existent to that purusha, but the facts of cognition will continue in an individual – he will see, hear, move and so on. That is the state of jivanmukti, in which one does not cease to exist. Jivanmuktas act in the realm of prakriti. In spite of their being liberated, prakriti goes on working because it is the common property of the mind, chitta, senses, etc. and, therefore, they go on experiencing the world and do not die soon after attaining jivanmukti. Thus purusha is liberated first, but prakriti survives and does its own work through the body of a jivanmukta.

The consciousness, or purusha, does not come in touch with prakriti, but after their separation, prakriti becomes dull. Just as a rider leaves the horse after his purpose is fulfilled and does not train, protect and take care of it, similarly, the liberated purusha does not care for prakriti. The horse thus becomes weak and one day it dies. Similarly, prakriti also becomes dull and feeble and leaves the jivanmukta because it is itself finished. This is called *videhamukti*.

Sutra 23: Why union?

स्वस्वामिशक्तयोः स्वरूपोपलब्धिहेतुः संयोगः ॥ २३ ॥

Svasvāmiśaktayoḥ svarūpopalabdhihetuḥ saṃyogaḥ

Sva: of one's own; *svāmi*: master; *śaktayoḥ*: of the two powers; *svarūpa*: one's essential nature; *upalabdhi*: acquirement; *hetuḥ*: purpose; *saṃyogaḥ*: coming together

The purpose of union of purusha and prakriti is to experience the essential nature and to achieve, in themselves, the powers of purusha and prakriti.

Purusha and prakriti come together for two purposes: one, to gain self-realization; two, to unfold the powers inherent in both of them. This is a very important sutra which says that realization is the purpose of the coming together of the purusha and prakriti. For prakriti, the purpose is to unfold the powers and the universe inherent in it. There are some powers inherent in the purusha also. Purusha is pure awareness. Prakriti is vibration, motion, inertia, the five elements, indriyas, etc., but the body, the mind, the gunas are all in prakriti.

The brain of an undeveloped person and the brain of a developed person are made up of the same grey matter, but there is some difference. The undeveloped person has not unfolded the powers inherent in him, but the developed person has unfolded these powers. The spiritually developed person has the highest degree of unfoldment, whereas the snake or the tiger have very little. The difference is due to a difference in the unfoldment of the inherent powers, and these powers always belong either to the realm of purusha or prakriti. There are certain spiritual powers and certain natural powers.

Spiritual powers are inherent in the purusha and natural powers belong to prakriti. By the evolution of purusha and prakriti unfoldment takes place, and thus every one of us has been spiritually and supernaturally evolved, although we may or may not be aware of it.

Sutra 24: Avidya is the cause

तस्य हेतुरविद्या ॥ २४ ॥

Tasya heturavidyā

Tasya: of it (union); *hetuh*: cause; *avidyā*: lack of inner awareness

The cause of union is avidya.

There must be a cause for the union of purusha and prakriti. The cause is avidya. Prakriti and purusha are both beginningless; they have been there since the beginning of the universe. Purusha is always liberated, but it may be asked, if purusha is always liberated, what is the sense in one attaining mukti again? This is a problem beyond logic; it can be solved only in a state of meditation.

Avidya is said to be the cause of union, but this avidya is not ignorance. It is not the avidya which was discussed while considering the kleshas. This avidya is the supreme power called maya, which they have not been able to define in the scriptures. It appears that this avidya is a primordial, effective cause of the mutual relationship between purusha and prakriti. This can be understood only through the philosophy of Adwaita because in Samkhya, purusha and prakriti are eternal. In Vedanta they are one, called Brahman, the highest.

It is the basis of all energies and all consciousness, but in that consciousness there is an effective power which is called maya. On account of that maya a veil is created and through that veil prakriti is born and then both prakriti and purusha become illusory processes. For dualistic Samkhya they are not illusory, but Vedanta is monistic and hence it can explain Brahman and maya as one entity.

Sutra 25: Definition of hana

तदभावात् संयोगाभावो हानं तद्दृशेः कैवल्यम् ॥ २५ ॥

Tadabhāvāt saṃyogābhāvo hānaṃ taddṛśeḥ kaivalyam

Tat: that (avidya); *abhāvāt*: by absence; *saṃyoga*: union; *abhāvaḥ*: absence; *hānaṃ*: avoidance; *tat*: that(state); *dṛśeḥ*: of the seer; *kaivalyam*: liberation

By the absence of avidya the union (between the purusha and prakriti) disappears. This is hana (avoidance), called liberation of the purusha.

With the removal of avidya, the cause of the contact of the purusha with prakriti is removed, and with the removal of the cause, the effect – namely, the contact, also ceases to exist. This is called *hana*, in which the purusha is isolated from everything else. It is liberation (*kaivalya*). This topic of kaivalya will be thoroughly discussed in the fourth chapter, so it is not necessary to give details here.

Sutra 26: The means for hana

विवेकख्यातिरविप्लवा हानोपाय: ॥ २६ ॥

Vivekakhyātiraviplavā hānopāyaḥ

Viveka: discrimination; *khyātih*: awareness; *aviplavā*: without fluctuation; *hānopāyaḥ*: the means of avoidance (hana)

The unfluctuating awareness of the real (vivekakhyati) is the means for avoidance of avidya.

There are different types of knowledge, such as knowledge through the indriyas, through the intellect, reasoning, through personal contact, hearing, imagination, and past memories. If we want to realize the real nature of purusha, we cannot depend on knowledge from these sources. That would need a different kind of knowledge altogether. That range of knowledge is called *vivekakhyati*. It is a process of knowing, not through the senses, nor intellect, nor higher perception. It is not possible to weigh the earth using scales, but you can do it through mathematical calculations. You cannot measure the distance between the sun and the moon using scales, but you can calculate it by the laws of physics. Similarly, if you want to know the supreme self, if you want to dispel avidya, you have to employ the process called knowledge through viveka (vivekakhyati).

Viveka usually means discrimination, knowing the difference, but in this sutra its meaning is different. As a result of the constant practice of self-knowledge, at a certain stage, awareness must develop in you. That awareness is a dual awareness.

Sutra 27: Stages of enlightenment

तस्य सप्तधा प्रान्तभूमिः प्रज्ञा ॥ २७ ॥

Tasya saptadhā prāntabhūmiḥ prajñā

Tasya: of it, the purusha; *saptadhā*: sevenfold; *prāntabhūmiḥ*: bordering province; *prajñā*: the cognizing consciousness

There are seven stages of enlightenment of that purusha.

Vivekakhyati brings about consciousness of seven stages, each one higher than the previous one. *Prantabhumi* means a particular range or province. It appears that during the process of vivekakhyati the purusha or consciousness goes through different stages of experience. Those experiences are contemplative: firstly, realization of what is to be avoided; secondly, awareness of the means for that removal; thirdly, awareness of spiritual evolution; fourthly, awareness of fulfilment and accomplishment; fifthly, awareness of the purpose of experience and liberation; sixthly, awareness of the fulfilment of the work of the gunas; and lastly, awareness of one's own self. Through these seven stages, a higher kind of awareness is developed which is called vivekakhyati.

Sutra 28: Necessity of yoga practice

योगाङ्गानुष्ठानादशुद्धिक्षये ज्ञानदीप्तिराविवेकख्यातेः ॥ २८ ॥

Yogāṅganuṣṭhānādaśuddhikṣaye
jñānadīptirāvivekakhyāteḥ

Yogāṅga: a part of yoga; *anuṣṭhānāt*: by practice; *aśuddhi*: impurity; *kṣaye*; destruction; *jñāna*: spiritual knowledge; *dīptih*: radiance; *āvivekakhyāteḥ*: till the awareness of reality

By the practice of the parts of yoga impurity diminishes until the rise of spiritual knowledge culminates in awareness of reality.

In order to know the higher self, we have to develop a true awareness of reality which is neither mental nor intellectual. That deeper awareness develops only by spiritual illumination, which goes on increasing with the gradual destruction of impurity. The impurity of the mind is destroyed by the practice of yoga.

Different aspects of yoga must be practised step by step, then the impurities are destroyed, giving rise to spiritual illumination which results in true, deeper awareness of reality. With the awareness of reality, avidya and prakriti both disappear. In this sense, therefore, yoga is not joining; yoga is disjoining.

It is usually argued that yoga is union, but it must be remembered that it is disunion first. It is a process of avoiding the conjunction between purusha and prakriti. Patanjali emphasizes the fact that yoga is disunion, disjunction, viyoga. So, Patanjali has really explained yoga in terms of viyoga. We must understand it properly.

Sutra 29: Eight parts of yoga discipline

यमनियमासनप्राणायामप्रत्याहारधारणाध्यानसमाधयोऽष्टावङ्गानि ॥ २९ ॥

Yamaniyamāsanaprāṇāyāmapratyāhāradhāraṇā-
dhyānasamādhayo'ṣṭāvaṅgāni

Yama: self-restraints; *niyama*: fixed rules; *āsana*: postures; *prāṇāyāma*: breath control; *pratyāhāra*: sense withdrawal; *dhāraṇā*: concentration; *dhyāna*: meditation; *samādhi*: samadhi; *aṣṭa*: eight; *aṅgāni*: parts

Self restraints, fixed rules, postures, breath control, sense withdrawal, concentration, meditation and samadhi constitute the eight parts of yoga discipline.

With this sutra we begin the topic of raja yoga. It is usually felt that meditation is yoga, but it actually includes a vast range of disciplines, conditioning and purification of the mental apparatus. The raja yoga of Patanjali is divided into eight limbs, and these eight limbs are interdependent and of similar value. Yama, niyama, asana, pranayama and pratyahara form the external aspect, *bahiranga*, or exoteric yoga. Dharana, dhyana, and samadhi form the internal aspect, *antaranga* yoga.

It is interesting to note that the entire range of yoga is divided into two: bahiranga and antaranga. Bahiranga means the yoga which is practised with the objects outside, in relation to the body, society and many other things outside oneself. Asana, pranayama, yama, niyama and pratyahara form bahiranga yoga. Dharana, dhyana and samadhi form esoteric yoga because in these practices you switch yourself off from the objective to the subjective method of contemplation.

The external and internal means are interdependent. It may be possible for a few people who are born with great samskaras to be able to practise meditation directly without going through the initial stages of yama and niyama. For most of us it is necessary to go ahead step by step, beginning from yama and niyama because in a life lacking restraint and discipline there is the possibility of an unconscious explosion, which might create mental derangement. Sometimes such explosions take place in meditation and there is a disturbance due to these impurities. It is one of the main reasons for failure in meditation.

Meditation should not be practised in a hurry; there should be no haste. Every stage of raja yoga makes way for the next higher stage, therefore, all these parts are interdependent. The boundaries cannot be previously known; they can be known through experience. It is one complete path leading the aspirant upwards. The eightfold division is made just to make the aspirant alert. Yama and niyama are universal in nature because they are respected everywhere.

The wisest way for the aspirant would be to practise all these stages as slowly as possible, so that there is no reaction due to suppression. The preliminary part of raja yoga must be practised in the presence of a group with whom the aspirant must live for some time.

When the entire mind is set into a pattern, you can go back to society and live with people. Society everywhere has been exploiting the individual, trying to take him away from the spiritual goal. Therefore, for some time the whole structure of the aspirant must be conditioned in the presence of the guru.

Sutra 30: The five yamas

अहिंसासत्यास्तेयब्रह्मचर्यापरिग्रहा यमाः ॥ ३० ॥

Ahiṃsāsatyāsteyabrahmacharyāparigrahā yamāḥ

Ahiṃsā: non-violence; *satya*: truthfulness; *asteya*: honesty; *brahmacharya*: sensual abstinence; *aparigrahā*: non-acquisitiveness; *yamāḥ*: self-restraints.

Non-violence, truth, honesty, sensual abstinence and non-possessiveness are the five self-restraints.

This sutra names the yamas. They will be discussed individually in the following sutras, so it is not necessary to explain them here.

Sutra 31: The great discipline

जातिदेशकालसमयानवच्छिन्नाः सार्वभौमा महाव्रतम् ॥ ३१ ॥

Jātideśakālasamayānavachchhinnāḥ sārvabhaumā mahāvratam

Jāti: class of birth; *deśa*: country, or place; *kāla*: time; *samaya*: circumstances; *anavachchhinnāḥ*: unconditioned, unlimited; *sārvabhaumā*: universal; *mahāvratam*: the great discipline

When practised universally without exception due to birth, place, time and circumstances they (yamas) become great disciplines.

It is observed that place, time, birth, etc. cause hindrances in the practice of the yamas. It is difficult to practise them without exception due to personal limitations, but it is recommended that they should be practised universally without exception. There should be no modification due to differences in country, birth, time, place and circumstances.

Sutra 32: The five niyamas

शौचसंतोषतपःस्वाध्यायेश्वरप्रणिधानानि नियमाः ॥ ३२ ॥

Śauchasantoṣatapaḥsvādhyāyeśvara praṇidhānāni niyamāḥ

Śaucha: cleanliness; *santoṣa*: contentment; *tapaḥ*: tapas, austerity; *svādhyāya*: self-study; *īśvara praṇidhānāni*: resignation to God; *niyamāḥ*: fixed rules

Cleanliness, contentment, austerity, self-study and resignation to God constitute fixed observances.

Sutra 33: Way to remove disturbances

वितर्कबाधने प्रतिपक्षभावनम् ॥ ३३ ॥

Vitarkabādhane pratipakṣabhāvanam

Vitarka: passions; *bādhane*: on disturbance; *pratipakṣa*: the opposite; *bhāvanam*: pondering over

When the mind is disturbed by passions one should practise pondering over their opposites.

During the practice of yama and niyama, evil passions come up due to old habits, evil tendencies and so on, and they create disturbances. Suppression will not do. The best thing is to ponder over the opposite tendencies. Thus hate is to be won over by love because they are the opposite of each other. So when there is vitarka, or disturbance due to evil thoughts, students should practise pratipaksha bhavana. For example, if one wants to be honest, one sometimes sees that dishonest people succeed in life, while honest people meet with failure. This may give rise to the evil thought that one should also be dishonest. This is vitarka; it is the wrong side of the argument. When this wrong side is advanced by the mind, it creates a disturbance and may mislead the aspirant. In this situation the opposite of dishonesty, which is honesty, should be cultivated through pondering over it.

When it comes to mind that honesty does not pay and nobody cares for an honest person, one should be ready with the opposite argument, namely, that it is only through honesty that one can succeed on the spiritual path. This is called *pratipaksha bhavana*.

Sutra 34: Their degree and nature

वितर्का हिंसादयः कृतकारितानुमोदिता लोभक्रोधमोहपूर्वका मृदुमध्याधिमात्रा दुःखाज्ञानानन्तफला इति प्रतिपक्षभावनम् ॥ ३४ ॥

Vitarkā hiṃsādayaḥ kṛtakāritānumoditā lobhakrodhamoha-pūrvakā mṛdumadhyādhimātrā duḥkhājñānānantaphalā iti pratipakṣabhāvanam

Vitarkā: evil passions; *hiṃsādayaḥ*: violence and others; *kṛta*: done by one's self; *kārita*: done through others; *anumoditā*; approved; *lobha*: greed; *krodha*: anger; *moha*: confusion; *pūrvaka*: preceded by; *mṛdu*: mild; *madhya*: medium; *adhimātrā*: intense; *duḥkha*: pain; *ajñāna*: ignorance; *ananta*: infinite; *phalāḥ*: results; *iti*: like that; *pratipakṣa*: opposite; *bhāvanam*: thinking

Thinking of evil thoughts such as violence, whether done through oneself, through others, or approved, is caused by greed, anger and confusion. They can be either mild, medium or intense. Pratipaksha bhavana is thinking that these evil thoughts cause infinite pain and ignorance.

Sometimes an individual does not practise violence himself, but he may have it done through others, or he may tolerate it being done by others. This is to be avoided in yoga because one is held responsible even when one tolerates violence or has it done through others. This also applies to other vitarkas such as falsehood, theft and so on.

Sometimes these vitarkas are done because of greed, or anger, or confusion, but all of them must be avoided. The vitarkas may be either mild, medium or intense, but they must be wiped out, irrespective of their cause, intensity and effect. All these evil passions beget two things ultimately – pain and ignorance. If this is realized or argued in the negative state of your mind, it becomes pratipaksha bhavana. One may think of eating or drinking prohibited things, but if one realizes it will do harm, the argument would be pratipaksha bhavana. When it is introduced, the mind overcomes evil passions, a positive complex is formed, and then the aspirant can follow the spiritual path of yama and niyama without difficulty.

Sutra 35: Fruits of (i) ahimsa

अहिंसाप्रतिष्ठायां तत्संनिधौ वैरत्यागः ॥ ३५ ॥

Ahiṃsāpratiṣṭhāyāṃ tatsaṃnidhau vairatyāgaḥ

Ahiṃsā: non-violence; *pratiṣṭhāyāṃ*: on being firmly established; *tatsaṃnidhau*: in its vicinity; *vaira*: hostility; *tyāgaḥ*: abandonment

On being firmly established in ahimsa, there is abandonment of hostility in his vicinity.

Ahimsa means love, harmlessness, non-killing, non-violence. It means absence of enmity, hostility and harm. For the spiritual aspirant it should mean absence of any harmful intention whatsoever. *Pratishtha* means being firmly established. When one is established in ahimsa, there develops a kind of magnetism around one that influences anybody who approaches. One becomes free of a very dangerous, evil complex – that of violence and hostility.

In Indian history there have been many great people who could convert even the most cruel and devilish hearts. Mahatma Gandhi, who was a devotee of ahimsa, did not harbour any ill will but he too had enemies and he was finally shot down. This shows how difficult it is to practise ahimsa. Lord Buddha had developed the practice of ahimsa so much that he converted any cruel person into a kind-hearted one. Once he faced a cruel dacoit (robber) who had come to kill him and by his mere look, the dacoit was converted. This is the power of ahimsa. In the ashram of Patanjali, the cow, goat and tiger could live, eat and drink together because of the ahimsa practised by the great sage.

It is very easy to say that we should be non-violent, that we should love each other, but the concept of love is too great for us to understand. For us love means security or defence against the fear of death, and nothing more. It is a psychological necessity but love is actually something much greater. Christ was crucified, Mohammed was stoned by his opponents, the great Sufi saint Mansoor was tortured by the Muslims and his skin was peeled off. All these men had enemies but in India there have been many who had no enemies because they practised ahimsa perfectly.

The most important thing is not to oppose even violent people. That is also ahimsa and if the whole thing is discussed more deeply, then it means that you practise elimination of the complex of enmity, disapproval. In India such a person is called *ajata shatru*, born without an enemy.

Thus it seems that even the great saints and prophets were not firmly established in ahimsa. For example, Buddha, Lord Krishna and Shankara used to criticize and oppose other schools of philosophy, but the yogic logic says that ahimsa must be practised completely. There should be a dignified way of facing the irregularities in society. That is what satyagraha means.

So, this sutra means that when the aspirant is firmly established in ahimsa, when even the last traces of hostility are finished, the soul unfolds itself from within in a magnetic form and that magnetic form is called *vairatyagah*, which is abandonment of hostility. Thus even the killing of animals should be given up. The Jain cult is famous for ahimsa in India.

Sutra 36: Fruits of (ii) satya

सत्यप्रतिष्ठायां क्रियाफलाश्रयत्वम् ॥ ३६ ॥

Satyapratiṣṭhāyāṃ kriyāphalāśrayatvam

Satya: truthfulness; *pratiṣṭhāyāṃ*: on being firmly established; *kriyā*: action; *phala*: result or fruit; *āśrayatvam*: basis

On being firmly established in truthfulness, the actions result in fruits, entirely depending on it.

When the aspirant becomes established in truthfulness by practising it as a universal law, unconditioned by time, country, birth and circumstance, then he develops a kind of divine buddhi in himself. Thereby he is able to acquire the result from his karma according to his wish. Usually the result of karma is independent of our wishes but it is not so with a person who has perfected truthfulness.

This sutra may also be interpreted to mean that the truthful aspirant develops truth of speech. Whatever he speaks will come true, whatever he says happens. In yoga this is called psychic speech. By the practice of truthfulness he develops a power in himself and his mind becomes so clear, like a mirror, that it reflects what is to happen through his speech. Thus, the result of any action is absolutely dependent on him, not on change or prarabdha. Or, it may be said that one who has developed truthfulness to such a high degree is able to perfectly weigh every word he utters.

Perhaps it is because he has complete control over his speech, but this is very difficult. Only that person can speak truth who knows how to weigh each word; it becomes a condition of his speech. He does not express anything without weighing the words with spiritual power. Through this he can put a great restraint on the vehicle of speech so that whatever comes from the mouth of such a person comes true. These are the two meanings of the sutra. Firstly, it means that whatever he speaks comes true and, secondly, it means that the result of actions follow from his will.

Sutra 37: Fruits of (iii) asteya

अस्तेयप्रतिष्ठायां सर्वरत्नोपस्थानम् ॥ ३७ ॥

Asteya pratiṣṭhāyāṃ sarvaratnopasthānam

Asteya: honesty; *pratiṣṭhāyāṃ*: on being firmly established; *sarva*: all; *ratna*: gems; *upasthānam*: self-presentation

On being firmly established in honesty, all gems present themselves.

When the spiritual aspirant is established in the yogic virtue of honesty, he develops within himself a power of cognition like clairvoyance or intuitive awareness. It is exactly the same faculty possessed by water diviners. Through this cognizing faculty the aspirant becomes aware of valuable stones and jewels nearby.

We have some persons, like Swami Sivananda, who could know how much wealth an approaching person had. This is a kind of intuitive awareness, possible on account of absolute, unconditional, universal honesty. Its aim is to render the entire life clean, in order to purify the entire structure of personality. When this is done, the personality becomes like a mirror in which the divine mind is reflected.

When the mirror is clean, you can see your face clearly in it. The virtue of asteya or honesty brings about a kind of awareness by which you become aware of hidden wealth.

Sutra 38: Fruits of (iv) brahmacharya

ब्रह्मचर्यप्रतिष्ठायां वीर्यलाभः ॥ ३८ ॥

Brahmacharyapratiṣṭhāyāṃ vīryalābhaḥ

Brahmacharya: sexual abstinence; *pratiṣṭhāyāṃ*: on being firmly established; *vīrya*: indomitable courage; *lābhaḥ*: gain

On being firmly established in brahmacharya, veerya is gained.

Brahma means supreme being and *charya* means living, but here the word brahmacharya means eight kinds of sexual contentment. Veerya means semen, about which it is said that one drop is made out of forty drops of blood. Veerya creates vitality. It is the essence of life which ultimately converts itself into energy. Many scientists have said that veerya is nothing but hormonal secretions; however, Patanjali does not agree with this. Veerya also means indomitable courage, which is essential for sadhana. Thus, when firmly established in brahmacharya, the yogi gains vigour, energy and courage, whereby he becomes free of the fear of death. Thus brahmacharya is an important way of overcoming the klesha called abhinivesha, which means fear of death. Brahmacharya is eightfold.

It is well known in yoga that there is an intimate connection between physical energy and spiritual energy. In order to bring about spiritual potentiality, it is necessary to conserve physical energy, known as *ojas*. It is formed by conservation of veerya. When the physical fluid called semen is conserved and converted into ojas, that is called reta or seminal energy. When it is sublimated and drawn inward, it produces energy and the whole body is filled with it. Such a man is called *urdhvareta*.

It is said in an Upanishad that by practising brahmacharya the gods completely killed the fear of death. Bhishma, for example, was without fear of death because he had practised brahmacharya. He was a great warrior; he had controlled death. He did not die on the battlefield, but he died according to his will. This was because he had not lost even a single drop of blood outside his body during his whole lifetime.

Sutra 39: Fruits of (v) aparigraha

अपरिग्रहस्थैर्ये जन्मकथन्तासम्बोधः ॥ ३९ ॥

Aparigrahasthairye janmakathantāsambodhaḥ

Aparigraha: non-possessiveness; *sthairye*: on becoming steady; *janma*: birth; *kathantā*: how and from where; *sambodhaḥ*: knowledge

On becoming steady in non-possessiveness, there arises the knowledge of how and from where birth (comes).

Aparigraha is one of the most important virtues. It means giving up the tendency to accumulate objects of utility and enjoyment. The aspirant keeps only those objects that are essential for living. This keeps the mind unoccupied and also he does not have to worry about anything because there in nothing there to be protected.

Many aspirants do not even touch fire and have only one set of clothes. They do not stay in one place. Their mind is so free and relaxed and they are always ready to do any duty anywhere. This is aparigraha. After deconditioning the mind sufficiently, the aspirant can have other comforts such as a chair, table and so on if he has to do special kinds of work. The samskaras of possessiveness must first be completely washed away and then one can start a new life.

Thus aparigraha is a temporary course of sadhana in an aspirant's life. If this particular sadhana is continued beyond reasonable limits, it gives rise to weakness and obsession. However, it is necessary to practise in the beginning in order to break the old habits. When they are broken, one can have different things which are needed for social work and service to humanity. When this sadhana is firmly established, the aspirant comes to know about the previous birth – its kind, its time and its reason. Similarly, one can even know the next birth. Just as by seeing a cloud you know that there will be rain, similarly, you know about the previous or the next birth by being firmly established in aparigraha.

Sutra 40: Fruits of (vi) shaucha

शौचात्स्वाङ्गजुगुप्सा परैरसंसर्गः ॥ ४० ॥

Śauchātsvāṅgajugupsā parairasaṃsargaḥ

Śauchāt: from cleanliness; *svāṅga*: one's own body; *jugupsā*: indifference; *paraih*: with others; *asaṃsargaḥ*: non-attachment

From cleanliness there comes indifference towards body and non-attachment to others.

From this sutra begins the discussion of the niyamas. These are fixed disciplines necessary for the practice of meditation and samadhi. All these are the means and not the end. The first rule, namely, cleanliness or purity, is described in this sutra. It is said that by practising bodily or physical cleanliness you develop in the course of time a kind of indifference towards your own body. At the same time a kind of non-attachment to others is also developed.

Sutra 41: Shaucha

सत्त्वशुद्धिसौमनस्यैकाग्र्येन्द्रियजयात्मदर्शनयोग्यत्वानि च ॥ ४१ ॥

Sattvaśuddhisaumanasyaikāgryendriyajayātma-
darśanayogyatvāni cha

Sattvaśuddhi: purity of internal being; *saumanasya*: cheerfulness; *ekāgrya*: one-pointedness; *indriyajaya*: control of senses; *ātmadarśana*: vision of the self; *yogyatvāni*: fitness; *cha*: and

By the practice of mental purity one acquires fitness for cheerfulness, one-pointedness, sense control and vision of the self.

This is also found described in the *Bhagavad Gita*. When the mind is purified or when mental purity is practised, one becomes fit to practise cheerfulness, concentration and sense control, and because of mental cleanliness, one is able to see the vision of one's self.

Sutra 42: Fruits of (vii) santosha

संतोषादनुत्तमसुखलाभः ॥ ४२ ॥

Santoṣādanuttamasukhalābhaḥ

Santoṣāt: from contentment; *anuttamah*: unexcelled; *sukha*: pleasure, happiness; *lābhaḥ*: gain

Unexcelled happiness comes from the practice of contentment.

Contentment is one of the fixed rules for a spiritual aspirant who is very serious about the higher aspect of yoga and realization. It is impossible for one who is dissatisfied with oneself or with anything else in life to realize the higher consciousness.

Dissatisfaction is one of the great veils of avidya and therefore it is to be removed, because it causes many undesirable complexes and brings about a state of psychic illness, and if the mind is ill, no sadhana is possible.

One who wants to attain meditation must practise yama and niyama. The awareness in meditation must be made free of all the mental errors, veils and complexes; therefore, one must practise *santosha* (contentment). The happiness that comes from it is unparalleled. As a result one can go very deep in meditation. In the absence of contentment, different mental complexes come into play and such a person is unfit for meditation.

Sutra 43: Fruits of (viii) tapas

कायेन्द्रियसिद्धिरशुद्धिक्षयात्तपसः ॥ ४३ ॥

Kāyendriyasiddhiraśuddhikṣayāttapasaḥ

Kāya: the body; *indriya*: sense organ; *siddhi*: perfection; *aśuddhi*: impurity; *kṣayāt*: destruction; *tapasaḥ*: by austerities

By practising austerities, impurities are destroyed and there comes perfection in the body and sense organs.

Meditation requires a perfect body and sense organs. All the organs must be healthy and perfect, otherwise meditation is disturbed. There may be pain in the joints or there may be toxins produced in the body. Those who practise meditation with an unhealthy body may suffer.

If you want to meditate for a long time every day, you must have a perfect body. It is not a joke to sit down for hours at a stretch, so in this sutra Patanjali recommends that the body and sense organs be perfected for meditation. The body should be held erect and there should be no uneasiness or discomfort in meditation due to weakness of an organ. All the functions of the body, such as breathing, circulation, digestion and excretion, must go on perfectly, and for this it is necessary to practise tapas.

This is not the tapas of kriya. It involves subjecting the body to hardships so that it can endure heat, cold, poisons and so on. For meditation a strong body is required.

Physical impurities should be removed from the brain, eyes, ears, nose, skin and so on. For this, austerities are very helpful. There are five types of austerities:

1. Exposing the body to the sun to make the skin hard.
2. Subjecting the body to the heat of fire to make it slim and brown.

3. Doing pranayama to create heat in the body.
4. Developing the fire of concentration on one point.
5. The fire of fasting.

These five fires remove toxins and harden the body so that it becomes fit for meditation.

Sutra 44: Fruits of (ix) swadhyaya

स्वाध्यायादिष्टदेवतासम्प्रयोगः ॥ ४४ ॥

Svādhyāyādiṣṭadevatāsamprayogaḥ

*Svādhyāyā*t: by self-awareness, self-observation; *iṣṭadevatā*: the deity of choice; *samprayogaḥ*: communion

By self-observation, union with the desired deity is brought about.

Swadhyaya means closing the eyes and observing one's own self, as in antar mouna. When it is practised, it gives rise to a faculty by which one is able to concentrate deeply on the god or goddess of choice.

Sutra 45: Fruits of (x) Ishwara pranidhana

समाधिसिद्धिरीश्वरप्रणिधानात् ॥ ४५ ॥

Samādhisiddhirīśvarapraṇidhānāt

Samādhi: trance; *siddhi*: perfection, *īśvara*: God; *praṇidhānāt*: self-surrender

Success in trance comes by complete resignation to God.

By complete resignation to God, which is very difficult, one is able to develop a state of trance. It is not exactly the samadhi which was described in the previous chapter. It is a kind of trance in which the aspirant loses body awareness and is able to start with deeper awareness and remain in a state of complete tranquillity and union. It is possible by complete resignation to God. Here God means the idea of the aspirant regarding the deity.

This technique of Ishwara pranidhana is also included in kriya yoga, but there its objective is different. Here it is described as a part of the discipline of fixed rules. It is employed here mainly for removing hindrances in the body and mind so that there is spiritual awareness of meditation. Thus the student has to undergo the practice of the five yamas and niyamas.

Sutra 46: Asana

स्थिरसुखमासनम् ॥ ४६ ॥

Sthirasukhamāsanam

Sthira: steady; *sukham*: comfortable; *āsanam*: posture

Steady and comfortable should be the posture.

The word *asana* is used for the meditation posture. Asana here does not mean the physical yoga exercises. Generally, this word asana is taken to mean yogic exercises, but here it only means a posture which is meant for meditation. For example, swastikasana, siddhasana, padmasana, sthirasana and sukhasana are the asanas meant for meditation, but there is no bar to other postures being counted as asanas.

Since the word literally means a method of sitting, we have to understand it that way. It is only later on that the rishis included other exercises in the system of asana, such as sirshasana, etc. There is no harm if a raja yogi practises these asanas. It does not mean that they are unnecessary just because they are not included in the sutras of Patanjali. Thus the asanas that bring about a state of equilibrium in the body should also be practised, though they are not mentioned by Patanjali.

Sutra 47: How to master asana

प्रयत्नशैथिल्यानन्तसमापत्तिभ्याम् ॥ ४७ ॥

Prayatnaśaithilyānantasamāpattibhyām

Prayatna: effort; *śaithilya*: looseness; *ananta*: the serpent called ananta; *samāpattibhyām*: by meditation

By loosening of effort and by meditation on the serpent ananta, asana is mastered.

In order to become perfect, steady and comfortable in the asana which one has selected for meditation, one has to overcome tension and effort. So there should be relaxation of effort; there should be perfect relaxation in the asana. Secondly, the mind must be concentrated on ananta.

The word *ananta* means endless. It also means the snake on which Lord Vishnu rests in the ocean of milk. So, symbolically, *ananta* means serpent, but in this sutra the serpent refers to the kundalini shakti. The student should concentrate on the serpent power in the mooladhara chakra, or any other method of concentrating on the kundalini should be employed.

The word relaxation or loosening of effort means that you should not struggle or apply any force. The asana must be perfectly relaxed and without any muscular or nervous tension. So, whichever asana one may be able to practise without effort, such as siddhasana or padmasana or swastikasana, should be taken up for meditation.

Sutra 48: Result of this mastery

ततो द्वन्द्वानभिघातः ॥ ४८ ॥

Tato dvandvānabhighātaḥ

Tatah: from that; *dvandva*: pairs of opposites; *anabhighātaḥ*: no impact

Thereby the pairs of opposites cease to have any impact.

Dvandvas (pairs of opposites) belong to the physical as well as the mental realms. Those belonging to the physical level are heat and cold, hunger and thirst, pain and so on. The psychic or mental dvandvas are happiness and sorrow. Every now and then our mind is subjected to them by circumstances. This causes a disturbance. On hot days we perspire and are restless and when winter comes it is very cold. Thus, in summer we want to be cold and in winter we like heat. This is how the pairs of opposites disturb the mind. A student must develop resistance to these, physical as well as mental, and that is only possible through yama, niyama and asana. These dvandvas must be overcome if we want to make progress in meditation, so our resistance must be increased to overcome the disturbance and hindrance caused by the dvandvas.

All the dvandvas, such as heat and cold, joy and sorrow, must be overcome. It must be possible to maintain mental and physical equilibrium. Moods should not change from moment to moment. The body should not be disturbed by heat and cold. Thus there should be physical and psychic resistance. Resistance plays a great role in counteracting micro-organisms. Thus, when there is an infectious disease in the family, like a cold or influenza, the family members are advised to keep away from the patient, whose resistance is lowered by this disease. Our mind becomes weak if we think about disease. There are many weaknesses in the personality which bring down the level of resistance, but a spiritual aspirant must have a high level of resistance, which can be brought about by the practice of asana.

Sutra 49: Pranayama

तस्मिन्सति श्वासप्रश्वासयोर्गतिविच्छेदः प्राणायामः ॥ ४९ ॥

Tasminsati śvāsapraśvāsayorgativichchhedaḥ prāṇāyāmaḥ

Tasmin: on that; *sati*: having been; *śvasapraśvāsayah*: inhalation, exhalation; *gati*: movement; *vichchhedaḥ*: break, cessation; *prāṇāyāmaḥ*

The asana having been done, pranayama is the cessation of the movement of inhalation and exhalation.

After he has perfected yama, niyama and asana sufficiently, the aspirant should take up pranayama. It is the cessation of inhalation and expiration. There is neither rechaka nor puraka, there is only kumbhaka.

It should be noted that pranayama is not deep breathing. Similarly, retaining the breath once only as long as one can do so is not the way of pranayama. *Prana* means breath, *ayama* is lengthening or widening through control. When breathing is controlled so as to retain the breath, it is *pranayama*. It is interesting to note that serpents, elephants, tortoises and so on live long lives because they perform the act of respiration fewer times per minute than human beings. The life of a human being can also be prolonged if the breath is retained, but this requires training as well as practice.

It is said that prana is like a wild elephant. If you want to tame the prana, you will have to take as much care as you would while taming a wild elephant. There must be steadiness and patience; there should be no hurry or haste. Retention must be practised slowly and with care. If there is any drawback, either physically or mentally, then the practice must be stopped for a few days or months. Atmospheric conditions, food habits, age, physical condition and other factors must be considered before beginning the practice. There should be sufficient caution. In hatha yoga it is clearly stated that breath control should not be practised in the physical asanas. It is wrong to control the breath in certain physical postures. There are certain other postures in which pranayama may be practised, but the student must know in which exercises to practise it and in which exercises to avoid it. For this, there should be a clear understanding of the meaning of prana. It has nothing to do with the lungs and much to do with the life current.

The ultimate aim of pranayama is to be able to retain the breath. There are three types of pranayama, namely, puraka, rechaka and kumbhaka. The fourth type, called kevala kumbhaka, is of two types: antaranga and bahiranga. Retention of breath brings about a certain condition in the brain, a certain change in the spinal cord, as well as in the physical body. Pranayama influences the nervous system and thereby the brain. It does not have much to do with the lungs. Puraka, kumbhaka and rechaka produce different effects in the body.

Thus, stopping the breath either inside or outside is the meaning of pranayama. The ayama – the distance or length of prana – is increased but the number of respirations per minute is decreased. Thus, if we breathe normally fourteen times per minute, in pranayama we breathe only once or twice per minute.

Sutra 50: Three kinds of pranayama

बाह्याभ्यन्तरस्तम्भवृत्तिर्देशकालसंख्याभिः परिदृष्टो दीर्घसूक्ष्मः ॥ ५० ॥

Bāhyābhyantarastambhavṛttirdeśakālasaṅkhyābhiḥ paridṛṣṭo dīrghasūkṣmaḥ

Bāhyah: outer; *abhyantara*: internal; *stambhavṛttih*: suppressed stage; *deśa*: place; *kāla*: time; *saṅkhyābhiḥ*: number; *paridriṣṭah*: measured; *dīrgha*: prolonged; *sūkṣmaḥ*: subtle

Pranayama is external, internal or suppressed, regulated by place, time and number and becomes prolonged and subtle.

Pranayama has three stages called puraka, kumbhaka and rechaka. Practice depends on the place of practice, whether it is a tropical or a temperate climate. It is also dependent on local diet. A detailed description of the rules are given in the hatha yoga books.

Time means the relative duration of puraka, rechaka and kumbhaka. It also means the time of the year or the season. Thus, if you practise twenty rounds during winter, you should practise ten rounds during summer. Samkhya means the number of rounds. This is determined by the number of matras or units of time. Thus, pranayama is regulated by desha, kala and Samkhya.

The technique of pranayama must be learnt from a guru. When you start, the relative duration should be 6:8:6 in the beginning. Finally, you can go 20:80:40. Here it becomes 1:4:2; that is, one unit of time for puraka, four units of time for kumbhaka, and two units of time for rechaka. A matra is the time taken for two claps and one snap. If an aspirant is able to practise pranayama for 20:80:40 matras, then he is supposed to be the best sadhaka. It is the best pranayama.

The quality depends upon the number of rounds; ultimately it becomes prolonged and subtle.

All the three stages, namely puraka, kumbhaka and rechaka, must be prolonged. Starting from 6:8:6 matras, one should ultimately go up to 20:80:40 matras. The pranas are prolonged in this way and retention is increased, thus the process becomes subtle.

Sutra 51: Fourth kind of pranayama

बाह्याभ्यन्तरविषयाक्षेपी चतुर्थः ॥ ५१ ॥

Bāhyābhyantaraviṣayākṣepī chaturthaḥ

Bāhya: external; *abhyantara*: internal; *viṣaya*: object; *ākṣepī*: transcending; *chaturtha*: fourth

The fourth pranayama is that which transcends the internal and external object.

In this fourth type of pranayama, you do not have to do either antaranga or bahiranga kumbhaka. This is exactly like the description in the *Bhagavad Gita* where it is said that apana should be joined with prana and prana joined with apana. Thereby, the student stops the incoming and outgoing sensation by joining the ingoing breath with the outgoing breath. Secondly, the ingoing breath should be joined with the ingoing breath itself. Thirdly, at the same time you should do kumbhaka. The sensations should not be allowed to penetrate. The outer experiences of objects should be left outside and the inner samskaras or experiences should be left inside. The outer manifestation should not be let inside and the inner samskaras should not be allowed to manifest outside. That is the fourth pranayama. You can do it by breathing in in ujjayi, breathing out in ujjayi, and trying to concentrate your mind on a particular psychic passage, without controlling or stopping the breath in the form of antaranga or bahiranga kumbhaka. Gradually you should be able to extinguish the experiences, block the path of sense experiences. That is the fourth kind of pranayama. In fact, it is ajapa japa.

Sutra 52: Removal of the veil

ततः क्षीयते प्रकाशावरणम् ॥ ५२ ॥

Tataḥ kṣīyate prakāśāvaraṇam

Tataḥ: thereby; *kṣīyate*: disappears; *prakāśa*: light; *āvaraṇam*: covering

Thereby the covering of light disappears.

By the practice of pranayama the psychic centres are activated and as a result, the covering of knowledge is removed. *Prakasha* here means the psychic centres. The psychic centres are usually covered or veiled due to sense experiences. The luminosity of these subtler vehicles is limited or covered by the physical matter of the brain. That covering is removed by pranayama. This kind of removal of the covering of physical matter over the psychic faculty is called the removal of the covering of light. It means that when you have practised pranayama, something happens in you by which the psychic powers are released from the veil or control or obstruction of the physical mechanisms of the brain.

Energy is released even when you switch on the light or the fan. Pranayama creates a similar condition in the brain by which the inherent psychic faculties are released.

Sutra 53: Mind becomes fit for dharana

धारणासु च योग्यता मनसः ॥ ५३ ॥

Dhāraṇāsu cha yogyatā manasaḥ

Dhāraṇāsu: in dharana; *cha*: and; *yogyatā*: fitness; *manasaḥ*: of the mind

And fitness of the mind for concentration (develops through pranayama).

By doing pranayama, there develops a capacity for concentration in the mind and one becomes qualified for concentrating the mind in the state of dharana. This is because the veil which covers the light of knowledge is removed. Next comes the stage called pratyahara.

Sutra 54: Pratyahara

स्वविषयासम्प्रयोगे चित्तस्यस्वरूपानुकार इवेन्द्रियाणां प्रत्याहारः ॥ ५४ ॥

Svaviṣayāsamprayoge chittasyasvarūpānukāra
ivendriyāṇāṃ pratyāhāraḥ

Sva: one's own; *viṣaya*: object; *asamprayoge*: not coming into contact; *chitta*: mind; *svarūpa*: own form; *anukārah*: imitating; *iva*: as if; *indriyāṇāṃ*: of the senses; *pratyāhāraḥ*: withdrawal

Pratyahara is, as it were, the imitation by the senses of the mind by withdrawing them from their respective objects.

It should be understood that *pratyahara* means withdrawing the mind from the objects of sense experience, then the senses function according to the mind, and not vice versa. The capacities of smell, taste, sight, touch and hearing are withdrawn from their objects and the senses begin to follow the mind inward and not outward. This is withdrawal of the mind from the sense activities so that the sense organs also become introverted with the mind; they imitate the mind and follow it inside.

Sutra 55: Mastery over the senses

ततः परमा वश्यतेन्द्रियाणाम् ॥ ५५ ॥

Tatah paramā vaśyatendriyāṇām

Tatah: thereby; *paramā*: highest; *vaśyate*: mastery; *indriyāṇām*: of the senses

There is highest mastery over the sense organs (by pratyahara).

It is felt by some scholars that controlling the senses only means suppressing the sense organs. They consider it to be an abnormal condition, but for one who wants to meditate and dive deep into the depths of the mind, it becomes very important to introvert oneself from the world of objects. To penetrate into the depths of the mind, the contact with the object must be cut off. When the mind is in contact with the external world, it is not aware of the deeper facets of consciousness. When one is aware of these deeper facets, one does not know the world of the senses.

It is important to remember that the consciousness, the atman or the self, does not actually evolve. There is no evolution of the atman, or soul. By the practice of pratyahara we do not actually evolve; it is a process of involution. It is not true to say that our souls have evolved from the primitive state to our present developed state. The supreme existence, or the soul, is the same as it was thousands of years ago. It does not undergo a change. The only difference is that our lower self or the individualized self becomes aware of that supreme form slowly, step by step.

When we turn our minds from the outer world to the inner world, we come to know that there is an infinite facet of existence in us which can only be experienced in samadhi.

It is not approachable through the intellect. Therefore, this chapter is aimed at giving a sadhana starting from yama and niyama and ending in pratyahara.

There are many kinds of pratyahara; for example, trataka, nada yoga, japa, music, kirtan and so on. They are all meant for purifying the sense awareness and making it turn inward. Some persons can get into it with just one nada yoga practice; others may find japa easier. Sometimes you are able to hold pratyahara for some time, then you find afterwards that it does not work even if you sincerely follow the sadhana, so this problem of pratyahara becomes very difficult. If you can master the technique of pratyahara, then concentration becomes very easy. It is impossible to go on to dharana and dhyana unless the field of pratyahara is crossed.

There are many sadhanas available for pratyahara. The guru selects a suitable sadhana for the disciple at the time of initiation.

Chapter Three

Vibhooti pada

(56 Sutras)

Sutra 1: What is dharana?

देशबन्धश्चित्तस्य धारणा ॥ १ ॥

Deśabandhaśchittasya dhāraṇā

Deśa: place; *bandha*: binding; *chittasya*: of the mind; *dhāraṇā*: concentration

Concentration (dharana) is binding the mind to one place.

Place here means a mental or physical spot. It is said in different scriptures that there are three bases available for a student, namely objective, subjective and visionary. So *dharana* means confinement of the mind to one point or one object or one area. There is a good example of one-pointed attention given in the *Mahabharata*. While teaching archery to the Pandavas, their guru Drona asked them what object they could see. Arjuna said that he could see only the eye of the bird which was the target and nothing else. This is an example of concentration.

When the mind is concentrated on a point, perception becomes intense. When the eyes are closed the object, which may be a thought, an idea or a word, appears intensely in the consciousness. The mind does not move or leave the point of concentration. If it moves, it is called vikshepa. *Vikshepa* means oscillation. In concentration there should not be awareness of anything but the desha. It is said sometimes that you can have two areas for concentration. For example, while doing japa, the mantra is one factor and form is another factor. For a beginner, concentration with japa on two factors is better. Later on one can concentrate without japa. While there is an influx of blood in the brain, there will be vibration, and concentration will be difficult. The influx of blood should be reduced and there should be no vibrations. For this, we utilize the optic system.

Through the optic system, the vibrations of the physical brain are reduced. If you look at one point with the eyes open, do not blink for some time and then close your eyes, you will fall asleep within five minutes. Just as you stop the waves or ripples on the surface of water in a vessel by keeping the water calm, similarly, the vibrations in the brain can be stopped if various disturbing factors are stopped. Even the physiological brain is to be stopped. For this, we fix the mind on a single point, such as a chakra in the body like mooladhara, manipura or ajna, etc. and the consciousness is fixed on this.

If the mind fluctuates, do not allow it to do so. Thus the cerebral activities cease for some time and during that time concentration takes place. In the beginning it is not possible to concentrate the mind for a long time.

Concentration is not a state of forgetfulness. If you forget everything, including the object, that is called *shoonya samadhi* or laya, but concentration must include awareness of a single object. If you are concentrating on a mantra, there should be awareness of it throughout, without a break. If there is a break, it is concentration; if there is no break, it becomes dhyana. It should be remembered that in concentration there is always the awareness that you are concentrating. Meditation is not different from concentration; it is a higher quality of it.

In dharana there is awareness of the object, which is broken from time to time in the process. The awareness may be broken by hearing an outside sound or by various thoughts coming into the mind. Thus dharana includes concentration of consciousness with breaks.

Sometimes the breaks become so powerful that it is difficult to concentrate again. This is called vikshepa. It is a disturbance, a distraction. A beginner always experiences this difficulty. Sometimes he is able to bring his mind back to the spot and sometimes he is not. This is because the physical body is not steady. With the slightest movement of the body the heart starts beating faster, respiration also increases and this gives rise to disturbance. When the body is absolutely steady like a stone, concentration becomes firm. This is why steadiness of posture is very essential.

Sutra 2: What is dhyana?

तत्र प्रत्ययैकतानता ध्यानम् ॥ २ ॥

Tatra pratyayaikatānatā dhyānam

Tatra: there (in the desha); *pratyaya*: basis or content of consciousness; *ekatānatā*: continuity; *dhyānam*: meditation

Uninterrupted stream of the content of consciousness is dhyana.

Pratyaya means the basis of consciousness which may be an idea, a sound, or any object, subtle or gross. If in dharana the consciousness becomes continuous so that there is no break or interruption due to any other thought, then dharana is replaced by or turned into dhyana. Sometimes we experience dhyana when we are practising dharana. In dhyana there is an uninterrupted flow of consciousness.

If you are visualizing a particular object, you should not visualize that object alone, but you should also visualize that you are practising dhyana. This is important. Sometimes you may become oblivious to the object also, but there is the awareness of dhyana, which is called *sakshi bhava*. Otherwise, what usually happens is that if your mind slips away during concentration, you do not know it. This should not happen. Thus *dhyana* includes two things: one, an unbroken continuous flow of consciousness of the single object, and two, the awareness of dhyana; that is, the awareness that you are practising unbroken concentration. These two kinds of awareness go hand in hand.

Sutra 3: What is samadhi?

तदेवार्थमात्रनिर्भासं स्वरूपशून्यमिव समाधिः ॥ ३ ॥

Tadevārthamātranirbhāsaṃ svarūpaśūnyamiva samādhiḥ

Tadeva: the same; *artha*: the object of dhyana; *mātra*: only; *nirbhāsaṃ*: appearing; *svarūpa*: one's own form; *śūnyam*: empty; *iva*: as if; *samādhiḥ*: samadhi

That state becomes samadhi when there is only the object appearing without the consciousness of one's own self.

It should be noted that dharana itself turns into dhyana, and dhyana itself turns into samadhi. In dharana the consciousness is broken, in dhyana it is continuous, whereas in samadhi it becomes one with the artha, that is, the object of concentration. It may be a gross object or a subtle one. In samadhi there is no consciousness that one is practising concentration.

It is sometimes said that in the state of deep concentration the object disappears, but this sutra tells us that the object does not disappear; on the contrary, it alone prevails. Thus, if you are concentrating on *Aum,* the symbol *Aum*, called artha, will be present in samadhi. It will not vanish, but it alone will shine completely in the awareness.

The object of meditation becomes clearer and clearer, its appearance becomes more and more vivid as you go deeper in the stages of samadhi. Then there is another important point: you do not remain aware of your own existence, there is not even the awareness that you are practising concentration. Thus there are two characteristics of samadhi: one, the object alone shines and, two, there is no awareness of the process or of the self. As there is no consciousness except of the object in samadhi, the mind appears not to be functioning, but it is not blank; therefore, the word *iva* is used.

As the student goes on making progress on the path of concentration, there is concentration in the beginning but it is broken time and time again. Thus concentration continues for some time and suddenly there is a break. This is the first stage. In the second stage there is more dhyana and fewer breaks. In the third stage you start with dharana and immediately go into dhyana, and suddenly there comes a void. This is the first stage of samadhi; you remember the object but there is no other awareness. The mind or consciousness is not annihilated, it only temporarily appears to be non-existent because you are not aware of yourself or of the process of concentration.

Sutra 4: What is samyama?

त्रयमेकत्र संयमः ॥ ४ ॥

Trayamekatra saṃyamaḥ

Trayam: the three; *ekatra*: together; *saṃyamaḥ*: samyama

The three (dharana, dhyana and samadhi) together constitute samyama.

Samyama is the totality of the three processes described above. It contains two parts: *sam* means perfect or thorough, *yama* means control. So *samyama* means complete mastery over the psychic process or a complete control of mental concentration. This is a very important topic of yoga. It reveals to us the secret of yogic powers. The application of samyama to different objects or thoughts will give rise to psychic powers called *vibhootis*.

The samyama cannot be said to be complete unless there is fusion of the three processes of concentration. The object of meditation must become extremely clear and there should be no personal consciousness. The object may pertain to the body or mind or society or personal possessions and so on, but there should be these two factors. The samyama starts with the subjective and objective awareness; that is a dual awareness. You are aware of your object of meditation within as well as in the outside world, but gradually the outer doors are closed and you see only the thing that is inside. That is dhyana. Then the thing seen inside becomes clearer and clearer and simultaneously you lose your personal consciousness; that is called samadhi. The three put together are known as samyama.

Sutra 5: Result of samyama

तज्जयात्प्रज्ञालोकः ॥ ५ ॥

Tajjayātprajñālokaḥ

Tat: that; *jayāt*: by mastering: *prajñā*: higher consciousness; *ālokaḥ*: illumination

By mastering it (samyama) the higher consciousness dawns.

When contemplation is continued on any object and when the object becomes very clear and there is no personal awareness for the time being, it is called the state of samyama. It gives rise to higher consciousness of the object of concentration. If meditating on *Aum*, it manifests itself most clearly in the higher consciousness.

When I see a thing with the eyes, it is sensual consciousness. When I close my eyes and try to see that object, it is mental consciousness. When that object, for example, *Aum*, comes in the form of a shadow, it is deeper consciousness. When suddenly it shines forth inside with all its clarity and vividness, it is called higher consciousness.

The student may be aware of his body, his existence, his consciousness and the things of the external world, but then again he blinks. The symbol or the object shines clearly, then again the consciousness returns. After that, the object again shines clearly in the chidakasha, but here the consciousness of the self is lost. In that state there is the manifestation of prajna. This is called *prajnaloka*, which means the arousal of the light of higher consciousness, in which the object of meditation shines in the clearest manner.

Sutra 6: Its application

तस्य भूमिषु विनियोगः ॥ ६ ॥

Tasya bhūmiṣu viniyogaḥ

Tasya: of that; *bhūmiṣu*: in the subtle states; *viniyogaḥ*: application

That (light of higher consciousness) should be applied to different, finer states of consciousness.

Hereafter the word samyama will be used for dharana, dhyana and samadhi. Samyama should be practised on different objects. They are the finer stages of consciousness called *bhumi*. In other words, they are the states of vitarka, vichara, ananda and asmita. This application of samyama to the finer stages must be done not only in the state of samadhi but in all stages of sadhana.

This application is a very difficult process. Supposing a scientist takes up a particular problem belonging to the world of the senses. He thinks about it in all stages during his work. There is continuous and intense thinking and awareness. This is a kind of samyama, through which he comes to know the truth lying behind that problem. It reveals itself to him in his deep state of absorption. He contemplates on that truth and further comes to know a still deeper truth. He takes that up and gives up the earlier one, then he thinks of nothing else. Ultimately he comes to a basic fact which is revealed to him in the third stage.

Similarly, a sannyasin or a student of yoga practises samyama first on the gross objects and slowly goes to the basic foundation of the problem. When a new idea, a new truth reveals itself, he catches hold of it and goes to a still finer, still deeper truth. Ultimately he comes to the central fact, which is beyond any relationship or maya. Behind the name and form, he comes face to face with the basic reality or truth. This is called application of samyama.

Thus samyama may be practised on an individual or a thing or its qualities and then on the underlying principle. Thus there is the application of samyama to gross and subtle states.

Sutra 7: These three are internal

त्रयमन्तरङ्गं पूर्वेभ्यः ॥ ७ ॥

Trayamantaraṅgaṃ pūrvebhyaḥ

Trayam: the three together; *antaraṅgaṃ*: internal; *pūrvebhyaḥ*: in relation to the earlier ones

The three together are internal in relation to the previous ones.

The trinity of dharana, dhyana and samadhi is internal as compared to the first five parts of yoga: that is yama, niyama, asana, pranayama and pratyahara. Internal means subtler or finer. The previous five parts belong to the realm of buddhi, character, habits, manners, mind, sense organs and prana. They belong to the annamaya kosha, pranamaya kosha and manomaya kosha; therefore, they are called the external parts or outward parts – *bahiranga*. They all belong to the external world.

Antaranga means internal, introverted. When you are standing at the threshold of the door, you are aware of both the outside and the inside. That is pratyahara. When you are not on the threshold but looking outside, then it is yama, niyama, asana and pranayama.

All the five parts up to pratyahara belong to your personal habits; they belong to the external world. They have nothing to do with the deeper layers of your consciousness and, therefore, it is said in this sutra that dharana, dhyana and samadhi together constitute the internal disciplines.

Sutra 8: Yet external to nirbeeja samadhi

तदपि बहिरङ्गं निर्बीजस्य ॥ ८ ॥

Tadapi bahiraṅgaṃ nirbījasya

Tadapi: that also; *bahiraṅga*: external; *nirbījasya*: of nirbeeja samadhi

That (three stages or trinity) also is external to nirbeeja samadhi.

Nirbeeja samadhi is the innermost or finest state, so even dharana, dhyana and samadhi are external as compared to nirbeeja samadhi. In nirbeeja samadhi there is no pratyaya, no object, no seed, but only pure awareness. Samyama belongs to sabeeja samadhi, so the four stages of samprajnata are to be considered external to nirbeeja samadhi.

Thus the first five parts, namely yama, niyama, asana, pranayama and pratyahara are external to dharana, dhyana and samadhi. The latter in their turn are external to nirbeeja samadhi.

There is an important purpose in mentioning that sabeeja samadhi is external to nirbeeja samadhi in that we must know that although we can obtain supernatural powers through samyama, it is not the highest state. The highest state, namely, nirbeeja samadhi, is altogether different. The psychic faculties which we possess through samyama are in the field of sabeeja samadhi, which is not the final stage. Therefore, the spiritual aspirant should not rest content with sabeeja samadhi but should try to go to the deepest level, that is, nirbeeja samadhi.

Samyama can be practised on any object which may be in the body or in the outside world; it may be gross or subtle or it may be a part of your body, such as the tip of the nose or tongue and so on. Samyama can be practised not only on present objects, but also on past objects such as a previous birth, or it can also be practised on a future birth, but it must be remembered that any kind of samyama is external to nirbeeja samadhi.

Sutra 9: Nirodha parinama

व्युत्थाननिरोधसंस्कारयोरभिभवप्रादुर्भावौ निरोधक्षणचित्तान्वयो
निरोधपरिणामः ॥ ९ ॥

Vyutthānanirodhasaṃskārayorabhibhavaprādurbhāvau
nirodhakṣaṇachittānvayo nirodhapariṇāmaḥ

Vyutthana: coming out; *nirodha*: stopping; *saṃskārayoh*: of the two impressions; *abhibhava*: suppression; *prādurbhāvau*: emergence; *nirodhakṣaṇa*: moment of suppression; *chitta*: the mind; *anvayah*: permeation; *nirodha*: suppression; *pariṇāmaḥ*: transformation

Nirodha parinama is that state of transformation of mind where it is permeated by the moment of suppression which appears and disappears between incoming and outgoing samskaras.

In this sutra, the fundamental state of mental transformation involved in the practice of yoga is explained. When you attain samadhi, you must know that your consciousness has undergone a definite state of transformation, and that change takes place in the realm of consciousness. *Parinama* is change. For example, curd is a parinama of milk. In samadhi or even in the preliminary sadhana, the mind undergoes transformations. They take place in different degrees and at different points. The whole range of transformation is classified into three. The present sutra describes the transformation in the form of suppression. There are two other forms which are described in the next two sutras. They are called transformation in the form of tranquillity and transformation in the form of concentration.

Thus the mind undergoes these three changes after attaining samadhi. It should be understood that samadhi parinama comes first, ekagrata parinama comes next and nirodha parinama comes last. It happens like this. When you have started the practice of samyama, the mind undergoes transformation in three stages. The first stage is samadhi, the second, ekagrata, and the third, nirodha. This is the order but in the sutra it is changed.

Nirodha is suppression of the object of meditation. This is a very interesting topic. When you practise samyama, for example, on *Aum* as the basis, you try to be aware of it and nothing else. All distractions are overcome, even your guru, or God, or any other idea. All else except *Aum* is suppressed. That is called samadhi parinama and thereby you attain the state of tranquillity. When you have finished that state, then *Aum* becomes clear and there is a continuous flow of it in your mind. If this continues for half and hour, every moment *Aum* will be in your awareness. In this process, one *Aum* is followed by another and there is continuity. It is like the continuity of the flame of an oil lamp. In that state, the mind undergoes a transformation which is called *ekagrata parinama*.

When you go ahead, suddenly another idea comes to you; that is not nirodha, that is called *vyutthana*, which is just the revival of the previous consciousness. Then there is suppression of it and again *Aum* emerges; that particular period of suppression is called nirodha. That is one parinama.

Now the student should know how to remove the pratyaya completely. In nirodha parinama, the pratyaya of disturbing factors is suppressed. Then there comes a period when your mind undergoes the second state of transformation in ekagrata parinama. Then, after that, instead of concentrating on *Aum*, you will have to concentrate on the intervening period and try to remove that *Aum* from the mind. It is very difficult to remove the pratyaya from the mind because the moment you try to make your awareness objectless, shoonya, *Aum* will come again. It has to be removed. Again it will come and again it has to be removed. With practice, the intervening period will go on increasing, the pratyaya will ultimately disappear. Then there will be absolute void. This is the period of nirodha parinama. This is a peculiar method of yoga which must be understood. Yoga first tries to remove one thorn with another thorn and when the thorn is removed, the other thorn is also thrown away. Yoga tries to bring about transformation in the awareness by introducing one particular pratyaya or symbol and then discarding it. So *nirodha parinama* is the dropping of the pratyaya, which one might have cultivated for years.

Vyutthana and nirodha are the two kinds of activities of consciousness. These two kinds of dynamic samskaras are the impressions of consciousness which are responsible for the stage of suppression and manifestation. Thus these two states of suppression and expression come and go, and with them, the pratyaya comes and goes. Thus, even when there is a single pratyaya coming into awareness, time and again there is nirodha parinama in between the expression of two pratyayas, but that pratyaya is also to be suppressed. There comes a condition of complete void, then the pratyaya comes up again.

Laya is different from nirodha. Sometimes while practising meditation there is momentary blankness in which everything disappears; that is laya and not nirodha. It is involuntary. Nirodha is voluntary suppression, which is different from laya. Transformation in the form of voluntary suppression is the last transformation of mind. The physical body also undergoes transformation; for example, childhood, youth, old age and death.

The mind undergoes a similar transformation from dharana to samadhi, through the three transformations or stages called samadhi parinama, ekagrata parinama and nirodha parinama. In samadhi parinama, you try to establish the pratyaya and diminish other thoughts. In ekagrata parinama, you try to continue that pratyaya because there are no distractions now, the mind is quiet. In nirodha parinama, you try to diminish the pratyaya which you have established and you now try to establish the shoonyata. Thereby you transcend the field of sabeeja samadhi and go into nirbeeja samadhi.

Sutra 10: Fruits of nirodha parinama

तस्य प्रशान्तवाहिता संस्कारात् ॥ १० ॥

Tasya praśāntavāhitā saṃskārāt

Tasya: of it; *praśānta*: peaceful; *vāhitā*: flow; *saṃskārāt*: by repeated impression

The flow of nirodha parinama becomes tranquil by repeated impression.

The final state of transformation of mind becomes tranquil and powerful by practising it again and again; then that state is not interrupted by any disturbance of the pratyaya. This is a very crucial point. If this nirodha is practised before ekagrata or before samadhi, you will enter laya, or darkness, and those who follow the path of *nirakara*, formless, will enter into double darkness. So this particular state of suppression should never be tried by any aspirant before he has finalized ekagrata parinama. Just as milk comes first, then curd, then butter, similarly samadhi parinama, ekagrata parinama and nirodha parinama should follow each other.

While you are practising deep meditation, the impression breaks sometimes and this breaking point is called nirodha. This will only come when there is practically continuous awareness. When it becomes continuous and then, in between two impressions suddenly there is blankness, shoonya, this is called nirodha. Suddenly your consciousness emerges into the next plane of one-pointed concentration, then there is a break again, there is no impression at all; hence it is called nirodha. Hereafter you have to change the whole pattern. Once the pratyaya becomes continuous, without any intervention, you have to wait for some time until there is a voluntary suppression. Then the pratyaya of the symbol, such as *Aum*, becomes clearer and then suddenly there is a break again. This is again nirodha; there is continuity of impression and suddenly after a few months of practice you find a break. Afterwards, suddenly the impression appears. Again by force you should break it. It disappears and automatically *Aum* will appear again. The moment it reappears, you should try to break it.

When you have come to a particular state where nirodha increases and vyutthana decreases, then samadhi comes, so you undo what you have already done. Therefore, yoga is called *viyoga*. We try to bring about a transformation in the mind and that transformation is brought about in three stages. It is not an imaginary circle but an actual change in the molecular structure of the mind. Even the brain is changed. This particular transformation in three stages is again subdivided into many stages, but we need not go into details here.

Sutra 11: Samadhi parinama

सर्वार्थतैकाग्रतयोः क्षयोदयौ चित्तस्य समाधिपरिणामः ॥ ११ ॥

Sarvārthataikāgratayoḥ kṣayodayau chittasya samādhipariṇāmaḥ

Sarvārthatā: a diverse state; *ekāgratayoḥ*: one-pointedness; *kṣayodayau*: disappearance and appearance; *chittasya*: of the mind; *samādhi*: tranquillity; *pariṇāmaḥ*: transformation

Samadhi parinama is the disappearance and appearance of distraction and one-pointedness of mind.

Samadhi parinama is a state when concentration and distraction of the mind appear and disappear. This is simultaneous; the distraction disappears and one-pointedness appears. Thus it is a state of mind, of transformation of consciousness. This is a higher state.

In this particular state an impression, for instance, *Aum*, appears then simultaneously distraction appears. Then you suppress the distraction and *Aum* reappears. The previous layer of samskaras tries to suppress concentration, but the latest layer of samskaras tries to suppress the distraction. Your effort to establish the one impression, *Aum*, suppresses all other distractions (vikshepa). This is exactly what happens in your daily practices. When you sit down, you are trying to practise ekagrata on a particular impression. Suddenly a particular thought comes up and disturbs the impression, then you bring the impression again to your mind and suppress the distraction. Again like an explosion some other thought comes from below and throws off the impression, and so on. This particular state is called samadhi parinama. This is the first stage of transformation in the realm of consciousness.

Sutra 12: Ekagrata parinama

ततः पुनः शान्तोदितौ तुल्यप्रत्ययौ चित्तस्यैकाग्रतापरिणामः ॥ १२ ॥

Tataḥ punaḥ śāntoditau tulyapratyayau
chittasyaikāgratāpariṇāmaḥ

Tataḥ: then; *punaḥ*: again; *śanta*: subsided; *uditau*: manifest; *tulya*: equal; *pratyayau*: content of the mind; *chittasya*: of the mind; *ekāgratā*: one-pointedness; *pariṇāmaḥ*: transformation.

Then again when the objects which subside and appear are similar, it is called one-pointed transformation of mind.

In ekagrata parinama the same impression rises and subsides time and again. The impression, for example, *Aum*, rises and subsides alternately. The quality of the subsiding impression and the rising impression must be the same, but the interval between is very short. When we see a film on the screen we cannot know the different pictures separately, for us there is continuity. It is the same in the case of ekagrata parinama. The rising and subsiding of the impressions is so quick that it escapes our attention and we may feel a continuous flow of pratyaya. The difference between the two states is difficult to perceive, yet it is not a single state.

The mind is steady in the state of concentration and in that case we do know the difference between the two states. Usually our mind keeps on moving from object to object and that is why it is said in the scriptures that the mind keeps on moving. In samadhi the mind is completely suppressed but in other stages, even if it is one-pointed, it keeps on moving. There is the movement of pratyaya; one pratyaya subsides and the same again arises. This process goes on for some time. This is known as ekagrata parinama of the mind.

Sutra 13: Application of these parinamas

एतेन भूतेन्द्रियेषु धर्मलक्षणावस्थापरिणामाः व्याख्याताः ॥ १३ ॥

Etena bhūtendriyeṣu dharmalakṣaṇāvasthāpariṇāmāḥ vyākhyātāḥ

Etena: by this; *bhūta*: elements; *indriyeṣu*: in the sense organs; *dharma*: quality, property; *lakṣaṇa*: characteristic; *avasthā*: condition; *pariṇāmaḥ*: transformations; *vyākhyātāḥ*: are explained

By this the three parinamas, namely, nature, character and condition in the elements and sense organs are explained.

We should understand the transformation or change in the elements and sense organs in the fashion of the transformations explained in the previous sutras. As the mind undergoes the threefold changes or transformations due to samyama in the form of samadhi, ekagrata and nirodha, similarly the elements and sense organs undergo three types of changes called dharma, lakshana and avastha. With the growth of the body certain changes take place. You become old and there are changes in the body and in the organs. These are the three types. This sutra means that when the mind undergoes a change or transformation, a similar change takes place in the sense perception and sense organs.

By analyzing the concepts deeply, the mind undergoes changes and corresponding to the transformations of the chitta, there are transformations in the body and in the objects of perception. These changes are as follows:

1. *Dharma parinama* – the chitta is transformed so far as its property (dharma) is concerned.
2. *Lakshana parinama* – the chitta is transformed so far as its character is concerned.

3. *Avastha parinama* – the chitta is transformed so far as its condition, that is, avastha, is concerned.

The first transformation is in samadhi. When you are trying to eliminate the distractions of the mind during the practice of samyama, the chitta undergoes a little change so far as its nature is concerned. In ekagrata, the chitta will have another change in its structure or property, character and condition. Then again, when the chitta undergoes nirodha parinama, it will have a third transformation in the property, character and condition. Thus, in all the three stages it undergoes dharma, lakshana and avastha parinama. The transformation in the senses and elements takes place exactly in the same manner.

There are five elements, such as earth, water, fire, air and ether, and ten sense organs, five of which are cognitive and five which are called motor organs. The cognitive organs have a connection with the corresponding bhuta; for example, the ears grasp sound, which is a quality of ether; the skin grasps touch, which is a quality of air and so on, but the senses do not work independently. The mind or chitta must be connected with them, otherwise the senses will not convey their impulses.

When the chitta undergoes the three kinds of changes, the sense organs and the five elements are also influenced by these changes. The elements and indriyas gradually undergo the changes called dharma, lakshana and avastha in the course of the practice of samadhi, ekagrata and nirodha. Perception is the dharma of the five senses and this dharma is modified with the transformation of the chitta.

The purpose of this sutra is to prove that in the course of time, by samyama, the yogi is able to perform many kinds of miracles. It is a kind of proof so that you may understand how, by concentration, the dharma, lakshana and avastha of the senses and the elements can be transformed. This will be made clear in the discussion of psychic powers.

Sutra 14: Dharmi – the common substratum

शान्तोदिताव्यपदेश्यधर्मानुपाती धर्मी ॥ १४ ॥

Śāntoditāvyapadeśyadharmānupātī dharmī

Śanta: peaceful, latent; *udita*: manifest; *avyapadeśya*: unmanifestable; *dharma*: the properties; *anupātī*: common; *dharmī*: substratum of properties

The dharmi (substratum) is common in all latent, active or unmanifestable properties.

While the transformations take place in the properties, characters and condition of the chitta, bhutas and indriyas, there must be something which remains unchanged, which is the common substratum of all these changes. In yoga philosophy, it is a common fact that under all conditions of change there is an underlying factor beyond any change.

The body changes with age, but the 'I' or the self remains unchanged, not only during this birth but throughout the whole series of births. My changing states from childhood to old age are all ascribed to me only because in me there is a principle which is unaltered, unchanged. This is called the *dharmi*. It is not the body or mind or the consciousness or the impressions.

Buddhists do not believe in anything permanent. They say that everything is undergoing a constant change throughout life, like the flame of a candle which burns continuously but changes every moment. Similarly, everything in the world changes every moment. Buddhists do not believe in the idea of dharmi, but yoga philosophy needs the idea of dharmi to show the possibility of miracles. So, it is said in this sutra that the dharmi is the substratum of all changes, past, present and future.

Sutra 15: Cause of difference

क्रमान्यत्वं परिणामान्यत्वे हेतुः ॥ १५ ॥

Kramānyatvaṃ pariṇāmānyatve hetuḥ

Krama: order; *anyatvaṃ*: difference; *pariṇāmāh*: transformation; *anyatve*: for difference; *hetuḥ*: cause

The difference in the process of succession is the cause in transformation.

There is a difference in the succession of events of various things. For example, a lump of mud can be developed into a pot; it will be destroyed and become a lump of mud again. In the same manner, a particular chitta undergoes transformations in a particular manner according to the underlying laws of its nature. This difference in the order of events gives rise to different transformations of the chitta, senses and elements.

Now the whole structure of chitta should undergo a change, a process called involution. Since the whole process of samadhi, ekagrata and nirodha is involved in the structure of chitta, this sutra says that any change which goes on in the structure of the mind is there because it must be there.

Even if you do not practise any sadhana and just leave yourself as you are, even then in the course of time your chitta will undergo this particular state of transformation, but it may take several births.

Sutra 16: Knowledge of past and future

परिणामत्रयसंयमादतीतानागतज्ञानम् ॥ १६ ॥

Pariṇāmatrayasaṃyamādatītānāgatajñānam

Pariṇāma: transformation; *traya*: three; *saṃyamāt*: by samyama; *atīta*: past; *anāgatah*: future; *jñānam*: knowledge

By performing samyama on the three transformations, knowledge of past and future (arises).

Samadhi, ekagrata and nirodha are the three transformations. To perform samyama on these three means to perform samyama first on samadhi, then on ekagrata and then on nirodha. It means you perform samyama in the form of awareness of the distractions and eliminate them. Then you practise samyama on the awareness of one-pointedness; similarly, samyama on nirodha means to become aware of it. These three samyamas eliminate the distractions of the mind. Side by side there is awareness of the state also, so, side by side with the removal of distractions, you must become totally aware of that removal. This is called samyama on the three transformations. Then the chitta becomes so fine that it transcends the barriers of time and knows the happenings of the past and the future.

Sutra 17: Knowledge of all speech

शब्दार्थप्रत्ययानामितरेतराध्यासात् संकरस्तत्प्रविभागसंयमात्
सर्वभूतरुतज्ञानम् ॥ १७ ॥

Śabdārthapratyayānāmitaretarādhyāsāt
saṅkarastatpravibhāgasaṃyamāt sarvabhūtarutajñānam

Śabda: word; *artha*: object; *pratyayānām*: mental content; *itaretarādhyāsāt*: because of mental superimposition; *saṅkara*: confusion; *tat*: that; *pravibhāga*: separate; *saṃyamāt*: by samyama; *sarvabhūta*: all living beings; *ruta*: speech; *jñānam*: knowledge

The word, object and mental content are in a confused state because of mutual superimposition. By performing samyama on them separately, knowledge of the speech of all beings (arises).

Usually our knowledge of objects is confused because of a confusion of shabda, artha and pratyaya. If we do samyama on them separately, we can know the speech of all animals. Thus sound should be separated from the object, the object from the idea, such as the word cow, the object cow and the pratyaya cow. Samyama should be done on these three factors separately, thereby the superimposition or confusion between the word, the object and the pratyaya or mental experience is removed.

Different people have different mental experiences from the object cow. For example, a Hindu will say it should be protected, while a Muslim will say that it should be slaughtered. This is the difference in pratyaya. Similarly, there is the difference between the words. For example, in different languages there are different words for the same object cow. When you make a difference between the form cow, the name cow and the idea of cow and do samyama separately on the three, this sutra says you will know the speech or language of the cow or any other animal or creature. These are the secrets of yoga which people do not practise because they are very difficult.

Every object in the world has three components or *vibhaga*, namely, sound or word, the form and the idea. You should be able to do samyama on the sound waves separately, on the form separately and also on the idea separately. This is very difficult.

Sutra 18: Knowledge of previous births

संस्कारसाक्षात्करणात् पूर्वजातिज्ञानम् ॥ १८ ॥

Saṃskārasākṣātkaraṇāt pūrvajāti jñānam

Saṃskāra: impression; *sākṣātkaraṇāt*: by direct perception; *pūrva*: previous; *jāti*: birth; *jñānam*: knowledge

By direct perception of the impressions, knowledge of previous births (arises).

Samskaras are to two types: memory and vasana. Memory is subconscious and vasana is unconscious. When in memory, the samskaras are arranged in a definite order; when in the unconscious, they are not so arranged. The samskaras which are giving rise to the fruits or effects are stored in the form of prarabdha, like sound in a gramophone record. By practising samyama on the impressions that can be seen during the deeper stages of consciousness, the subconscious as well as the unconscious can be probed. By practising samyama on these samskaras, the yogi can have access to past births.

Sutra 19: Knowledge of others' minds

प्रत्ययस्य परचित्तज्ञानम् ॥ १९ ॥

Pratyayasya parachittajñānam

Pratyayasya: of the content of the mind; *para*: another; *chitta*: mind; *jñānam*: knowledge

By performing samyama on the pratyayas, knowledge of another's mind (arises).

The clairvoyant contact between two individuals can take place only when the objective perception of the personality is clearly acquired in all the three stages.

Sutra 20: But not of the mental image

न च तत् सालम्बनं तस्याविषयीभूतत्वात् ॥ २० ॥

Na cha tat sālambanaṃ tasyāviṣayībhūtatvāt

Na: not; *cha*: and; *tat*: that; *sālambanaṃ*: with support; *tasya*: its; *aviṣayībhūtatvāt*: because of not being the subject of samyama

But the knowledge of that (other mental factors) is not gained with support of the mental image because that is not the object of samyama.

The knowledge of others' minds gained through samyama does not include the mental image of that mind because it is of a general nature. The different contents of that mind are not the object of samyama. If you are aware of a particular image or pratyaya prevailing in others' minds, then you can have the knowledge of that mind but the thought can be read only generally. You cannot know any particular thought in that mind – only the nature of the thoughts can be known, so the pratyaya is of a general nature. For example, you can know greed, raga, dwesha and so on.

There are two stages. In the first stage there is general thought reading, and in the second stage there can be particular thought reading. When we look at a particular person, through samyama over his mind we know in a general way which vrittis, such as hate, anger, love, passion, fear, anxiety, etc., are arising in his mind. It is done through understanding the pratyaya and not through reading the face. The pratyaya can be understood through dhyana or through dreams or through observation or behaviour. These are other methods of understanding other people's minds.

So, for understanding another person's mind, you have to give him some negative suggestions and understand his response. Then, after you have been able to do samyama on his response, you can know the general nature of his mind. In the second stage, you have to start with particular thoughts working in his mind. You will have to give him a few symbols and ask him to work with them. That creates a sort of connection between your mind and his mind, and whatever takes place in his mind, every particular thought or reaction, can be directly seen through samyama.

It is said in this sutra that particular thoughts in the mind of another person cannot be read or seen. That is the first stage we have described above; it is very difficult and requires a very special capacity of the mind.

Sutra 21: Invisibility

कायरूपसंयमात् तद्ग्राह्यशक्तिस्तम्भे चक्षुःप्रकाशसम्प्रयोगेऽन्तर्धानम् ॥ २१ ॥

Kāyarūpasaṃyamāt tadgrāhyaśaktistambhe chakṣuḥ prakāśāsamprayoge'ntardhānam

Kāya: body; *rūpa*: form; *saṃyamāt*: by doing samyama; *tat*: that; *grāhya*: receptive; *śakti*: power; *stambhe*: on suspension; *chakṣuh*: the eye; *prakāśa*: light; *samprayoga*: absence of contact; *antardhānam*: being invisible

By performing samyama on the form of the body and suspending receptivity of the form, there being no contact between the eye and the light (the yogi can become) invisible.

When the yogi performs samyama on his own body, then suddenly the power of receiving the form stops and there in no contact between the eyes of observers and the body of the yogi. He thus becomes invisible. This is a well-known siddhi or psychic power. It is a frightening practice. When a form dissolves before one's eyes, it is as frightening as the coming of death. An object becomes visible when the light rays reflected from its surface enter the eye of an observer. If the light is stopped by the power of samyama, then one can become invisible.

In yoga there are five tanmatras or subtle forms of the elements. The roopa tanmantra becomes the object of the yogi's samyama. First the yogi practises samyama on his body with a mirror, then there is suspension of the power of receiving roopa, or form. For some time there is no contact between the observer and the body of the yogi. Thus, the physical body first becomes invisible to the yogi himself and afterwards through practice it becomes invisible to others.

This is because there is no connection between the object and the observer. Thus this involves meditation on the physical form as seen in a mirror. This is different to what you do in kriya yoga.

Sutra 22: Disappearance of the tanmatras

एतेन शब्दाद्यन्तर्धानं उक्तम् ॥ २२ ॥

Etena śabdādyantardhānaṃ uktam

Etena: by this; *śabdādi*: sound and others; *antardhānaṃ*: disappearance; *uktam*: said

By what has been said the disappearance of sound and other tanmatras can be understood.

By practising samyama on your own form, you can make yourself invisible. Now in this sutra it is said that in the same manner, by performing samyama on sound, touch, taste, etc. those faculties can be made to disappear. In a similar way, the yogi can stop other sensations also and control the phenomena concerning them.

Sutra 23: Knowledge of time of death

सोपक्रमं निरुपक्रमं च कर्म तत्संयमादपरान्तज्ञानमरिष्टेभ्यो वा ॥ २३ ॥

Sopakramaṃ nirupakramaṃ cha karma
tatsaṃyamādaparāntajñānamariṣṭebhyo vā

Sopakramaṃ: the karma with activity; *nirūpakramaṃ*: the karma that is dormant; *cha*: and; *karma*: action; *tat*: that; *saṃyamāt*: by performing samyama; *aparānta*: death; *jñānam*: knowledge; *ariṣṭebhyah*: by omens; *vā*: or

Karma is of two kinds, active and dormant. By performing samyama on them knowledge of death is gained, also by omens.

Karma is of two kinds. *Sopakrama* means that karma which has started giving its fruits. *Niroopakrama* karma is that which is dormant at present and would be exhausted after some time. The first kind of karma is also called *prarabdha*, and the second kind *sanchita*, that which remains in store. Now, as a matter of fact, the karmas can be divided into three, but in this sutra they are divided into two. Patanjali does not include *kriyamana karma* because it has to go into the store of niroopakrama karma.

By performing samyama on these two types of karma, the time of death can be known beforehand. Birth and death are the effects of karma and if we can do samyama on karma, we can know when there will be death. There have been many such cases in history. There is also another way of knowing the time of death, which is called *arishta*. By knowing the arishta, people can know death six months in advance. It is a very common thing: even ordinary people can know this. There are certain symptoms, such as not being able to look at the nose, not seeing the left ear when you look at the shadow, not seeing the shadow at all, and so on. These are called arishtas. They are studied in swara yoga and in chhaya upasana. Thus there are two ways of knowing death beforehand.

Sutra 24: Powers of friendliness, etc.

मैत्र्यादिषु बलानि ॥ २४ ॥

Maitryādiṣu balāni

Maitri: friendliness; *ādiṣu*: etc.; *balāni*: powers

By performing samyama on friendliness, etc. there come those particular powers.

Friendliness, compassion, happiness and indifference are the four tendencies that a yogi has to cultivate. These were described in the first chapter. It is said that when samyama is performed on these four tendencies, certain powers are developed. Thus different kinds of power are developed by practising samyama on each one of the four tendencies, namely, maitri, karuna, mudita and upeksha.

Sutra 25: Attainment of strength

बलेषु हस्तिबलादीनि ॥ २५ ॥

Baleṣu hastibalādīni

Baleṣu: by samyama on the powers; *hasti*: elephant; *bala*: strength; *ādīni*: etc.

By samyama on the strength of an elephant, etc. the corresponding strength (is developed).

One can make anything – a person, an animal or an event – the object of his samyama. When strong animals like the elephant, lion or tiger are made the objects for practising samyama, the strength of that animal can be acquired. The strength of these animals is to be meditated upon while doing samyama, then the same strength can be developed in the student of yoga. If he does samyama on the mental alertness of a tiger, he can develop that mental alertness in himself. Similarly, if samyama is practised on the agility of a tiger, that agility can be developed by the yogi in himself.

Sutra 26: Hidden knowledge

प्रवृत्त्यालोकन्यासात् सूक्ष्मव्यवहितविप्रकृष्टज्ञानम् ॥ २६ ॥

Pravṛttyālokanyāsāt
sūkṣmavyavahitaviprakṛṣṭajñānam

Pravṛtti: superphysical faculty; *āloka*: light; *nyāsāt*: by projecting; *sūkṣma*: fine; *vyavahita*: hidden; *viprakṛṣṭa*: distant; *jñānam*: knowledge

The knowledge of subtle, obscure or distant (objects) is gained by dilating the light of the superphysical faculty.

It is said in sutra 36 of the first chapter that a faculty called *vishoka* can be developed in the mind. The mind can also develop a superphysical faculty, which is called *jyotishmati pravritti*, the illuminating faculty. In this sutra, the word pravritti is used to indicate that faculty. By developing this illuminating faculty in the mind, which is capable of penetrating anywhere, the yogi can see hidden, obscure or distant objects.

When the illuminating faculty is directed towards a person or an object which is missing, it can immediately be known where that person or thing is. Thus, treasures which are buried underground, or objects which are very distant can be directly observed. Even subtle things like atoms or individual cells in the body can be observed. There are two methods of practising this.

One is the vedic method, the other is the yogic method. The vedic or tantric method need not be discussed here because it is an absolutely ritualistic method. In yogic practices, the crystal plays a very important part. In South India there is a particular science called anjnanam, meaning not known. It consists of different methods of projecting the illuminating superphysical faculty through a crystal. The same thing can be done by reflection of light from any shining surface, but it is necessary for the person to have developed the superphysical faculty called jyotishmati pravritti.

Sutra 27: Knowledge of the solar system

भुवनज्ञानं सूर्ये संयमात् ॥ २७ ॥

Bhuvanajñānaṃ sūryesaṃyamāt

Bhuvana: solar system; *jñānaṃ*: knowledge; *sūrye*: on the sun; *saṃyamāt*: by performing samyama

Knowledge of the solar system is gained by performing samyama on the sun.

Knowledge of the solar system has three parts as follows:

1. The structure of the solar system, which is a unit in the cosmos.
2. The arrangement of stars in the groups called galaxies.
3. The law which governs the movements of planets and stars.

This knowledge can be gained by practising samyama on the sun. The word sun may mean various things, such as the surya nadi, sushumna, the physical sun and so on. In ancient times the modern techniques of astronomy were not available, yet the rishis were able to calculate various astronomical facts very correctly.

They could arrive at their astonishing discoveries only in one of two ways. They could either develop their mind through samyama, or else they had developed some apparatus like a telescope, otherwise they could not have calculated correctly. We do not know of any apparatus they used, so we must believe that they knew the universe through practising samyama on the sun.

When you try to perform samyama on the physical sun, or on the mental image of the sun, then gradually, in the deepest state of ekagrata, you are able to locate the microcosmic sun within you. When you are able to do this, then certainly you will know everything about the structure and arrangement of the universe, as well as the laws underlying these structures.

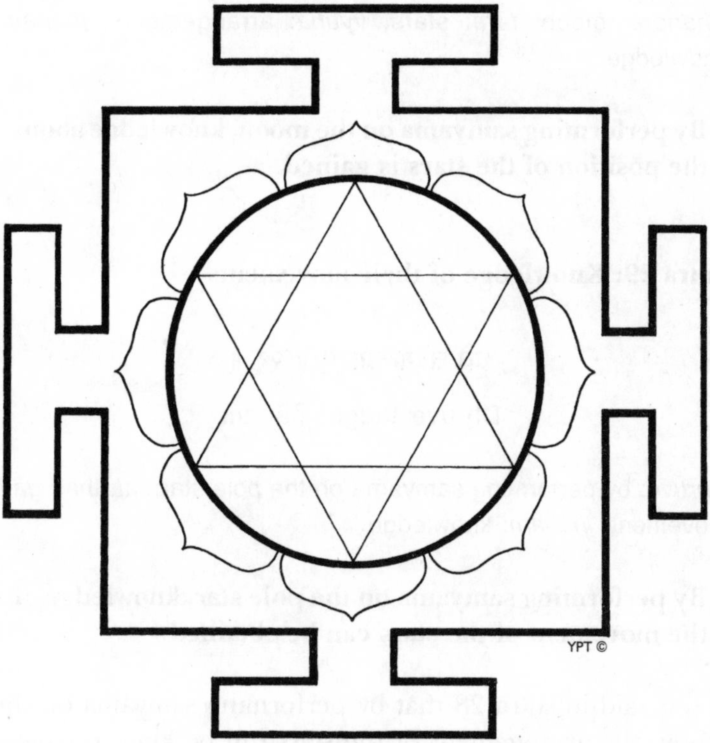

Shiva Yantra

Sutra 28: Knowledge of the stars

चन्द्रे ताराव्यूहज्ञानम् ॥ २८ ॥

Chandre tārāvyūhajñānam

Chandre: moon; *tārā*: stars; *vyūha*: arrangements; *jñānam*: knowledge

By performing samyama on the moon, knowledge about the position of the stars is gained.

Sutra 29: Knowledge of their movements

ध्रुवे तद्गतिज्ञानम् ॥ २९ ॥

Dhruve tadgatijñānam

Dhruve: by performing samyama on the pole star; *tat*: that; *gati*: movement; *jñānam*: knowledge

By performing samyama on the pole star, knowledge of the movement of the stars can be obtained.

It was said in sutra 28 that by performing samyama on the moon, the arrangement of the stars can be known. Now if you want to know about their absolute and relative movement, you have to do samyama on the pole star. Our ancient rishis knew a lot of things very accurately about the stars and the heavenly bodies. This must have been due to samyama on the sun, moon and the pole star.

Sutra 30: Knowledge of the body

नाभिचक्रे कायव्यूहज्ञानम् ॥ ३० ॥

Nābhichakre kāyavyūhajñānam

Nābhi: navel; *chakre*: centre; *kāya*: body; *vyūha*: arrangement; *jñānam*: knowledge

By performing samyama on the navel centre, knowledge of the arrangement in the body is gained.

It should be noted that *nabhi chakra* here does not mean manipura chakra but the centre of the navel from where different nadis emerge and go to different parts of the body.

Sutra 31: Cessation of hunger and thirst

कण्ठकूपे क्षुत्पिपासानिवृत्तिः ॥ ३१ ॥

Kaṇṭhakūpe kṣutpipāsā nivṛttiḥ

Kaṇṭhakūpe: by performing samyama on the throat pit; *kṣut*: hunger; *pipāsā*: thirst; *nivṛttiḥ*: retirement

By performing samyama on the throat pit, hunger and thirst retire.

The gullet or the throat pit is the centre of the gland that secretes the fluid which causes dryness in the throat, resulting in thirst, and burning in the stomach which causes hunger. By performing samyama on that particular centre of the gland, the secretion can be checked and thereby the student obtains mastery over thirst and hunger.

Sutra 32: Power of steadiness

कूर्मनाड्यां स्थैर्यम् ॥ ३२ ॥

Kūrmanāḍyāṃ sthairyam

Kūrmanāḍyāṃ: by performing samyama on the kurma nadi; *sthairyam*: steadiness

Steadiness is achieved by samyama on the kurma nadi.

Steadiness here means both in an ordinary capacity and a miraculous capacity. The student may become so immovable that you cannot move him even with the application of great force. Steadiness may also mean steadiness of the body during the state of meditation. It may also mean perfect mental stability. All these can be developed by samyama on the kurma nadi.

The *kurma nadi* is supposed to be situated just below the throat pit. It has a shape resembling a tortoise, hence it is called kurma nadi. The easiest method to practise samyama on kurma nadi is to meditate on the point where the chin touches the chest in jalandhara bandha, or else in the pose of sarvangasana. In these two positions the chin touches the chest near the kurma nadi, hence it becomes easy to locate this nadi for practising samyama.

Sutra 33: Spiritual vision

मूर्धज्योतिषि सिद्धदर्शनम् ॥ ३३ ॥

Mūrdhajyotiṣi siddhadarśanam

Mūrdha: crown of the head; *jyotiṣi*: on the light; *siddha*: adept; *darśanam*: spiritual vision

By performing samyama on the light of the crown of the head (sahasrara), a spiritual vision of the masters of yoga is gained.

Murdha here means sahasrara. The light is connected rather with ajna chakra, situated at the centre of the eyebrows. Samyama on ajna chakra can bring about the result much more quickly. When this light flashes before the mind, it gives rise to spiritual visions in which the student has direct perception of various masters of yoga. The masters are able to live even without a body because they have full control over their voluntary and involuntary mental psychic functions, so they can disconnect themselves from the body. They can live without a physical body, hence they are called siddhas. We cannot see them ordinarily because they have no physical body like us but when samyama is practised on ajna chakra or sahasrara chakra, the yogi can meet and communicate with them, so that he can obtain guidance and inspiration from them.

Sutra 34: Intuitive knowledge

प्रतिभाद् वा सर्वम् ॥ ३४ ॥

Pratibhād vā sarvam

Pratibhāt: from pratibha; *vā*: or; *sarvam*: everything

Or everything by virtue of pratibha (intuition).

All the psychic powers mentioned so far can be attained by one distinct faculty called pratibha. Thus the psychic powers can be either individually or collectively acquired through pratibha.

This idea of *pratibha* will be made clearer in sutra 45 of this chapter. It means a kind of superior intuition. It is a process of knowledge devoid of reasoning. As the higher consciousness unfolds, a kind of light is thrown on everything which the mind confronts. This is called knowledge through pratibha. This particular superior quality is the first stage of *viveka jnana*, that is, knowledge gained through the separation of matter and energy. Just as the sunlight makes everything manifest from darkness, similarly, this superior faculty becomes capable of understanding anything and everything.

Sutra 35: Awareness of chitta

हृदये चित्तसंवित् ॥ ३५ ॥

Hṛdaye chittasaṃvit

Hṛdaye: by performing samyama on the heart; *chittasaṃvit*: awareness of the consciousness

By samyama on the heart, awareness of chitta dawns.

Heart here means the lotus called anahata chakra. By meditation or samyama on anahata chakra, the student gains knowledge about the nature of his mind. When matter and mind are associated, that consciousness is known as *chittasamvit*.

Sutra 36: Knowledge of purusha

सत्त्वपुरुषयोरत्यन्तासङ्कीर्णयोः प्रत्ययाविशेषो भोगः परार्थत्वात्
स्वार्थसंयमात् पुरुषज्ञानम् ॥ ३६ ॥

Sattva puruṣayoratyantāsaṅkīrṇayoḥ pratyayāviśeṣo bhogaḥ parārthatvāt svārthasaṃyamāt puruṣajñānam

Sattva: chitta; *puruṣayoh*: of the purusha; *atyanta*: extremely; *asaṅkīrṇayoḥ*: distinct; *pratyaya*: awareness; *aviśeṣah*: not distinct; *bhogaḥ*: experience; *parārthatvāt*: from objective consciousness; *sva*: one's own; *artha*: subjective awareness; *saṃyamāt*: by samyama; *puruṣajñānam*: knowledge of purusha

Chitta and purusha are extremely distinct. On account of non-difference of the awareness of both there is objective or subjective experience. By samyama on subjective awareness apart from objective awareness, the knowledge of purusha is obtained.

It is a basic principle of Samkhya and yoga that chitta and purusha are extremely different and separate by nature, but they appear to be one due to avidya. When we realize or feel that purusha and chitta are one, there is what is called *bhoga* or experience. This is a product of avidya. Due to it, the knowledge that purusha and chitta are totally different is forgotten or veiled. By performing samyama on self-awareness as distinct from subjective awareness, the knowledge of purusha is gained.

We must understand what objective awareness is and what subjective awareness is. Objective awareness is based on the mistaken unity of purusha and chitta, but when there is the realization of their distinctness, then subjective awareness replaces objective awareness. During samyama we meditate on this difference. Purusha is constant, while chitta is fluctuating. By practising samyama, the nature of the purusha is understood.

To realize purusha, you must go beyond the realm of prakriti. That is subjective awareness or self-awareness. Self-awareness arises after you transcend prakriti. Then the distinctness of purusha and prakriti is realized completely. Then there is no bhoga, that is, objective awareness, because avidya is finished.

Sutra 37: Intuitive perception

ततः प्रातिभश्रावणवेदनादर्शास्वादवार्ता जायन्ते ॥ ३७ ॥

Tataḥ prātibhaśrāvaṇavedanādarśāsvādavārtā jāyante

Tataḥ: therefrom; *prātibha*: the faculty of superior consciousness; *śrāvana*: the faculty of hearing; *vedanā*; touch consciousness; *darśa*: visualization; *āsvāda*: faculty of taste; *vārtā*: the olfactory faculty: *jāyante*: are produced

Therefrom are produced transcendental audition, sensation, perception, taste and olfactory knowledge.

The transcendental faculties concerning the sense organs are called the pratibha faculties, such as *pratibhashravan*, *pratibhadarshan* and so on. The word pratibha is common to all the five faculties. By practising samyama on the purusha or subjective awareness as described in the previous sutra, the transcendental faculties pertaining to the sense organs of hearing, touch, seeing, taste and smell arise. Sometimes we come across people who have these faculties, but they should not be confused with telepathy, clairvoyance, etc. These faculties are the product of samyama on the subjective awareness. They are the faculties of Ishwara, such as omniscience, omnipotence and so on. They are obtained through samyama on purusha.

Sutra 38: Psychic powers are obstacles

ते समाधावुपसर्गा व्युत्थाने सिद्धयः ॥ ३८ ॥

Te samādhāvupasargā vyutthāne siddhayaḥ

Te: they; *samādhau*: in samadhi; *upasargā*: obstacles; *vyutthāne*: in the state of consciousness of the world; *siddhayaḥ*: psychic powers

These psychic powers (mentioned in the previous sutra) are obstacles in samadhi, but in the state of consciousness of the world they are psychic powers.

In the extroverted position they are psychic powers, but so far as samadhi is concerned, they act as hindrances. The mind of a yogi does not remain permanently in samadhi. It fluctuates and there is consciousness of the world. In that state these powers can be manifested, but when he is in samadhi, these powers create disturbance if they are allowed to become manifest. The yogi can use them when he comes out of meditation.

The first state of siddhi is there when the student is in samadhi. Even if he may not want to practise or achieve siddhis, they will come to him automatically due to the development of the higher consciousness in deep meditation. When they manifest themselves, they create disturbance in samadhi by generating a kind of psychic vibration. This disturbs the peaceful state of samadhi, but their effects can be seen or observed or tried when the student comes out of samadhi.

Sutra 39: Entering another's body

बन्धकारणशैथिल्यात्प्रचारसंवेदनाच्च चित्तस्य परशरीरावेशः ॥ ३९ ॥

Bandhakāraṇaśaithilyātprachārasaṃvedanāchcha chittasya paraśarīrāveśaḥ

Bandha: bondage; *kāraṇa*: cause; *śaithilyāt*: by loosening; *prachāra*: passage; *saṃvedanāt*: by knowledge; *cha*: and; *chittasya*: of the subtle body; *para*: of others; *śarīra*: body; *āveśaḥ*: entry

By loosening of the cause of bondage and by knowledge of the passage, the subtle body enters another person's body.

This particular psychic power is of a very high order. The aspirant steps out of his body and enters the body of another person. For this, the aspirant can also utilize the help of his disciple. We hear this in the case of many liberated persons and advanced students of yoga, such as Adi Shankaracharya. For this, two conditions must be fulfilled: one, loosening of the cause of bondage; two, knowledge of the path or passage of entry.

The causes of bondage are love for the physical body, fear of death, and the kleshas. This cause of bondage must be loosened, which is done through meditation and samyama. The *sukshma sharira* or subtle body is to be separated from the gross body just as two pieces of cloth glued or stitched together are removed from each other by breaking or loosening the stitches or glue. Similarly, the subtle body is removed and separated from the physical body by loosening the kleshas, fear, etc. While the subtle body is out and away from the physical body, the physical body must be properly taken care of, otherwise it will be impossible to come back, so the causes of bondage must be relaxed and the body should be preserved in good condition.

There should be knowledge of the passage, that is, the nadi along which the chitta has to enter into the body of another person. Only then the entry into another body becomes possible.

Sutra 40: Levitation

उदानजयाज्जलपङ्ककण्टकादिष्वसंग उत्क्रान्तिश्च ॥ ४० ॥

Udānajayājjalapaṅkakaṇṭakādiṣvasaṅga utkrāntiścha

Udāna: one of the five pranas; *jayāt*: by mastery; *jala*: water; *paṅka*: mud; *kaṇṭakādiṣu*: with thorns, etc.; *asaṅga*: no contact; *utkrāntih*: levitation; *cha*: and

By mastery of udana there is non-contact with water, mud, thorns, etc. and the body levitates.

The centre of udana is in the throat, but moves upwards in the region of the head. At the time of death this prana, udana, makes the subtle body free from the physical body. The method of mastery over udana is not given in the scriptures. It is not known whether it is a kind of pranayama or samyama, or a nadi, etc., but it is true this particular nadi has its specialized function and if that is mastered, then you can work against the gravitational pull of the earth.

Levitation is a well-known phenomenon. It is done through the practice of pranayama; therefore, it may be said that mastery over udana can be had by practising pranayama.

Sutra 41: Aura

समानजयाज्ज्वलनम् ॥ ४१ ॥

Samānajayājjvalanam

Samāna: the samana vayu; *jayāt*: by mastery; *jvalanam*: blaze

By mastery of the samana vayu the body blazes.

The samana vayu produces the digestive fluid and is related to the fire which digests food in the stomach. Its range of operation is from the heart to the navel. When the samana vayu is mastered by developing the fire principle, the body develops an aura around itself. This is also possible through pranayama, by brahmacharya and by other purificatory practices.

Sutra 42: Divine hearing

श्रोत्राकाशयोः सम्बन्धसंयमाद्दिव्यं श्रोत्रम् ॥ ४२ ॥

Śrotrākāśayoḥ sambandhasaṃyamāddivyaṃ śrotram

Śrotra: ear; *ākāśayoḥ*: space; *saṃbandha*: relation; *saṃyamāt*: by samyama; *divyaṃ*: divine; *śrotram*: organ of hearing

By samyama on the relation of the ear and space (there is) divine hearing.

Akasha is the medium through which sound travels; the ear is the organ which grasps the sound. Samyama on the relationship of this gives rise to superphysical sounds which are no different from the sounds of the physical plane. Continuity of the sounds is always there but the plane may be physical or superphysical. For example, in nada yoga there are four stages of sound, namely, physical, audible, mental and transcendental, or *vaikhari*, *madhyama*, *pashyanti* and *para*. These are the four planes of sound.

Our ears have the capacity to hear sounds within a particular range, but akasha, as the medium, has the capacity to conduct all sounds. Sound waves take some time to move from place to place, but once generated they exist somewhere in gross or subtle form; they are never finished. Similarly, there is the concept in yoga that the sound of the superphysical plane is not cut off from the sound of the physical plane; it is continuous. By performing samyama on the ear and its relation with akasha, one can have the superphysical properties of hearing sounds, called superphysical sounds. Divine hearing is becoming sensitive to those subtle sounds which are beyond the range of normal mental capacity.

When a gross sound stops you can hear a still finer sound. When that also stops you can hear a still finer sound.

Ultimately the mind becomes so sensitive that it can hear the finest sounds. When that also stops, you may hear your heart beat. After that you can catch the vibration of very subtle sounds, and by practising samyama on akasha and its relationship with the ears, you can start hearing divine sounds.

Sutra 43: Moving through space

कायाकाशयोः सम्बन्धसंयमाल्लघुतूलसमापत्तेश्चाकाशगमनम् ॥ ४३ ॥

Kāyākāśayoḥ sambandhasaṃyamāllaghutūla-
samāpatteśchākāśagamanam

Kāyā: body; *ākāśayoḥ*: of space; *saṃbandha*: relation; *saṃyamāt*: by samyama; *laghu*: light; *tūla*: cotton, wool; *samāpatteh*: by fusion of mind; *cha*: and; *ākāśa*: space; *gamanam*: going through

By samyama on the relation of body and akasha and by fusing the mind with the lightness of cotton, there is going through space.

Toola means the finest fibres of cotton which are extremely light and so float in the air. Similarly, a yogi can float in the air if he does samyama on the relation of his body with akasha, and also concentrates on the lightness of cotton fibres. Here going through space does not mean shifting or moving the physical body through space. When the samyama described in this sutra is practised, there comes a stage when the subtle body is made to move through space. It does not involve movement of the physical body but rather that of the psychic body. The physical body will remain in a particular place, but the subtle body is separated from it and moves through space. It seems that just by performing samyama on akasha, on the body and on light cotton, one cannot move into akasha, but the technique depends more upon the knowledge of the particles that constitute the physical and mental bodies.

Just as a carpenter can reassemble a piece of furniture if he notes the structure of the constituents, similarly, the yogi can disintegrate or dismantle his body if he knows the constitution of the physical and psychic bodies. This siddhi requires a clear-cut understanding of the components of the body and mind, then it is possible that a yogi may resolve his body. Lightness of the physical body can be felt by concentrating on cotton fibres, but that lightness is subjective lightness. It is only a feeling.

The spiritual aspirant should slowly, mentally resolve the physical body in space and gradually the concept of the physical body dissolves, but that is only a subjective feeling.

Sutra 44: Univeral state of mind

बहिरकल्पिता वृत्तिर्महाविदेहा ततः प्रकाशावरणक्षयः ॥ ४४ ॥

Bahirakalpitā vṛttirmahāvidehā tataḥ
prakāśāvaraṇakṣayaḥ

Bahih: external; *akalpitā*: unimaginable; *vṛttih*; state of mind; *mahāvidehā*: existence without body; *tataḥ*: therefrom; *prakāśa*: light; *āvaraṇa*: covering; *kṣayaḥ*: distraction

In the state of mahavideha the vrittis are inconceivable and outside the scope of the body, whereby the covering of light is destroyed.

The word *mahavideha* means the great or universal state of mind which functions without the physical body. The content of our mind is made up of two things:

1. Those that we learn and experience in everyday life, the impressions of many lives and so on. This content of the mind is dependent on the store of past impressions.
2. In addition there is a state called the universal mind. This should be already understood. The individual mind is made up of impressions of various kinds. It depends on contact with the external world via the sense organs but has its basis in the universal mind. The universal mind is original; it is the common foundation of the personality of all human beings.

If all the impressions of experiences could be taken out of the mind, what would remain would be the universal mind, which is infinite and limitless. The state of mahavideha is to be aware of that universal mind. When this is contacted by samyama, one exists without a body.

This mahavideha state is a vritti. It is a state of mind. When this state is established the covering of light is destroyed. When you go on negating the impressions gained through your contact with the senses and the external world, then you arrive at a state of mind in which the universal mind functions independently of the body, mind and senses. Also, in that state the spiritual light shines clearly because of the removal of its covering, but this is different from the covering of light which is removed by practising pranayama.

Sutra 45: Mastery of the bhutas

स्थूलस्वरूपसूक्ष्मान्वयार्थवत्त्वसंयमाद् भूतजयः ॥ ४५ ॥

Sthūlasvarūpasūkṣmānvayārthavattvasaṃyamād bhūtajayaḥ

Sthūla: gross; *svarūpa*: real form; *sūkṣma*: subtle; *anvaya*: interpenetrating; *arthavattva*: serving the purpose; *saṃyamāt*: by samyama; *bhūtajayaḥ*: mastery over elements

By samyama on the gross, basic, subtle and interpenetrating states and the purpose of the bhutas, mastery over them is obtained.

There are five states of the five elements, namely, their gross form, their real form, their subtle form, their universal form and their purpose. Samyama on these states of the elements gives mastery over them. *Tattwa* here does not mean a quality; it means thatness. It means the principal components. It refers to the states of existence and functions and nature of an object.

In Samkhya and yoga there are innumerable tattwas. Although they are different from each other, they are derived from one supreme principle. The five tattwas mean the elements called earth, water, fire, air and ether. These are made the object of samyama. Thus samyama is to be performed not only on the gross form but on the subtle, basic and universal forms as well. The basic nature of earth is smell, that of water is liquidity, of fire it is heat, of air it is motion, and of akasha, ether, it is sound. Samyama is practised on these basic qualities. Their subtle states mean their tanmatras, which are called smell, fluid, form, touch and sound. Samyama is practised on them also. Similarly, samyama is practised on their universal form, which is common for all. The purpose or function of the bhutas is next meditated upon. Their function means the twenty-five tattwas of Samkhya, namely: purusha, prakriti, three internal organs, five cognitive organs, five motor organs, five tanmatras, and the five elements. These twenty-five tattwas of Samkhya are the functions of the bhutas.

Sutra 46: Attainment of anima, etc.

ततोऽणिमादिप्रादुर्भावः कायसम्पत्तद्धर्मानभिघातश्च ॥ ४६ ॥

Tato'ṇimādiprādurbhāvaḥ
kāyasampattaddharmānabhighātaścha

Tatah: therefrom; *aṇimādi*: anima, etc.; *prādurbhāvaḥ*: appearance; *kāyasaṃpat*: bodily well; *tat*: that; *dharma*: function; *anabhighātah*: non-obstruction; *cha*: and

From that the appearance of anima (and other powers), perfection of the body and non-obstruction from the functions of the body (follows).

By having mastery over the five elements as declared in the previous sutra, the yogi develops the eight psychic powers: anima, laghima, mahima, garima, prapti, prakamya, vashitwa, ishitva. His body becomes perfect and he overcomes all the obstructions due to limitations of the body and the bhutas. Thus there are three factors: appearance of anima and other powers, perfection of the body, and overcoming all the obstructions.

There are eight kinds of psychic powers which go together and are called the ashta siddhis:

1. *Anima* – the yogi can make his body small like an atom.
2 *Laghima* – the body can be made light.
3. *Mahima* – the body can be made large.
4. *Garima* – the body can be made heavy.
5. *Prapti* – capacity to reach anywhere.
6. *Prakamya* – unobstructed fulfilment of desire.
7. *Vashitwa* – control over all objects, organic or inorganic.
8. *Ishitva* – the capacity to create and destroy at will.

These eight siddhis appear as a result of complete mastery over the five mahabhutas. In addition to these powers there is also the achievement of perfection of the body. The third achievement is that the yogi is not influenced by the obstructions of prakriti or the elements.

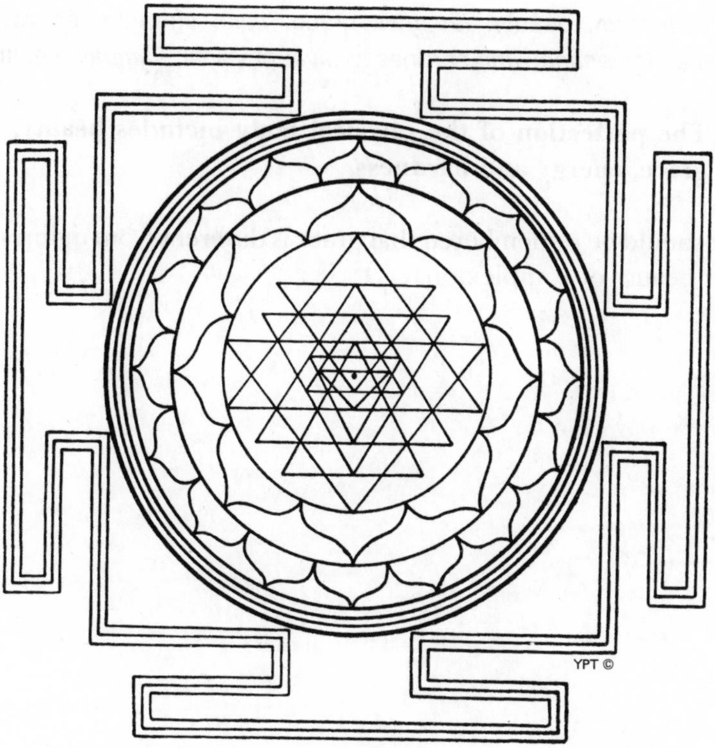

Sri Yantra

Sutra 47: Perfection of the body

रूपलावण्यबलवज्रसंहननत्वानि कायसम्पत् ॥ ४७ ॥

Rūpalāvaṇyabalavajrasaṃhananatvāni kāyasampat

Rūpa: form, beauty; *lāvaṇya*: grace; *bala*: strength, energy; *vajrasaṃhananatvāni*: hardness; *kāya*: physical; *saṃpat*: wealth

The perfection of the physical body includes beauty, grace, energy and hardness.

It should be remembered that grace is different from ugliness or beauty of complexion.

Sutra 48: Mastery of sense organs

ग्रहणस्वरूपास्मितान्वयार्थवत्त्वसंयमादिन्द्रियजयः ॥ ४८ ॥

Grahaṇasvarūpāsmitānvayārthavattvasaṃyamādindriyajayaḥ

Grahaṇa: power of cognition; *svarūpa*: real nature; *asmitā*: egoism; *anvayārthavatva saṃyamāt*: by samyama; *indriyajayaḥ*: mastery over the sense organs

Mastery over the sense organs is gained by samyama on the power of cognition, real nature, egoism, all-pervasiveness and purposefulness.

To have control and mastery over the sense organs it is necessary to perform samyama on these five items:

1. The power of cognition of the particular sense organ.
2. The essential quality of the sense organ.
3. Egoism or the individuality of the person which expresses itself through the sense organs.
4. All-pervasiveness, which means the co-relationship of the sense organs with each other. This means the simultaneous functioning of many sense organs; for example, when you see an animal, you can know through the eyes whether it is a dog or an elephant; you can hear its noise, feel its touch and so on. The knowledge arising in the mind is a combination of the impacts of all the organs. The knowledge is one, but it depends equally and simultaneously on the various sense organs.
5. Purpose. Every sense organ has a definite purpose in the scheme of human life. There are two purposes: *bhoga*, or experience, and *apavarga*, or liberation.

Samyama is to be performed on all five stages of the indriyas, sense organs, separately. For example, you meditate upon the essential nature of the eyes; that is perception. The egoism of the eyes means the awareness that I see. Then the knowledge gained through perception is dependent upon other organs as well. Thus samyama on the sense organs is practised.

Prana Shakti

Sutra 49: Conquest of prakriti

ततो मनोजवित्वं विकरणभावः प्रधानजयश्च ॥ ४९ ॥

Tato manojavitvaṃ vikaraṇabhāvaḥ pradhānajayaścha

Tatah: therefrom; *manojavitvaṃ*: speed of mind; *vikaraṇabhāvaḥ*: freedom from sense organs; *pradhānajayah*: conquest of prakriti; *cha*: and

Therefrom follows speed like that of mind, freedom from any medium of instrumentality and conquest of the limitations of prakriti.

By becoming master of your sense organs, the great qualities which develop are as follows:

1. Attainment of speed of the mind.
2. Capacity to function without any instrument.
3. Complete control over prakriti.

The yogi sees without eyes and moves without legs; he does not require the instrumentality of any cognitive or motor organ. He transcends the indriyas completely. This is the meaning of *vikaranabhavah*.

Pradhana means prakriti, including its transformations. Through this a psychic power called *madhupratika* is obtained; one enjoys siddhas as one enjoys honey.

The attainment of yogic powers is full of great responsibilities. It is like keeping a cobra around your neck or a tiger in your room. The siddhis can become enjoyable, like honey, only when you have complete control over the transformations of prakriti, otherwise they create agitation and disturbance. It is like a person having a lot of money and being in the company of many robbers. Just as he cannot maintain peace of mind unless he has the robbers completely under his control, so it is with the yogi who has the siddhis.

Sutra 50: Omnipotence and omniscience

सत्त्वपुरुषान्यताख्यातिमात्रस्य सर्वभावाधिष्ठातृत्वं सर्वज्ञातृत्वं च ॥ ५० ॥

Sattvapuruṣānyatākhyātimātrasya
sarvabhāvādhiṣṭhātṛtvaṃ sarvajñātṛtvaṃ cha

Sattva: chitta; *puruṣa*: self; *anyatā*: difference; *khyāti*: awareness; *mātrasya*: only; *sarva*: all; *bhāva*: states of existence; *adhiṣṭhātṛtvaṃ*: supremacy; *sarvajñātṛtvaṃ*: omniscience; *cha*: and

Just by knowledge of the awareness of the difference between chitta and purusha comes supremacy over all states and forms of existence and omniscience.

Ishwara has three qualities, namely, omnipotence, omniscience and omnipresence. When samyama is done on the difference between chitta and purusha, and when the difference between chitta and purusha is known completely, the aspirant realizes purusha as wholly different from chitta. Then Ishwara comes to function in man.

The aspirant then comes to function as omnipotent and omniscient. That is why many persons having these qualities come to be known as prophets or incarnations of God. The purusha becomes free from the binding effects of chitta and is able to manifest its essential nature in the form of omnipotence and omniscience.

Sutra 51: Vairagya and knowledge

तद्वैराग्यादपि दोषबीजक्षये कैवल्यम् ॥ ५१ ॥

Tadvairāgyādapi doṣabījakṣaye kaivalyam

Tat: that; *vairāgyāt*: by vairagya; *api*: even; *doṣa*: defect; *bīja*: seed; *kṣaye*: due to destruction; *kaivalyam*: isolation

By vairagya, even regarding that (the powers), the seed of defect is destroyed and kaivalya is attained.

When, by realization of the difference between chitta and purusha, vivekakhyati is attained and also the two powers of omnipotence and omniscience are obtained, the yogi is completely detached and he renounces the effects and influences so far achieved. Thereby the seed of bondage (avidya) is destroyed. That is the state of kaivalya.

Kaivalya is translated as liberation or freedom, but it is really not that. God realization is also different from that state. The word kaivalya is derived from the word *keval*, which means absolutely one, without others. *Kaivalya* therefore means isolation, aloneness. It is as state of non-duality.

Much has been said about kaivalya and much will be said about it. It is not a state of realization of any positive knowledge of God or the supreme being. This notion of kaivalya must be properly understood by a student of yoga. It is not a state which can be explained. It can be had only by losing or giving up everything else. It is a state of absoluteness, of only-ness, or of *adwaita*. It is at this point, kaivalya, that Vedanta comes into yoga.

Sutra 52: Causes of downfall

स्थान्युपनिमन्त्रणे संगस्मयाकरणं पुनरनिष्टप्रसङ्गात् ॥ ५२ ॥

Sthānyupanimantraṇe saṅgasmayākaraṇaṃ punaraniṣṭaprasaṅgāt

Sthāni: gods (devata); *upanimaṇtraṇe*: on being respectfully invited; *saṅga*: attachment; *smaya*: pride; *akaraṇaṃ*: by not doing; *punah*: once again; *aniṣṭa*: undesirable; *prasaṅgāt*: by revival

On being invited by the devatas there should be no attachment and pride, because of the possibility of revival of the undesirable.

After the manifestation of siddhis, the yogi becomes the object of respectful invitation from the powers in charge of different actions, for example, the devatas. In such circumstances he should not show any attachment or pride, otherwise there is the possibility of revival of undesirable reactions. The yogi suffers from physical or mental troubles; therefore, it is said in this sutra that he should be careful and should not show any attachment or pride.

Yogis are of four types:

1. *Prathama kalpika*, or beginners in samadhi.
2. *Madhubhumika*, or one who has tasted the honey of yogic powers.
3. *Prajnajyoti*, who sees the light of pure consciousness.
4. *Atikranta bhavaniya*, who becomes absolutely detached and renounces even the highest achievement. He has finished the entire course of spiritual practices.

In different stages, the yogis are invited by authorities of higher astral planes and it is here that the yogi should exercise absolute restraint. He should avoid attachment and pride, then he can go ahead and reach the goal from where there is no return, but if he does not take this precaution, then he has to undergo a punishment. It also means that when one has any spiritual power in hand, one should first of all try to fulfil these two conditions, that is, freedom from attachment and freedom from pride. Until these two conditions are fulfilled, he should decide not to use his occult or psychic powers. Once he has become free from these two, he can easily go ahead.

Sutra 53: Awareness of ultimate reality

क्षणतत्क्रमयोः संयमाद्विवेकजं ज्ञानम् ॥ ५३ ॥

Kṣaṇatatkramayoḥ saṃyamādvivekajaṃ jñānam

Kṣaṇa: moment; *tatkramayoḥ*: its order of succession; *saṃyamāt*: by samyama; *vivekajaṃ*: born of realization; *jñānam*: knowledge

By samyama on moment and its order of succession is born the knowledge of realization of the ultimate reality.

Kshana means the smallest unit of time, a moment. Time is a perpetual succession of moments and samyama is practised on this succession of moments. The knowledge that arises from it is called *viveka jnana*; it is born of discrimination between purusha and prakriti. Viveka is a very crucial idea in Samkhya and yoga. It means the correct understanding of the purusha and prakriti.

Thus viveka involves the knowledge of the absolute difference between purusha and prakriti. By the realization of the difference, ultimately the yogi attains complete isolation for his supreme self. Vivekaja jnana is the knowledge born of the awareness of ultimate reality. It is the highest plane of superconsciousness. To achieve it, one should close the eyes and try to be aware of the ceaseless flow of moments, and practise samyama on that flow of moments.

Sutra 54: Knowledge of distinctions

जातिलक्षणदेशैरन्यतानवच्छेदात् तुल्ययोस्ततः प्रतिपत्तिः ॥ ५४ ॥

Jātilakṣaṇadeśairanyatānavachchhedāt
tulyayostataḥ pratipattiḥ

Jāti: birth; *lakṣaṇa*: characteristic; *deśayoh*: by place; *anyatā*: difference; *anavachchhedāt*: on account of no definition; *tulyayoh*: of the two similar objects; *tataḥ*: therefrom; *pratipattiḥ*: knowledge

Therefrom comes knowledge of two similar objects which are indistinguishable by class of birth, characteristic or position, because of no definition.

By the knowledge of ultimate reality, one develops a faculty by which one can make a clear distinction between two different states of an object. It is by this that the previous and present and future birth and the continuity of consciousness is determined. The characteristics, positions and places of an individual change from birth to birth but the self remains the same. However, this is difficult to understand. Just as different objects like bricks or pots are made out of mud and ultimately return to the same state of mud, similarly, the self, although looking different in different births, is actually one and the same. This is known through the superior consciousness.

Through vivekaja jnana, the knowledge between two similar objects which are indistinguishable by class of birth, character or position is gained. By this the yogi knows the various transformations taking place in the jiva and knows the substance of matter perfectly.

Sutra 55: Transcendental knowledge

तारकं सर्वविषयं सर्वथाविषयमक्रमं चेति विवेकजं ज्ञानम् ॥ ५५ ॥

Tārakaṃ sarvaviṣayaṃ sarvathāviṣayamakramaṃ
cheti vivekajaṃ jñānam

Tārakam: transcendental; *sarvaviṣayam*: all subjects; *sarvathāviṣayam*: object of every place; *akramaṃ*: beyond the order of succession; *cha*: and; *iti*: that is all; *vivekajaṃ jñānam*: knowledge born of viveka

Transcendental knowledge includes the knowledge of all objects beyond all orders of succession and is born of viveka. That is all.

The highest knowledge is the knowledge of the ultimate reality. By attaining this stage one crosses over the field of ordinary existence, that is why the word *akrama* is used here. It means the knowledge by which one can cross. The knowledge of the ultimate reality saves the aspirant from pain forever. By the attainment of this knowledge, the individual self transcends the barriers of time and space. The jiva who was involved in the limitations of maya is completely liberated on the attainment of this knowledge.

Sutra 56: Attainment of kaivalya

सत्त्वपुरुषयोः शुद्धिसाम्ये कैवल्यमिति ॥ ५६ ॥

Sattvapuruṣayoḥ śuddhisāmye kaivalyamiti

Sattva: chitta; *puruṣayoḥ*: of the purusha; *śuddhi*: purification; *sāmye*: on becoming equal; *kaivalyam*: isolation; *iti*: end

Kaivalya is achieved by equalizing and purifying the illumination of purusha and chitta.

Kaivalya comes when the whole structure of chitta is completely purified and its superimposition on the purusha is removed. The realization of their difference comes gradually. Purification of chitta means this progressive and gradual realization.

When the awareness of ultimate reality increases in the framework of chitta, then we can say that it is being purified or illumined. When there are distractions, then the chitta is full of impurities. The external world is reflected in the impure chitta in a distorted fashion but when the chitta is purified it shows everything as it is, including the purusha. This is like cleaning a mirror so that it shows the reflection very accurately, without distortion.

In that state the purusha is free of the influence of prakriti. There is a process of division and discrimination. It is the state of kaivalya. When the purusha acts through the mind, intellect and sense organs, it is not free. It becomes affected by the senses and the intellect. It is the purusha in bondage.

The purpose of yoga is to give a method of involution by which the purusha functions in isolation, independent of the chitta or prakriti. At different stages of psychic achievement, the purusha can see without eyes and can act without the medium of the senses.

Therefore, kaivalya is achieved when the chitta is purified and the purusha is made free from the binding or colouring effect of the chitta. When this process of illumination in the sphere of chitta and in the sphere of purusha is attained through sadhana, purusha becomes completely isolated from the sphere of prakriti. That is not emotional isolation but spiritual isolation, in which the subjective consciousness in an individual can function at all stages without any hindrance due to chitta or the external world. That state of kaivalya is the goal of yoga.

Chapter Four

Kaivalya Pada

(34 Sutras)

Sutra 1: Sources of siddhis

जन्मौषधिमन्त्रतपःसमाधिजाः सिद्धयः ॥ १ ॥

Janmauṣadhimantratapaḥsamādhijāḥ siddhayaḥ

Janma: birth; *auṣadhi*: herbs; *mantra*: mantra; *tapaḥ*: austerity; *samādhi*: samadhi; *jāḥ*: born of; *siddhayaḥ*: siddhis

The siddhis are born of birth, herbs, mantras, austerities or samadhi.

Psychic powers can be obtained in five ways. There are people who are born with certain powers, such as telepathy. This manifestation of the powers is an outcome of the sadhana done in previous births. This is clearly explained in the *Bhagavad Gita*. It is said there that when a sadhaka achieves something through sadhana and dies, in the next birth he receives that ready in accumulated form and starts his progress from that point onward. Such persons are born with spiritual qualities. They do not have to do any sadhana for that in the present birth. Shankaracharya is a good example. He renounced everything at the early age of eight years and wrote wonderful commentaries on sacred scriptures. He destroyed the Buddhist empire in India before he was thirty-two. Another boy, called Gyaneshwar, who died at an even earlier age, did tremendous spiritual work and became a liberated person. This does not happen by chance, but is due to samskaras accumulated in previous births.

Siddhis can also be had from herbs, but things like LSD and ganja are not to be included here because they cause disease and nervous disorders. These things cause depression of certain nerve centres and give rise to effects like samadhi, but they are not to be included in the herbs causing siddhis because they are of a lower type. Traditionally, *aushadhi* means the juice of certain herbs, such as anjana, rosayana, etc., but not LSD or ganja. The method of preparation is known to only a few responsible persons. These herbs are available in the Himalayas and nowhere else and bring about supramental states of consciousness.

The effects of these herbs can be controlled through higher mental phenomena. There are certain preparations of mercury which are of great importance and use to the body, but they are not to be included with the herbs, because of their properties and the demands of yoga.

The third way of obtaining siddhis is by mantra. This is a very great siddhi of the highest spiritual quality. It is a very powerful means of developing spiritual powers. This method belongs to a very high order. Siddhis obtained through birth or aushadhi are not in one's hands or under one's control, but those developed by mantras are very important because they can be developed through will, with full conscious effort. There are many mantras available and in tantra shastra a study of them is scientifically made. The mantra unfolds the latent spiritual, psychic and occult faculties.

The fourth means for the attainment of yogic powers is tapas, or austerities, but the most important and highest means for developing siddhis is samyama or samadhi. This we have already discussed in detail.

Sutra 2: Fundamental transformation

जात्यन्तरपरिणामः प्रकृत्यापूरात् ॥ २ ॥

Jātyantarapariṇāmaḥ prakṛtyāpūrāt

Jātyantara: another birth; *pariṇāmaḥ*: transformation; *prakṛti*: nature; *āpūrāt*: by making up, overflowing

By the overflow of natural potentiality occurs the transformation from one substance (or birth) into another.

The logical process by which the speed of natural tendencies can be increased is here described, whereby an ordinary mind suddenly takes a leap into an extraordinary state. It happens by compensation and by overflowing the differences in the law of nature.

For example, one person is born as a human, another as an animal, a third as a plant and so on. Here the word *jati* means the group or substance to which a person belongs. A change in the jati involves a fundamental transformation in substance. If water changes into ice or vapour, or when an ornament of gold is changed into another ornament, it is not a fundamental transformation, but when a mind full of avidya, kleshas and impurities is changed into pure consciousness, it would mean a fundamental change or *jatyantara parinama*.

Prakriti means nature, the inherent dharma, and apurat means compensating. Thus, *prakrityapurat* means overflowing the gap in nature. For example, when wood is put into fire it is reduced to ashes. This jatyantara parinama is the result of prakrityapurat; there is complete transformation of form and nature. If, however, a brick is put into fire it will not undergo a fundamental transformation, it will only change its colour and hardness.

Fundamental change is not brought about from outside; it must be inherent in the material. For example, the mind can be developed into superconsciousness only because the self or atman is already there. Only avidya needs to be removed. Thus, development of superconsciousness is inherent in the nature of the mind. The potentiality should exist in the substance and only then can it undergo a fundamental change. The change from avidya to pure knowledge may take many births. For this there should be some process of transmigration or some law deciding it. It is the samskaras which are responsible for a swift movement of prakriti in order to bring about jatyantara parinama. If you know how to speed up the process of evolution – for example from a dog to an elephant – then it can be brought about in a smaller number of births, or it may even be brought about in the very next birth. The law which decides the transformation in the fundamental order of a substance is called prakrityapurat, the overflow of prakriti.

Sutra 3: Instrumental cause

निमित्तमप्रयोजकं प्रकृतीनां वरणभेदस्तु ततः क्षेत्रिकवत् ॥ ३ ॥

Nimittamaprayojakaṃ prakṛtīnāṃ varaṇabhedastu tataḥ kṣetrikavat

Nimittam: instrument; *aprayojakaṃ*: indirect; *prakṛtīnāṃ*: of various natural tendencies; *varaṇa*: obstacles; *bhedhah*: removal; *tu*: but; *tataḥ*: therefore; *kṣetrikavat*: like the farmer

The instrumental cause does not stir up the various natures but merely removes the obstacles like a farmer.

The various sadhanas and methods of obtaining siddhis are not the real instrumental cause of awakening the potentialities. No sadhana or spiritual practice can have a direct effect, but the transformation brought about is indirect, by fulfilling certain conditions of prakriti. Just as a farmer irrigating a field removes the obstacle so the water can flow of its own accord through the channels, similarly, these sadhanas remove the obstacles in the way of prakriti, and thus prakriti does the rest of the job of its own accord. The sadhanas work only indirectly.

The spiritual practices bring about a transformation in the order of consciousness, or chitta. The obstacles preventing the aspirant from observing his true nature and reality have first to be removed. Sadhanas are meant for this purpose. Shankaracharya says in his commentary on the *Vedanta Sutra* that the individual consciousness has three defects: impurity (mala), oscillation (vikshepa) and ignorance of truth (avarana). To remove them, different methods are used; for example, impurities of the mind are removed by bhakti or love for God. The vikshepas are corrected through concentration, and ultimate knowledge is attained through pure awareness.

Karma yoga, bhakti yoga or jnana yoga cannot give mukti directly. They act in an indirect manner. They only remove the obstacles in the way of prakriti. It is in this context that the sutra should be understood. If there is any delay in realization, that is because of the obstacles. To remove the obstacles the spiritual practices should be continued with vigour and earnestness.

When you remove the obstacles from a water channel, the water flows automatically through the channel because it is in the nature of water to flow to a lower level. Similarly, it is in the nature of prakriti to create experiences for the purusha and to bring about the state of liberation. The obstacles in the way of prakriti are removed by sadhana. Thus all kinds of sadhana are instrumental; they do not bring about realization directly. They are very powerful methods of removing impurities from the passage of consciousness and creating a free passage for the divine nature to act unhindered.

Sutra 4: Created mind

निर्माणचित्तान्यस्मितामात्रात् ॥ ४ ॥

Nirmāṇachittānyasmitāmātrāt

Nirmāṇa: creation; chittāni: minds; asmitā: egoism; mātrāt: alone

Created minds are free from egoism alone.

The yogi can create out of his asmita various minds through which he can experience the various fruits of past karmas simultaneously. These new minds or new vehicles of consciousness can be created by asmita only. *Nirmana chitta* means the consciousness that is made or created or that is put into operation separately. These artificial vehicles of consciousness are created by manipulating the forces of the higher planes through samyama. Through these created minds the yogi operates in different spheres of his consciousness at the same time. He is full of awareness in all the chittas simultaneously. This is done by samyama on mahatattwa, which is called ahamkara or asmita both in Samkhya and in yoga.

In yoga, *mahatattwa* means the centre of individuality in man around which the individual functions during different states of consciousness, such as waking, dream, sleep and so on. The created minds give him experience at the same time. These experiences are transferred to the natural mind of the yogi and that mind becomes free of karmashaya due to enjoyment of its fruits.

The artificial minds are completely under the control of the aspirant. He can create them and again fold them according to his will. For an ordinary person, God is supreme, but for a yogi, the supreme is inside himself. Thus his individuality has a support in himself. In ordinary people, the individuality is dependent upon so many factors of life. This topic of artificially created minds is very interesting and useful for the finishing of karmashaya.

Lord Shiva: the first exponent of yoga

Sutra 5: Natural mind directs

प्रवृत्तिभेदे प्रयोजकं चित्तमेकमनेकेषाम् ॥ ५ ॥

Pravṛttibhede prayojakaṃ chittamekamanekeṣām

Pravṛtti: activity; *bhede*: in connection with the difference; *prayojakaṃ*: moving; *chittam*: mind; *ekam*: one; *anekeṣām*: of many

The one mind directs the many in connection with the difference of activities.

The one mind that is the original mind of the yogi is the natural mind, and this natural mind is the director, mover and controller of the many created minds. It decides, directs and moves the created minds in various activities in different spheres of consciousness.

The yogi multiplies his consciousness in different planes and with regard to different activities with the help of his original natural mind. The created minds are entirely dependent on the natural mind and have to work according to the consciousness of the natural mind. Sometimes they exhibit wonderful capacities in various respects. In many cases the intelligence working in the mind of a guru plays the part of the natural mind and it works through the disciple if he has been able to create artificial vehicles of consciousness.

Sutra 6: And is free from impressions

तत्र ध्यानजमनाशयम् ॥ ६ ॥

Tatra dhyānajamanāśayam

Tatra: there, of them; *dhyānajam*: born of meditation; *anāśayam*: without the store of past impressions

Of these, the one born of meditation is free of impressions.

When the yogi creates several minds artificially, his own original natural mind becomes progressively free of past impressions. The artificial minds do not have their separate karmashaya, but they depend upon and serve the natural mind. It is something like a business concern with branches at different places. The branches are open or closed according to decisions taken in the head office or at headquarters. Similarly, the created mind may be considered as the temporary branch offices of the head office, that is, the natural mind. They have no independence because they have only one purpose, that of serving the natural mind.

Yogis are able to operate in different minds, in different bodies and different places, and they also do karma. The impressions are wiped out from the natural mind and it becomes progressively free of its karmashaya.

Sutra 7: Influence of karma

कर्माशुक्लाकृष्णं योगिनस्त्रिविधमितरेषाम् ॥ ७ ॥

Karmāśuklākṛṣṇaṃ yoginastrividhamitareṣām

Karma: action; *aśukla*: not white; *akṛṣṇaṃ*: not black; *yoginah*: of the yogis; *trividham*: threefold; *itareṣām*: of others

The actions of yogis are neither white nor black; of others they are threefold.

White karma means the action which involves virtue, that is, good karma. Black karma means bad actions, those actions which involve vice. The yogi acts in such a way that his actions cannot be classified as good or bad; they are called neither good nor bad. This is because the mind of the yogi is clarified through sadhana and thus he has no selfish motive underlying his actions. Yogis do not operate through the lower mind; they operate through nirmana chitta. While a yogi does karmas which are neither good nor bad, the karmas of all others are of three types.

The other people in this world operate through the lower mind and senses, and our mind and body are the vehicles or media of karma. When the karmas are performed through the indriyas, mind and body, then they bring about these threefold effects, namely, good karmas, bad karmas and mixed karmas. So, ordinary people who live in the world of the senses, body and mind, who do not know the secrets of nishkama karma, have to undergo suffering.

Sutra 8: Manifestation of vasanas

ततस्तद्विपाकानुगुणानामेवाभिव्यक्तिर्वासनानाम् ॥ ८ ॥

Tatastadvipākānuguṇānāmevābhivyaktirvāsanānām

Tatah: therefrom; *tadvipāka*: the ripening of those; *anuguṇānām*: accordingly; *eva*: only; *abhivyaktih*: manifestation; *vāsanānām*: of potential desires

Therefrom the manifestation of potential desires according to their ripening only.

The manifestation of vasanas in different lives depends upon the possibility, the conditions and the ripening of the karma. Usually it happens that in this life we do not suffer even though we may not do good karmas, or we may suffer even if we do good karmas. This is due to the possibility of manifestation of the potential desires according to those conditions available for ripening of the fruits. The prarabdha karma of an individual comes to fruition not according to the karmas but according to their suitability. Just as there are early and also late varieties of vegetables, similarly, some karmas fructify very soon, whereas others ripen after a long time. For example, if you plant spinach today, you will have the vegetable in two or three months. A guava tree will bear fruit after three years, while a mango tree may take five to ten years. It is the same with the karmas.

Thus the experiences one may have in this life may be the effects of actions done in past lives. Ordinary people have to suffer because they have no control over the fruition of karmas. The yogi, on the other hand, has complete control over the conditions which give rise to effects of the karmas. There is one consciousness, one karma, one mind that undergoes suffering and enjoyment and is operated by the natural law of karma, but there is another mind in him which is absolutely free. This is the decisive point of yoga and hence must be understood very clearly.

Thus a yogi has two minds, one of which undergoes the effects of prarabdha in daily life. He enjoys the good and bad results of his past karmas, like ordinary people but because of meditation on mahatattwa, or asmita, the yogi develops in himself another channel called *nirmana chitta*, which is the higher vehicle of consciousness. Through this, there is no enjoyment of pain or pleasure. The average person has only the lower mind, hence he suffers. The yogi, on the other hand, has neither good nor bad karmas because of the nirmana chitta.

Kabir has said that nobody is an exception to the rule, that one who has a body has to undergo pain and pleasure, but still there is a difference. While the foolish man of the world undergoes the laws of karma with sorrow, cries and wailing, the yogi and the jnani undergo suffering with absolute knowledge, understanding and power.

This is the secret about which most people are confused. They do not understand that even a yogi cannot go beyond prarabdha. No one can break the law of karma, but the yogi can remain unaffected even if he is in the stream of karmas and their effects. This is because of his nirmana chitta. Thereby the yogi discovers the door through which he escapes the cruelties of life and then he evolves a new method to face this life.

Sutra 9: Memory and impressions

जातिदेशकालव्यवहितानामप्यानन्तर्यं स्मृतिसंस्कारयोरेकरूपत्वात् ॥ ९ ॥

Jātideśakālavyavahitānāmapyānantaryaṃ
smṛtisaṃskārayorekarūpatvāt

Jāti: class of birth; *deśa*: place; *kāla*: time; *vyavahitānām*: separated; *api*: even; *anantaryaṃ*: sequence; *smṛtisaṃskārayoh*: of memory and impressions; *ekarūpatvāt*: because of sameness in form

Because memory and impression are the same in form there is a sequence although they may be divided by class of birth, place and time.

When the jiva migrates from one body to another in countless births, there is continuity between the various births, and the memory and impressions of all the past births are also continued in this birth. This is because there is an uninterrupted sequence of one personality throughout these incarnations. The present birth is divided from the previous births insofar as it takes place in a different class of birth (*jati*), in a different place and at a different time, but the births are all of one single jiva.

After departing from the body, when reincarnation takes place in another body, the body, place and time cannot be the same. Moreover, the knowledge of the conscious mind does not link itself with any previous birth at all. It is very difficult to understand the sameness of the two births. This very important topic concerns the theory of transmigration of jivatma. Thus, the memory and impressions being the same in different incarnations, the difference in birth, place and time does not matter.

Sutra 10: Source of vasanas

तासामनादित्वं चाशिषो नित्यत्वात् ॥ १० ॥

Tāsāmanāditvaṃ chāśiṣo nityatvāt

Tāsām: there is; *anāditvaṃ*: beginninglessness; *cha*: and; *āśiṣah*: of the will to live; *nityatvāt*: by permanence

There is no beginning to them and the desire to live is eternal.

The law of cause and effect binds the mind of ordinary people and hence there is continuity in memory and impressions. This sutra describes the source of the vasanas. The process of accumulating impressions is without a beginning. It is eternal, hence vasanas are called *anadi*. They are the latent potentialities of desires. They can manifest in the form of desire whenever an opportunity arises.

Vasanas form a part of the causal or subtle body. Usually they are supposed to mean subconscious desires, but in yoga, *vasana* means the latent potentialities which give rise to karmas. The causal body is also called vasana deha, because the vasanas are a part of it.

The beginninglessness of the vasanas is proved by the eternity of the will to live. The will to live is found in human beings from birth, as also in all other living beings. There is no creature free of the will to live, hence vasanas also become beginningless.

Vasanas are found in the subtle spheres of this body, and even in the cosmic mind which undergoes different modifications. There is another stream of consciousness of which the individual willpower is a manifestation; that stream is also present in every being. When a yogi is able to develop the nirmana chitta, it is a manifestation of that universal stream present in him. It is the divine mind. It has often been used by inspired thinkers of East and West. Apart from the lower individual mind and the cosmic mind, there is the third one, which is called the divine mind. The nirmanakayachitta is the microcosmic manifestation of the discovery of that supreme mind.

Sutra 11: Disappearance of vasanas

हेतुफलाश्रयालम्बनैः संगृहीतत्वादेषामभावे तदभावः ॥ ११ ॥

Hetuphalāśrayālambanaiḥ saṅgṛhītatvādeṣāmabhāve tadabhāvaḥ

Hetu: cause; *phala*: effect; *āśraya*: support; *ālambanaiḥ*: object; *saṅgṛhitatvāt*: because of being bound together; *eṣām*: of these; *abhāve*: on the disappearance; *tadabhāvaḥ*: their disappearance

Since cause and effect, support and object are bound together, by their disappearance that also disappears.

The vasanas are beginningless, but they come to an end when their cause or support disappears. Cause and effect are bound together. Similarly, the substratum and the object are bound together, so if one of the two disappears, the other one will also vanish. The cause of vasanas is the kleshas, namely, avidya, asmita, raga, dwesha, and abhinivesha. The effect is birth, experience and life. The substratum of all these experiences is the chitta. It is the substratum of vasanas, and the alambana, or basis of vasanas, are the objects of enjoyment. So the cause, the effect, the support and the object of vasanas go together to make them continuous throughout the cycle of rebirth.

If these four factors are removed, then naturally vasanas will also come to an end. If there is no cause, there can be no effect; similarly, if there is no support, there will be no object. If the kleshas are finished, there can be no life, birth and experience because these are the effects of the kleshas, and if there is no birth, there cannot be any question of the chitta. If the chitta is not there, there is no support for the vasanas. The chitta can be eliminated by the process of meditation; then, although the objects of enjoyment are there, there can be no vasana. However, when the substratum and objects are eliminated, then vasanas will disappear completely. Thus, through knowing the fact that vasanas are dependent on four factors, vasanas are also made to disappear through elimination of these four factors.

Sutra 12: Past and future exist

अतीतानागतं स्वरूपतोऽस्त्यध्वभेदाद्धर्माणाम् ॥ १२ ॥

Atītānāgataṃ svarūpato'styadhvabhedāddharmāṇām

Atīta: past; *anāgataṃ*: future; *svarūpatah*: in its essential form; *asti*: exists; *adhvabhedāt-dharmāṇām*: of inherent properties

Past and future exist in their own form by difference of paths.

The world process in terms of time is past, present and future. There are different states of this world in the form of events or processes. That which is today will become yesterday, and, after some time, a happening in the remote past. This today will exist and will continue to exist even after a year, but it will not exist in the present. It will exist in the past. At the same time, the world which is yet to come, the world of future time, is already there. After a day or two or after a few years, the future will become the world of today and also the world of the past.

So, we come to know that the world exists in the past, in the present, as well as in the future, and the past, present and future exist in their own real form. They are not contaminated or confused; they are not mixed up or lost. Their essential form and their identity are not lost. There are people who are able to enter this world of time that you call the future, and they become prophets and tell you what is to come.

Thus it is said in this sutra that the world of time, in the form of past and future, may be considered as separate. This is the classical view of yoga philosophy. The essential form of the world of time is a matter of controversy. What is more important is the difference of inherent properties. There are two paths: one is determination, the other is free will. Determination is like a film being projected on the screen. It will project only what is in the film, it cannot project anything else. The other path is that of free will. There are many happenings that can be changed, according to our will.

On account of these two different paths, there is difference in the inherent properties. The past and future remain different. It can be changed. According to yoga every happening is absolutely preplanned in space and time. Everything goes on like a film projected on the screen but there is difference in the inherent properties (*dharmas*). That difference is due to the difference of path, and the difference of path is what we call determination and free will. When you discuss determinism, then the future becomes the present, the present becomes the past. You cannot change it because that is beyond your powers. The second point is that the future becomes the present and the present becomes the past, but there is change every moment because you have the capacity to change it. You are able to know the secret of the world of time.

Sutra 13: Factor of existence

ते व्यक्तसूक्ष्मा गुणात्मानः ॥ १३ ॥

Te vyaktasūkṣmā guṇātmānaḥ

Te: they; *vyakta*: manifest; *sūkṣmā*: subtle; *guṇātmānaḥ*: of the nature of gunas

Whether manifest or unmanifest they are of the nature of gunas.

'They' means the inherent property of the world of time (dharmas). These dharmas are sometimes manifest in the form of the present; sometimes they are unmanifest in the form of the past and future. They are not merely events, but they are the different combinations of dharmas and the objects that you perceive and are pervaded by the three gunas: sattwa, rajas and tamas. The gunas are the fundamental principle in the individual as also in the cosmos. They combine in various proportions to give rise to the objects in the world.

So, the manifest qualities and the unmanifest states of the world are both derived from the three gunas. It should be understood that time is as important a part of the world as is the object. Usually the world is considered to be just the creation of material, mental and spiritual objects, but the factor of time is also involved. This sutra makes the point very clearly that the dharmas are not just imagination, but they have a definite existence because they are made up of the three gunas.

When the three gunas are eliminated either in an individual or in the cosmos, one can understand and transcend the time process of the world.

Sutra 14: Essence of object

परिणामैकत्वाद्वस्तुतत्त्वम् ॥ १४ ॥

Pariṇāmaikatvādvastutattvam

Pariṇāma: transformation; *ekatvāt*: due to oneness; *vastu*: object; *tattvam*: the essence

The essence of the object is due to the uniqueness of transformation of the gunas.

The gunas undergo the process of transformation and this transformation has peculiarity and uniqueness. The mental perception in daily life is due to the uniqueness of transformation of the three gunas.

The three gunas, which are part of prakriti, undergo transformation from avyakta to vyakta, from unmanifest to manifest. The three gunas not only produce and control matter but make it different from another. The gunas produce the organic, inorganic, physical, mental and psychic as well as the astral fields of the universe.

It is very difficult to have a metaphysical concept or knowledge of the three gunas. It is such a fine process, that from within its structure time and space are produced. Naturally, the uniqueness of the transformation of the gunas is accepted by Patanjali.

Due to the uniqueness of transformation, various combinations of the gunas arise, and result in various objects, gross as well as subtle. It is an absolutely unique transformation. The reality of the object inheres in the three gunas because of this uniqueness of transformation.

Sutra 15: Theory of perception

वस्तुसाम्ये चित्तभेदात्तयोर्विभक्तः पन्थाः ॥ १५ ॥

Vastusāmye chittabhedāttayorvibhaktaḥ panthāḥ

Vastusāmye: by sameness of the object; *chittabhedāt*: by the difference of mind; *tayoh*: of these two; *vibhaktaḥ*: separate; *panthāḥ*: path of manifestation

Because of the sameness of object and difference of mind their paths are separate.

This sutra explains the yogic theory of perception. Even though the object is one, its perception becomes different according to the difference of the chitta. The same object is perceived differently at different times because of the difference in the mental condition or the instrument of cognition. The object may be one, but it looks different due to a difference in degree and also in time concerning the cognizing faculty. This particular difference in the order of chitta is responsible for the difference of cognition.

Sutra 16: Mind and object

न चैकचित्ततन्त्रं वस्तु तदप्रमाणकं तदा किं स्यात् ॥ १६ ॥

Na chaika chittatantraṃ vastu tadapramāṇakaṃ
tadā kiṃ syāt

Na: not; *cha*: and; *eka*: one; *chitta*: mind, *tantraṃ*: dependent; *vastu*: object; *tat*: that; *apramāṇakaṃ*: non-cognized; *tadā*: then; *kiṃ*: what; *syāt*: would happen

The object of perception is not dependent on the chitta; what would happen to the object of perception when the medium of cognition is not there?

The perception of an object takes place through the medium of the indriyas, but it is not dependent on one mind or one form of knowledge of chitta. If it were so, then the cognition would not continue in the absence of the medium of cognition.

There are two theories about this. The idealistic theory denies the very existence of the world. The realistic theory is that the world exists in its objective form as we see it. Vedanta is idealistic, while the Charvaka school of philosophy is realistic. Yoga seems to be a middle path. It does not dispose of the higher side of the world of perception and it also does not dispose of the objective side. It believes in existence of objects as well as in the higher side of existence. Therefore, when even chitta is withdrawn, the world will continue to exist because the world as a whole is existing in matter, in mind, in the indriyas and in time and space.

The object is not dependent on one mind. It means that the phenomenal world is subjective to each mind, but it does not disappear when one person obtains kaivalya; it continues for other people who have not attained kaivalya. If you think that the object of perception is dependent on one mind which has been eliminated, then, it may be asked, what happens to the object of perception when it is not cognized by the mind? The reply is that the object continues to exist for other persons.

Sutra 17: Reflection of object

तदुपरागापेक्षित्वाच्चित्तस्य वस्तु ज्ञाताज्ञातम् ॥ १७ ॥

Taduparāgāpekṣitvāchchittasya vastu jñātājñātam

Taduparāga: the reflection of the object in chitta; *apekṣitvāt*: because of necessity; *chittasya*: of the mind; *vastu*: object; *jñāta*: known; *ajñātam*: unknown

The mind needs the reflection of the object for its cognition.

The mind needs the object of cognition for its reflection and only then can the knowledge of that object take place. So long as the object of conception is not reflected in the chitta, the chitta does not have knowledge or cognition of that particular object.

If an object is placed before the chitta but no reflection takes place, then there will be no knowledge, there will be no cognition, even though the object and the chitta are face to face. Moreover, the knowledge of an object does not take place just because the object is there. Knowledge arises only when there is reflection of the object in the chitta.

Thus this sutra means that an object is either known or unknown, according to the presence or absence of the reflection of the object in the mind.

Sutra 18: Purusha knows the mind

सदाज्ञाताश्चित्तवृत्तयस्तत्प्रभोः पुरुषस्यापरिणामित्वात् ॥ १८ ॥

Sadā jñātāśchittavṛttayastatprabhoḥ
puruṣasyāpariṇāmitvāt

Sadā: always; *jñātāh*: are known; *chittavṛttayah*: modifications of mind; *tatprabhoḥ*: on its master; *puruṣasya*: of the purusha; *apariṇāmitvāt*: due to changelessness

Purusha, the master of chitta, is changeless, therefore, he always knows the modifications of the mind.

The purusha never changes; it is constant although everything else changes. The world of time and space, qualities and cognitions, etc. undergoes constant change, but this change has a permanent changeless background, a permanent basis, which is the soul. Therefore, whatever takes place in the chitta is automatically known to the soul because he is the master of chitta.

Sutra 19: Chitta not self-illuminative

न तत्स्वाभासं दृश्यत्वात् ॥ १९ ॥

Na tatsvābhāsaṃ dṛśyatvāt

Na: not; *tat*: that; *svābhāsaṃ*: self-illumined; *dṛśyatvāt*: of perceptibility

That chitta is not self-illumined because it is the subject of knowledge and perception.

The sun shines of its own accord but the moon is not self-illumined. Similarly, the soul is self-illumined but not the chitta. When yogis vividly perceive the various spheres of chitta during different states of samadhi, then it becomes a subject of perception and knowledge, but the purusha is changeless.

The moment the mind is introverted and it transcends the limits of the senses, one is aware that purusha is other than the chitta. The purusha illumines the chitta.

The purusha is not realized through the mind. For its realization, the mind as a whole is completely separated and is thrown out of the field of experience. While an ordinary person depends on his indriyas for knowledge, or a scientist on his instruments, the yogi depends upon the highest faculty of self-knowledge. It is only after the changing instrument of knowledge, that is, chitta, is eliminated that the purusha can be realized. Therefore, the supreme being or purusha is not the subject of knowledge through the mind, but it is the subject of knowledge by itself. The whole process of yoga sadhana is not so much the awareness of purusha, as the elimination of the lower forms, the lower vehicles of awareness. Though the purusha illumines itself, it is not perceptible by the chitta.

Sutra 20: Limitation of mind

एकसमये चोभयानवधारणम् ॥ २० ॥

Ekasamaye chobhayānavadhāraṇam

Ekasamaye: simultaneously; *cha*: and; *ubhaya*: both; *anavadhāraṇam*: non-comprehension

And there cannot be the comprehension of both simultaneously.

The chitta has its own limitations. It is pointed out here that you cannot have a simultaneous comprehension of the perceiver and the perceived, the cognizer and the cognized. You can have the knowledge of one of them at one time because the mind can perceive only certain experiences.

When the mind is the perceiver, it cannot be perceived. This dual faculty of perception and perceived is not there in the mind, and that is its limitation.

Sutra 21: Confusion of memories

चित्तान्तरदृश्ये बुद्धिबुद्धेरतिप्रसंगः स्मृतिसंकरश्च ॥ २१ ॥

Chittāntaradṛśye buddhibuddheratiprasaṅgaḥ smṛtisaṅkaraśćha

Chittāntaradṛśye: in one mind being cognized by the other; *buddhibuddheh*: cognition of cognitions; *atiprasaṅgaḥ*: absurd superfluity; *smṛti*: memory; *saṅkarah*: confusion; *cha*: and

If cognition by one mind of the other be accepted, then there will be cognition of cognitions leading to absurdity and confusion of memory.

Buddhism does not recognize the purusha. It says that the mind can itself perceive another mind, but in that case there would be the necessity of an endless chain of minds, one seeing the other, the other being seen by a third one, and so on. So this doctrine of the Buddhists is very faulty. Chitta cannot be the cognizer, the purusha is the real cognizer. The purusha cannot be cognized by the mind or anything else.

Yoga is of the opinion that instead of accepting the chitta itself as the cognizer of another chitta, we should accept the basis of purusha as the cognizer who remains unchanged while everything else undergoes a constant change.

Sutra 22: Knowledge of its own nature

चित्तेरप्रतिसंक्रमायास्तदाकारापत्तौ स्वबुद्धिसंवेदनम् ॥ २२ ॥

Chitterapratisaṅkramāyāstadākārāpattau
svabuddhisamvedanam

Chitteh: of the consciousness; *apratisaṅkramāyāh*: not passing from one to another; *tadākāra*: own form; *āpattau*: have accomplished; *svabuddhi*: self-cognition; *saṃvedanam*: knowing of

Knowledge of its own nature through self-cognition is accomplished when consciousness assumes that form in which it does not pass from one stage to another.

Cognition through the chitta depends on different levels of consciousness, because the consciousness assumes that particular form of buddhi through which the mind is passing. When the consciousness assumes that pratyaya in which one's experience does not pass from one level to another, due to the absence of the mental vehicle, then self-cognition takes place. Thereby the knowledge of one's own nature is obtained.

This has a connection with the state of purusha called swaroopavasthanam. That state comes into being when the chitta assumes pratyaya which is a product of ritambhara, in which the experience does not change. So long as meditation continues in the field of mind, experiences go on changing. There is *pratisankram*. These experiences go on changing. When the mental awareness is evolving or becoming subtler and subtler, the experiences also go on changing. The mind is not steady; it is ever developing, changing. The psychological and physiological structure of the mind keeps on changing. The inner structure of the mind undergoes a tremendous change in meditation.

The experiences in meditation are not ultimate because there is constant change. In the final stage, the chitta has a constant unchanging pratyaya; there would be no change. There is a stage of samadhi where the process of experiences stops and there is no longer the possibility of transcending the limitations of the chitta. Then the seer accomplishes his own form. In the beginning there may be different forms such as shivalingam or Aum, but in the final stage there is only one form which does not change. This is called *tadakarapatti* and belongs to the last category of samadhi. This final state is described in the Upanishads and in the *Bhagavad Gita*. It is the state of pure consciousness which has the attributes of sat, chit, ananda. It gives a homogeneous experience which is not limited by the mind.

It comes when one transcends the limits of chitta and establishes oneself in unfluctuating pure consciousness, which is absolutely homogeneous and static. In that state there is *swabuddhi samvedanam*, that is, complete knowledge of one's mind. The knowledge of the body, senses and mind completely stops and there is only the unchanging knowledge of swaroopa, that is, one's own form.

The knowledge of buddhi is the knowledge of your inner nature. Here buddhi does not mean intellect or mind; it means awareness. In yoga, buddhi means intellect as supreme awareness.

It is said in the *Gita* that supreme reality is beyond the buddhi or self-awareness. The word buddhi is being used in this sutra for that state of supreme awareness. It is there when you are not functioning through the medium of the mind but through the medium of supreme awareness. Just when the level of consciousness stops fluctuating, a single unchanging awareness of one's own inner nature arises. Then there is self-cognition or supreme knowledge of the self.

Sutra 23: Apprehension of mind

द्रष्टृदृश्योपरक्तं चित्तं सर्वार्थम् ॥ २३ ॥

Draṣṭṛdṛśyoparaktāṃ chittaṃ sarvārtham

Draṣṭṛ: the seer (of the seer); *dṛśya*: prakriti; *uparaktaṃ*: coloured; *chittaṃ*: mind; *sarvārtham*: all inclusive

The mind which is coloured by the seer and the seen is all-apprehending.

The word chitta here does not stand for the ordinary functions of the mind but for a higher expression of consciousness through which the higher spheres of atman become perceived. In this sutra the word chitta is used in relation to the transcendental purusha. We must understand the vast scope of chitta, which includes not only prakriti but purusha also. It should be remembered that the mind of an ordinary sadhaka continues to be the same, even after he has made considerable progress on the spiritual plane. The only difference is that while in the beginning the mind was coloured by prakriti, by objective awareness and the three gunas, the mind now throws off its limitations and becomes pure so as to reflect the purusha in itself. Thus it becomes all-apprehending.

This word *sarvartham*, all-apprehending, must be understood well. Even in the primary stages of spiritual practices the chitta has the capacity of being all-apprehending, but it is not functioning in actuality. At that time the mind can only perceive what is knowable, but when it becomes pure, it develops higher awareness and can see the drashta also. Thus it becomes sarvartham in actuality. It is a very high state of spiritual life. The chitta becomes capable of reflecting back the subject and the object at the same time. When this state remains constant, the aspirant should know that the state of kaivalya will be achieved very soon but if this state of all-inclusive awareness is not maintained constantly and if there is fluctuation of awareness, then it should be understood that kaivalya is far away.

Sutra 24: It works for purusha

तदसंख्येयवासनाभिश्चित्रमपि परार्थं संहत्यकारित्वात् ॥ २४ ॥

Tadasaṅkhyeyavāsanābhiśchitramapi parārthaṃ saṃhatyakāritvāt

Tat: that; *asaṅkhyeya*: innumerable; *vāsanābhih*: by the vasanas; *chitram*: variegated; *api*: although; *parārthaṃ*: for the sake of purusha; *saṃhatyakāritvāt*: because of associated action

Though variegated by innumerable vasanas it acts for the purusha because it works in association.

The mind is made of innumerable vasanas and is variously coloured by them, but it is not for itself. It always works for the purusha; it is meant wholly for the purpose of the purusha. Just as a factory worker works for his family and not for the machines and the other factory workers, similarly, the chitta, although coloured by innumerable impressions and desires, is really meant for purusha.

The innumerable vasanas do not form the objective or purpose of the mind. Just as we eat many things of which some portion is retained in the body and the rest thrown out, so too in this case our eating is not for the purpose of those various things that are eaten. Similarly, the chitta is not for the vasanas but for the purusha. Although purusha is the master or objective purpose of the mind, the mind has so many vasanas only because it has to produce various enjoyments for purusha.

Vasana is the original, primitive unconscious vehicle of desire. It is not a hidden desire; it is beginningless. It is the main incentive for all creations on the lower plane. They do not act on the higher plane of supreme awareness. Thus it should be understood that our mind, which always clings to the objects of the lower world, is full of all kinds of attachments, sufferings, desires and so on. The mind has for its aim or object the purusha, and nothing else; therefore, spiritual aspirants who are tortured by vasanas and attachment should not feel pessimistic. They should not be depressed when the vasanas work in the mind. They should understand the ultimate purpose of the pilgrim, namely, the purusha, and it should be noted that the various vasanas are ultimately serving an essential purpose of the purusha.

Life after life, birth after birth, the mind keeps on migrating from one sphere of consciousness to another sphere, from one plane of evolution to the next higher plane until ultimately there comes a point where it is able to reflect back the seer and the seen, the knower and the known at the same time. Then there is an end to the vasanas because they have served their purpose of creating bhoga for the purusha.

Sutra 25: Cessation of distinction

विशेषदर्शिनः आत्मभावभावनाविनिवृत्तिः ॥ २५ ॥

Viśeṣadarśinaḥ ātmabhāvabhāvanāvinivṛttiḥ

Viśeṣa: the distinction; *darśina*: of one who sees; *ātmabhāva*: self-consciousness; *bhāvanā*: feeling; *vinivṛttiḥ*: complete cessation

The awareness of self-consciousness ceases completely for one who sees the distinction.

The differentiating faculty of consciousness of the self ceases completely after the entire range of mental consciousness is achieved. There are two interpretations of this rather confusing sutra. According to the first, when the yogi becomes capable of perceiving mental awarenesses which are opposite to each other, then he can understand the distinction between the two points of any process. The process begins with prakriti and terminates at purusha. After the yogi has covered this entire range of the process, he visualizes the distinction between the two points: one, purusha consciousness and two, prakriti consciousness. Then there arises in him the resolution (*sankalpa*) to retire from the awareness of the self. This happens when he becomes aware of prakriti and purusha with their distinction, when he wants to transcend even this consciousness.

According to the second interpretation, when the yogi acquires the highest state of consciousness of the self, he can make a distinction between prakriti and purusha by which he is able to see purusha as different from prakriti. There the awareness of the self is transcended. The first interpretation appears to be more correct. We know that in the highest state of samadhi the consciousness does not change;

it becomes static. In that state the difference between the seer and the seen is known perfectly. Moreover, the vasanas which constitute the general structure of mental consciousness are not the end but just the means. Therefore, the ultimate purpose of the mind is to transcend itself. *Atmabhava* is the finest point where the mind as an entity dissolves itself. At this stage there comes the experience of kaivalya.

Sutra 26: Heading to kaivalya

तदा विवेकनिम्नं कैवल्यप्राग्भारं चित्तम् ॥ २६ ॥

Tadā vivekanimnaṃ kaivalyaprāgbhāraṃ chittam

Tadā: then; *vivekanimnaṃ*: inclined towards discrimination; *kaivalyaprāgbhāraṃ*: inclined towards kaivalya; *chittam*: the mind

Then verily the mind is inclined towards discrimination and heading on towards kaivalya.

When the yogi realizes that even ritambhara and atma bhava, the awareness of the highest point of the self, are also inadequate for the realization of the absolute, and when he is determined to cast off even the highest features of the mental factors, then he develops a peculiar unconscious sense of renunciation of the bliss and knowledge, which is born of the higher atmic plane. When he attains the perfected state of samadhi, then he forgets everything about him and around him, but at the same time he is able to visualize the entire range of consciousness which he has transcended.

At that time, the entire movement from the lowest to the highest spiritual point comes before him. He remembers all the spiritual experiences he has had from the beginning of his spiritual life. Then he is able to create a sense of distinction between experiences of different dimensions. He then realizes that all of them, including meditation and even bliss, are relative, not absolute. It is said that the bliss and jnana born of the supreme consciousness is unchanging and permanent, but during periods of sadhana, over many births the quality of experience changes. Even the quality of trance and consciousness of self and supreme knowledge are not absolute.

As such, the aspirant feels that all those experiences should be transcended because they are inadequate. It is a peculiar experience if you sit down quietly and look back over your life; you do not remember how your physical body has been developing. You remember only one thing – how you have been progressing materially, academically, socially and politically. You take just one of these and start thinking about it. When the mind is introverted, you will see the whole continuity of experiences. You can just feel the experiences. However, if you compare the last one with the first one, you can always see the difference. Then you see the developing factors. You can then transcend the whole path of the mental sphere.

Then you come to know that all these experiences were on the plane of prakriti. This is the point of purusha. Until it is achieved, all the experiences are within the range of prakriti, even the finest ones. It is the plane of mental consciousness, sensual consciousness. It includes the supramental consciousness as well as visions, subtle currents, vibrations in telepathy, clairvoyance, clairaudience and so on. The whole thing forms a continuous process, starting from the grosser plane and going down to the deeper planes.

Here the mind is inclined towards viveka through discriminatory analysis and sees all the happenings in the past with a bird's-eye view. There is a tendency of the consciousness to gravitate towards kaivalya. This is described by the wonderful word *kaivalyapragbharam*.

We know in physics that everybody is gravitating towards the centre of the earth and so we have heaviness or weight. In the same way, during the final stages of sadhana the mind is drawn towards the centre of gravity, that is, kaivalya. Thus, when all the superfluous agents of consciousness are taken away, the purusha becomes filled with absolute consciousness and is drawn towards the state of kaivalya by a force or pull.

Sutra 27: Pratyayas still arise

तच्छिद्रेषु प्रत्ययान्तराणि संस्कारेभ्यः ॥ २७ ॥

Tachchhidreṣu pratyayāntarāṇi saṃskārebhyaḥ

Tachchhidreṣu: in the intervals of that; *pratyayāntarāṇi*: other pratyayas; *saṃskārebhyaḥ*: by samskaras

In between the state of discrimination (viveka) other pratyayas arise due to past impressions.

After the yogi achieves the state of vivekakhyati, it so happens that he cannot maintain the conditions of unfluctuating consciousness of viveka because the relaxation of effort is followed by an intervening pratyaya. Even after the mind becomes full of vairagya and, leaving the sphere of prakriti, starts being pulled towards the state of kaivalya, there are intermediate stages when it reverts back to places from where it had entered the plane of nirbeeja samadhi.

This is due to traces of ignorance (*avidyaklesha*), which are nothing but traces of past samskaras which break through the state of viveka. Here the pratyaya stands for the last trace that has been left after complete scorching of the karma and samskaras, but this condition is not constant. It only intervenes between the flow of viveka. When a yogi is established in the highest form of meditation, his meditation is broken up only slightly and temporarily before he reaches the point of final experience, but that interval does not take him to a lower stage. He establishes himself firmly in it on the highest stage. Just as when we sleep during the night there may be short periods when we are awake or half-awake, similarly, in the case of the mind which is being attracted towards kaivalya, the traces of impressions break through viveka, but viveka again continues. There should be no misunderstanding about this point. It is felt by some people that when a yogi finally attains the final state, he is not able to look back and he merges completely, but actually it is not so. As long as the seeds are present, they give rise to vyuthana from the state of viveka, but this does not cause any disturbance because the seeds are almost scorched or burned.

Sutra 28: Their removal

हानमेषां क्लेशवदुक्तम् ॥ २८ ॥

Hānameṣāṃ kleśavaduktam

Hānam: destruction; *eṣāṃ*: of these; *kleśavat*: like the kleshas; *uktam*: is said

The removal of these (pratyayas) is prescribed like the destruction of the kleshas.

The process of revival of previous consciousness must be stopped completely. This is done by removing the pratyayas arising due to traces of personality like the kleshas. The kleshas are removed by understanding their nature and their relation to karma. The pratyayas in samadhi are also due to the past karma and its impressions. These impressions are rooted in the kleshas and the kleshas are rooted in avidya. This is how these pratyayas are to be traced back to their root.

When avidya is removed, the kleshas vanish, the power of discrimination evolves and due to past impressions the conscious pratyayas also arise. Just as kleshas are removed through meditation (*dhyana*) and through making the vivekakhyati state more stable and firm, similarly, the pratyayas during vivekhyati can also be removed through making the vivekakhyati very firm and unshakable.

Sutra 29: Dharmamegha samadhi

प्रसंख्यानेऽप्यकुसीदस्य सर्वथा विवेकख्यातेर्धर्ममेघः समाधिः ॥ २९ ॥

Prasaṅkhyāne'pyakusīdasya sarvathā
vivekakhyāterdharmameghaḥ samādhiḥ

Prasaṅkhyāne: in the highest meditation; *api*: even; *akusīdasya*: of one who has no interest left; *sarvathā*: in every way; *vivekakhyāteh*: by discrimination; *dharmameghaḥ*: the showering of dharma; *samādhiḥ*: samadhi

When there is no interest even in the highest meditation, dharmamegha samadhi develops on account of complete discrimination.

When the state of vivekakhyati is completely established and the impressions causing interruption are also subdued, the meditation culminates in the finest type of samadhi, called *dharmamegha samadhi*. This is interesting because here the yogi develops an aversion even for enlightenment. There is complete vairagya even regarding vivekakhyati and the yogi becomes free of the desire to attain kaivalya. So far, he has been guided by the ambition for kaivalya; now even that is left behind. Once he is near the culminating point, the thirst for reaching that point is completely lost.

Akusida means not expecting any discount. This is a state in which the yogi gives up the idea of gaining anything or reaching anywhere through the meditation he is doing. The ambition and interest are left behind. Sadhana is practised, but there is no idea of achieving anything. In that state there is no attachment even to the state of kaivalya. It is very interesting to note that the urge for kaivalya, which guides the aspirant from the lowest point of consciousness to the development of supreme consciousness, is automatically given up just at the time of attaining kaivalya. This gives rise to dharmamegha samadhi. In that state all the seeds of past impressions are completely burned, every karma is finished and the gates of reality are opened up. The mysteries and curiosities remain no more.

The word *dharma* here does not mean religion or duty. It means the inherent property or characteristic function. The dharma here involved is sat, chit and ananda, which is a universal characteristic or function of the higher consciousness. *Megha* is a technical term meaning a mystical condition, which may be described as a very superior state of drowsiness through which we have the experience of satchidananda. Megha in Sanskrit means a cloud. It is a cloud which showers on the yogi a homogeneous experience of sat, chit and ananda. It cannot be described through language, through words. It may be said that it is a very high state of homogeneous experience of satchidananda.

This becomes possible when the last stage of nirbeeja samadhi is reached. To take an example; when a man dies, the last moment of his life is the moment when he sees his whole life passing in front of him in a mystic way. He does not see everything clearly, but he has a kind of mystic awareness of all that which has happened in his life. He looks at it as if he is looking at a landscape. Similarly, the great experience in dharmamegha samadhi is the last moment before liberation. This brings about an end of all efforts, all the sadhana, meditation or samadhi.

Liberation means breaking off, and dharmamegha samadhi is the ultimate point of the aim of yoga abhyasa. After it is reached, the yogi enters into a new field of existence and activities.

Sutra 30: Freedom from kleshas

ततः क्लेशकर्मनिवृत्तिः ॥ ३० ॥

Tataḥ kleśakarmanivṛttiḥ

Tataḥ: thereafter; *kleśa*: affliction; *karma*: actions: *nivṛttiḥ*: cessation

Thereafter (arises) freedom from kleshas and karmas.

When the yogi attains the state of satchidananda through dharmamegha samadhi, he is no longer affected by kleshas and karmas. These two instruments of bondage, which keep the jiva tied down to the world of experience, are completely dissolved by the influence of dharmamegha samadhi. Once these twin instruments are destroyed, yogic sadhana ends.

It should be understood that the immediate purpose of yoga is to eliminate avidya and the kleshas. Realization of kaivalya is not the direct effect but an indirect effect through the removal of the kleshas. We do not have to develop it. It is only the discovering of a state that is already there by the very nature of purusha. Jivanmukti is the ultimate root of yoga. It means the state of freedom from the clutches of prakriti and the three gunas. The province of prakriti begins with avidya and ends in jivanmukti. It is a state beyond the realm of prakriti where the jivanmukta experiences eternal bliss. The jivanmukta can look at prakriti from outside because he himself is not in its fold. He has a practical understanding of both prakriti and mukti at one and the same time.

Though it is true that the ultimate state of mukti is already in us, it must be understood that it is hidden by layers of avidya and the impressions of the past actions. When these layers are removed through yoga, the state which is already there is discovered anew.

So, the spiritual aspirant should never give up his sadhana until he has finally achieved the experience of bliss, by virtue of elimination of prakriti and the three gunas. He should continue the path of yoga until he becomes a separate centre of pure consciousness in the supreme reality and becomes completely separate from prakriti. After achieving dharmamegha samadhi, the kleshas and karmas no longer bind the yogi. For him they become non-existent.

The process of mukti is twofold: namely, individual mukti and cosmic mukti (prakriti moksha). The latter is the liberation of prakriti and purusha as a whole. When an individual becomes free of kleshas and karma, they exist somewhere in prakriti, although for him they come to an end. When there is the end of a vast cycle, everything merges into prakriti. That is prakriti moksha. A rich person in an air-conditioned room while the heat of summer is everywhere outside may be compared to a jivanmukta. The elimination of heat from every corner after heavy rains may be compared to prakriti moksha. So these are the two aspects of mukti: one individual, the other universal. The efforts made by individuals in this country and elsewhere are meant for individual liberation. Prophets like Christ, Buddha and Shankara are also examples of individual liberation. Universal liberation cannot be brought about by any single individual, but one can practise intense sadhana so as to bring about liberation for oneself.

There are two approaches to liberation: one is the escapist approach, the other is the practical approach. The approach of a yogi should be practical and not escapist. The practically liberated jivanmukta works for the good of humanity; he does not escape into the realm beyond prakriti even when he is liberated. He works for bringing solace and peace to the suffering. Thus he remains in dharmamegha samadhi and does not escape into kaivalya, although that is just at hand for him. When he feels that he has done his job, he goes beyond into the state of kaivalya.

Individual liberation is no liberation at all. Of course, academically it is liberation but practically it is not. The liberated individual has to fight. He has to continue his fight against pain, against misery, against the cause of pain and so on. So he goes on spreading the message of good living on earth. Ultimately, when he feels he has shown a way to the millions who are suffering, he transcends the realm of prakriti and becomes videha mukta.

Sutra 31: Infinity of knowledge

तदा सर्वावरणमलापेतस्य ज्ञानस्यानन्त्याज्ज्ञेयमल्पम् ॥ ३१ ॥

Tadā sarvāvaraṇamalāpetasya
jñānasyānantyājjñeyamalpam

Tadā: then; *sarva*: all; *āvaraṇa*: covering; *mala*: impurity; *apetasya*: of one from which it is removed; *jñānasya*: of knowledge; *anantyāt*: infinity; *jñeyam*: knowable; *alpam*: but little

Then by the removal of all veils and impurities little remains to be known because of the infinity of knowledge.

Dharmamegha samadhi brings about two things. Firstly, it removes the veil or covering of knowledge and, secondly, it completely removes all impurities. There are three things that are removed. In addition to the above two, vikshepa is also removed, but vikshepa has already been eliminated through abhyasa and hence only two errors are mentioned in this sutra.

It is said in the Upanishads and other scriptures that darkness and fear do not leave an individual until the light of knowledge (*jnanasurya*) rises on the horizon of the superconscious. It is said here that after dharmamegha samadhi, the great event of removal of impurities and the veils of knowledge takes place and the yogi sees that little remains to be seen or known.

In the beginning, the aspirant constantly feels that he has known very little and much has yet to be known, but when the veil of knowledge is removed there remains little to be known or acquired. The yogi becomes aptakama, aptajnana and antasankalpa. Nothing remains to be known or fulfilled, won or desired. This becomes his personal nature, but until this enlightenment he has to make steady progress through rigorous discipline and constant sadhana. He is a seeker in the beginning. When he becomes established in sadhana he is called a sadhaka, but when he attains dharmamegha samadhi he becomes a siddha. His thirst for knowledge, steadiness and peace is quenched by the showers of the cloud of dharma. For him anything and everything becomes known whenever he desires it because there is no veil or covering for his knowledge. He comes to experience the *mahavakyas*, the great sayings, in his personal life. These great sayings can be summarized as follows:

1. *Prajnanam Brahma*: The ultimate truth, the cosmic reality is consciousness.
2. *Ahambrahmasmi*: I am Brahman.
3. *Tatwamasi*: Thou art that (Brahman).
4. *Ayamatma Brahma*: This individual soul is Brahman.

These are the four immortal utterances which sum up the whole philosophy of the Upanishads. They are to be understood not only intellectually, but in actual experience and realization, and that is possible only in dharmamegha samadhi.

After attaining dharmamegha samadhi, the purusha remains in its own form and nature. It is freed of the superimpositon of the vrittis of the mind.

Sutra 32: Gunas retire

ततः कृतार्थानां परिणामक्रमसमाप्तिर्गुणानाम् ॥ ३२ ॥

Tataḥ kṛtārthānāṃ pariṇāmakramasamāptirguṇānām

Tataḥ: thereafter; *kṛtārthānāṃ*: having fulfilled their purpose; *pariṇāma*: of the changes; *krama*: process; *samāptih*: end; *guṇānām*: of the gunas

Thereafter, having fulfilled their purpose and after the end of the process of change, the gunas retire.

The yogi becomes kritartha by attaining dharmamegha samadhi, because for him nothing remains to be achieved. The process of change in the mind and the gunas also comes to an end. The law of cause and effect comes to an end with the law of change, so far as the yogi is concerned. The entire process of the gunas has one object, that of creating experiences for the purusha and ultimately bringing about liberation. Both these purposes being fulfilled, the gunas retire.

Sutra 33: Krama apprehensible

क्षणप्रतियोगी परिणामापरान्तनिर्ग्राह्यः क्रमः ॥ ३३ ॥

Kṣaṇapratiyogī pariṇāmāparāntanirgrāhyaḥ kramaḥ

Kṣaṇa: moment; *pratiyogī*: corresponding; *pariṇāma*: change; *aparānta*: in the end; *nirgrāhyaḥ*: entirely apprehensible; *kramaḥ*: process

Krama is the process corresponding to moments, apprehensible in the end.

A process is a series of occurrences. It can be known only when it is complete. For instance, the end of this body becomes apprehensible only at the end of the process that is death and, therefore, the process of death is taking place constantly. However, it does not stop there because the moments of transformation are immediately succeeded by another form of existence. Things go on becoming old every moment, but we call them old only after the end of the process. That particular process in relation to time and in relation to event is called *krama*. It is true of everything that is a product of the three gunas because the gunas go on changing every moment. Only the soul or purusha is beyond the scope of these transformations.

There are five states of parinama:

1. From unmanifest to manifest.
2. From mineral to vegetable.
3. From vegetable to animal.
4. From animal to human.
5. From human to superhuman.

In these different classes there are also various stages of evolution. We do not usually notice the individual changes from stage to stage because they are not very pronounced.

When we meet a person after ten or twenty years, we can see a change in him. That change was actually going on every moment, but we cannot know it separately every moment.

This process of change comes to an end in dharmamegha samadhi, which is the final point of transformation of the three gunas. Beyond that there is no transformation. With this, there comes the end of transformation in all realms of existence, so there is no rebirth after moksha is attained because the transformations in the physical and mental realms also stop thereafter.

Just as we do not know when a child becomes a young man or when a young man becomes an old man, similarly, the transformations of the jiva from one kingdom to another, that is, from vegetable to animal, from animal to human and so on, from one incarnation to another, from one birth to another birth, are not apprehensible. Therefore, there are people in the world who do not believe in rebirth or reincarnation, but that is because they cannot see it. It may be said that it is not possible to see it; it is apprehensible only at the end of the process and not in-between. Thus this sutra gives a scientific and logical reasoning for the theory of rebirth.

Sutra 34: Kaivalya

पुरुषार्थशून्यानां गुणानां प्रतिप्रसवः कैवल्यं स्वरूपप्रतिष्ठा वा चित्शक्तेरिति ॥ ३४ ॥

Puruṣārthaśūnyānāṃ guṇānāṃ pratiprasavaḥ kaivalyaṃ svarūpapratiṣṭhā vā chitśakteriti

Puruṣārtha: purpose of the purusha; *śūnyānāṃ*: devoid of; *guṇānāṃ*: of the gunas; *pratiprasavaḥ*: involution; *kaivalyaṃ*: liberation; *svarūpa*: one's own nature; *pratiṣṭhā*: establishment; *vā*: or; *chitśakteḥ*: purusah; *iti*: that's all (denotes the end of the book)

Kaivalya is the involution of the gunas because of the fulfilment of their purpose; or it is the restoration of the purusha to its natural form which is pure consciousness.

The state of kaivalya is defined here in two ways: one in terms of involution of the gunas, the other in terms of the purusha. This is because in nature a twofold process can take place: one is evolution, the other is involution. In the process of evolution, the objects of experience manifest through various stages such as asmita, tanmatra, bhutas, etc. for the enjoyment of the purusha. The process of involution is the opposite, where objects merge into their cause progressively, so that ultimately the gunas remain in an undisturbed condition. This happens when the purpose of the gunas, namely, bhoga and kaivalya of purusha is achieved. Thus kaivalya can be defined as involution of the gunas by fulfilment of their purpose – *purushartha*. The process of *pratiprasava* or involution of the gunas ends in kaivalya of the purusha.

According to the other definition, kaivalya is the state of purusha in its own pure nature of pure consciousness. The individual tries to purify consciousness through various sadhanas such as meditation, samadhi, samyama and so on. Due to this, the veils covering the real nature of the purusha are removed until at last, through dharmamegha samadhi, the consciousness becomes extremely pure and attains its real nature (swaroopa pratishtha).

Kaivalya is thus the highest point of the combination of all sadhanas. This is the belief of yoga as well as of the Jains, but there are some other thinkers, such as those rishis to whom the Upanishads were revealed, who believe that kaivalya is only a stage in the unfoldment of consciousness. We do not know how much more of the consciousness remains unfolded and remains beyond the point of realization.

Lord Buddha has also written in one place that kaivalya is reached when veil after veil of ignorance is removed through the practices of dhyana, etc., but even then it is possible that some veils remain to be lifted. It seems for the time being that kaivalya is the highest stage so far as we are concerned and, therefore, the whole of yoga sadhana is said to be directed towards this goal, directly or indirectly. Yoga is thus a means and not an end in itself.

Appendices

Phonetic Pronunciation Guide

अ		a	*as in* mica
आ	ा	ā	far
इ	ि	i	hill
ई	ी	ī	police
उ	ु	u	pull
ऊ	ू	ū	nude
ऋ	ृ	ṛ	clarity
ॠ	ॄ	ṝ	marine
ऌ		lṛ	rivalry
ॡ		lṝ	rivalry (*prolonged*)
ए	े	e	prey
ऐ	ै	ai	aisle
ओ	ो	o	go
औ	ौ	au	cow
.		ṃ	rum
:		ḥ	bah
क्		k	meek
ख्		kh	inkhorn
ग्		g	go
घ्		gh	yoghurt
ङ्		ṅ	sing
च्		ch	check
छ्		chh	churchhill
ज्		j	jab
झ्		jh	hedgehog
ञ्		ñ	canyon
ट्		ṭ	true
ठ्		ṭh	anthill
ड्		ḍ	do
ढ्		ḍh	redhead
ण्		ṇ	gong
त्		t	water (*dental*)
थ्		th	nuthook
द्		d	bud
ध्		dh	adhere (*more dental*)
न्		n	not
प्		p	pay
फ्		ph	photo
ब्		b	rub
भ्		bh	abhor
म्		m	map
य्		y	yoga
र्		r	red
ल्		l	bull
व्		v	vice
श		ś	shield
ष		ṣ	assure
स्		s	sin
ह्		h	hit
क्ष्		kṣ	kshatriya
त्र्		tr	track (*dental*)
ज्ञ्		jñ	jnana

Appendix B

Freedom in a Nutshell

समाधि पाद

१. अथ योगानुशासनम्
२. योगश्चित्तवृत्तिनिरोधः
३. तदा द्रष्टुः स्वरूपेऽवस्थानम्
४. वृत्तिसारूप्यमितरत्र
५. वृत्तयः पञ्चतय्यः क्लिष्टाक्लिष्टाः
६. प्रमाणविपर्ययविकल्पनिद्रास्मृतयः
७. प्रत्यक्षानुमानागमाः प्रमाणानि
८. विपर्ययो मिथ्याज्ञानमतद्रूपप्रतिष्ठम्
९. शब्दज्ञानानुपाति वस्तुशून्यो विकल्पः
१०. अभावप्रत्ययालम्बना वृत्तिर्निद्रा
११. अनुभूतविषयासम्प्रमोषः स्मृतिः
१२. अभ्यासवैराग्याभ्यां तन्निरोधः
१३. तत्र स्थितौ यत्नोऽभ्यासः
१४. स तु दीर्घकालनैरन्तर्यसत्कारासेवितो दृढभूमिः
१५. दृष्टानुश्रविकविषयवितृष्णस्य वशीकारसंज्ञा वैराग्यम्
१६. तत्परं पुरुषख्यातेर्गुणवैतृष्ण्यम्
१७. वितर्कविचारानन्दास्मितानुगमात् सम्प्रज्ञातः
१८. विरामप्रत्ययाभ्यासपूर्वः संस्कारशेषोऽन्यः
१९. भवप्रत्ययो विदेहप्रकृतिलयानाम्
२०. श्रद्धावीर्यस्मृतिसमाधिप्रज्ञापूर्वक इतरेषाम्
२१. तीव्रसंवेगानामासन्नः

२२. मृदुमध्याधिमात्रत्वात् ततोऽपि विशेषः
२३. ईश्वरप्रणिधानाद्वा
२४. क्लेशकर्मविपाकाशयैरपरामृष्टः पुरुषविशेष ईश्वरः
२५. तत्र निरतिशयं सर्वज्ञबीजम्
२६. पूर्वेषामपि गुरुः कालेनानवच्छेदात्
२७. तस्य वाचकः प्रणवः
२८. तज्जपस्तदर्थभावनम्
२९. ततः प्रत्यक्चेतनाधिगमोऽप्यन्तरायाभावश्च
३०. व्याधिस्त्यानसंशयप्रमादालस्याविरतिभ्रान्तिदर्शनालब्ध-
भूमिकत्वानवस्थितत्वानि चित्तविक्षेपास्तेऽन्तरायाः
३१. दुःखदौर्मनस्याङ्गमेजयत्वश्वासप्रश्वासा विक्षेपसहभुवः
३२. तत्प्रतिषेधार्थमेकतत्त्वाभ्यासः
३३. मैत्रीकरुणामुदितोपेक्षाणां सुखदुःखपुण्यापुण्यविषयाणां
भावनातश्चित्तप्रसादनम्
३४. प्रच्छर्दनविधारणाभ्यां वा प्राणस्य
३५. विषयवती वा प्रवृत्तिरुत्पन्ना मनसः स्थितिनिबन्धनी
३६. विशोका वा ज्योतिष्मती
३७. वीतरागविषयं वा चित्तम्
३८. स्वप्ननिद्राज्ञानालम्बनं वा
३९. यथाभिमतध्यानाद्वा
४०. परमाणुपरममहत्त्वान्तोऽस्य वशीकारः
४१. क्षीणवृत्तेरभिजातस्येव मणेर्ग्रहीतृग्रहणग्राह्येषु तत्स्थतदञ्जनता समापत्तिः
४२. तत्र शब्दार्थज्ञानविकल्पैः संकीर्णा सवितर्का समापत्तिः
४३. स्मृतिपरिशुद्धौ स्वरूपशून्येवार्थमात्रनिर्भासा निर्वितर्का
४४. एतयैव सविचारा निर्विचारा च सूक्ष्मविषया व्याख्याता
४५. सूक्ष्मविषयत्वं चालिङ्गपर्यवसानम्
४६. ता एव सबीजः समाधिः
४७. निर्विचारवैशारद्येऽध्यात्मप्रसादः
४८. ऋतम्भरा तत्र प्रज्ञा
४९. श्रुतानुमानप्रज्ञाभ्यामन्यविषया विशेषार्थत्वात्

५०. तज्जः संस्कारोऽन्यसंस्कारप्रतिबन्धी

५१. तस्यापि निरोधे सर्वनिरोधान्निर्बीजः समाधिः

साधना पाद

१. तपःस्वाध्यायेश्वरप्रणिधानानि क्रियायोगः

२. समाधिभावनार्थः क्लेशतनूकरणार्थश्च

३. अविद्यास्मितारागद्वेषाभिनिवेशाः क्लेशाः

४. अविद्याक्षेत्रमुत्तरेषां प्रसुप्ततनुविच्छिन्नोदाराणाम्

५. अनित्याशुचिदुःखानात्मसु नित्यशुचिसुखात्मख्यातिरविद्या

६. दृग्दर्शनशक्त्योरेकात्मतेवास्मिता

७. सुखानुशयी रागः

८. दुःखानुशयी द्वेषः

९. स्वरसवाही विदुषोऽपि तथारूढोऽभिनिवेशः

१०. ते प्रतिप्रसवहेयाः सूक्ष्माः

११. ध्यानहेयास्तद्वृत्तयः

१२. क्लेशमूलः कर्माशयो दृष्टादृष्टजन्मवेदनीयः

१३. सति मूले तद्विपाको जात्यायुर्भोगाः

१४. ते ह्लादपरितापफलाः पुण्यापुण्यहेतुत्वात्

१५. परिणामतापसंस्कारदुःखैर्गुणवृत्तिविरोधाच्च दुःखमेव सर्वं विवेकिनः

१६. हेयं दुःखमनागतम्

१७. द्रष्टृदृश्ययोः संयोगो हेयहेतुः

१८. प्रकाशक्रियास्थितिशीलं भूतेन्द्रियात्मकं भोगापवर्गार्थं दृश्यम्

१९. विशेषाविशेषलिङ्गमात्रालिङ्गानि गुणपर्वाणि

२०. द्रष्टा दृशिमात्रः शुद्धोऽपि प्रत्ययानुपश्यः

२१. तदर्थ एव दृश्यस्यात्मा

२२. कृतार्थं प्रति नष्टमप्यनष्टं तदन्यसाधारणत्वात्

२३. स्वस्वामिशक्त्योः स्वरूपोपलब्धिहेतुः संयोगः

२४. तस्य हेतुरविद्या

२५. तदभावात् संयोगाभावो हानं तद्दृशेः कैवल्यम्

२६. विवेकख्यातिरविप्लवा हानोपायः

२७. तस्य सप्तधा प्रान्तभूमिः प्रज्ञा

२८. योगाङ्गानुष्ठानादशुद्धिक्षये ज्ञानदीप्तिराविवेकख्यातेः

२९. यमनियमासनप्राणायामप्रत्याहारधारणाध्यानसमाधयोऽष्टावङ्गानि

३०. अहिंसासत्यास्तेयब्रह्मचर्यापरिग्रहा यमाः

३१. जातिदेशकालसमयानवच्छिन्नाः सार्वभौमा महाव्रतम्

३२. शौचसंतोषतपःस्वाध्यायेश्वरप्रणिधानानि नियमाः

३३. वितर्कबाधने प्रतिपक्षभावनम्

३४. वितर्का हिंसादयः कृतकारितानुमोदिता लोभक्रोधमोहपूर्वका मृदुमध्याधिमात्रा दुःखाज्ञानानन्तफला इति प्रतिपक्षभावनम्

३५. अहिंसाप्रतिष्ठायां तत्संनिधौ वैरत्यागः

३६. सत्यप्रतिष्ठायां क्रियाफलाश्रयत्वम्

३७. अस्तेयप्रतिष्ठायां सर्वरत्नोपस्थानम्

३८. ब्रह्मचर्यप्रतिष्ठायां वीर्यलाभः

३९. अपरिग्रहस्थैर्ये जन्मकथन्तासम्बोधः

४०. शौचात्स्वाङ्गजुगुप्सा परैरसंसर्गः

४१. सत्त्वशुद्धिसौमनस्यैकाग्र्येन्द्रियजयात्मदर्शनयोग्यत्वानि च

४२. संतोषादनुत्तमसुखलाभः

४३. कायेन्द्रियसिद्धिरशुद्धिक्षयात्तपसः

४४. स्वाध्यायादिष्टदेवतासम्प्रयोगः

४५. समाधिसिद्धिरीश्वरप्रणिधानात्

४६. स्थिरसुखमासनम्

४७. प्रयत्नशैथिल्यानन्तसमापत्तिभ्याम्

४८. ततो द्वन्द्वानभिघातः

४९. तस्मिन्सति श्वासप्रश्वासयोर्गतिविच्छेदः प्राणायामः

५०. बाह्याभ्यन्तरस्तम्भवृत्तिर्देशकालसंख्याभिः परिदृष्टो दीर्घसूक्ष्मः

५१. बाह्याभ्यन्तरविषयाक्षेपी चतुर्थः

५२. ततः क्षीयते प्रकाशावरणम्

५३. धारणासु च योग्यता मनसः

५४. स्वविषयासम्प्रयोगे चित्तस्यस्वरूपानुकार इवेन्द्रियाणां प्रत्याहारः

५५. ततः परमा वश्यतेन्द्रियाणाम्

विभूति पाद

१. देशबन्धश्चित्तस्य धारणा

२. तत्र प्रत्ययैकतानता ध्यानम्

३. तदेवार्थमात्रनिर्भासं स्वरूपशून्यमिव समाधिः

४. त्रयमेकत्र संयमः

५. तज्जयात्प्रज्ञालोकः

६. तस्य भूमिषु विनियोगः

७. त्रयमन्तरङ्गं पूर्वेभ्यः

८. तदपि बहिरङ्गं निर्बीजस्य

९. व्युत्थाननिरोधसंस्कारयोरभिभवप्रादुर्भावौ निरोधक्षणचित्तान्वयो निरोधपरिणामः

१०. तस्य प्रशान्तवाहिता संस्कारात्

११. सर्वार्थतैकाग्रतयोः क्षयोदयौ चित्तस्य समाधिपरिणामः

१२. ततः पुनः शान्तोदितौ तुल्यप्रत्ययौ चित्तस्यैकाग्रतापरिणामः

१३. एतेन भूतेन्द्रियेषु धर्मलक्षणावस्थापरिणामाः व्याख्याताः

१४. शान्तोदिताव्यपदेश्यधर्मानुपाती धर्मी

१५. क्रमान्यत्वं परिणामान्यत्वे हेतुः

१६. परिणामत्रयसंयमादतीतानागतज्ञानम्

१७. शब्दार्थप्रत्ययानामितरेतराध्यासात् संकरस्तत्प्रविभागसंयमात् सर्वभूतरुतज्ञानम्

१८. संस्कारसाक्षात्करणात् पूर्वजातिज्ञानम्

१९. प्रत्ययस्य परचित्तज्ञानम्

२०. न च तत् सालम्बनं तस्याविषयीभूतत्वात्

२१. कायरूपसंयमात् तदग्राह्यशक्तिस्तम्भे चक्षुःप्रकाशसम्प्रयोगेऽन्तर्धानम्

२२. एतेन शब्दाद्यन्तर्धानं उक्तम्

२३. सोपक्रमं निरुपक्रमं च कर्म तत्संयमादपरान्तज्ञानमरिष्टेभ्यो वा

२४. मैत्र्यादिषु बलानि

२५. बलेषु हस्तिबलादीनि

२६. प्रवृत्त्यालोकन्यासात् सूक्ष्मव्यवहितविप्रकृष्टज्ञानम्

२७. भुवनज्ञानं सूर्ये संयमात्

२८. चन्द्रे ताराव्यूहज्ञानम्
२९. ध्रुवे तद्गतिज्ञानम्
३०. नाभिचक्रे कायव्यूहज्ञानम्
३१. कण्ठकूपे क्षुत्पिपासानिवृत्तिः
३२. कूर्मनाड्यां स्थैर्यम्
३३. मूर्धज्योतिषि सिद्धदर्शनम्
३४. प्रतिभाद् वा सर्वम्
३५. हृदये चित्तसंवित्
३६. सत्त्वपुरुषयोरत्यन्तासङ्कीर्णयोः प्रत्ययाविशेषो भोगः परार्थत्वात् स्वार्थसंयमात् पुरुषज्ञानम्
३७. ततः प्रातिभश्रावणवेदनादर्शास्वादवार्ता जायन्ते
३८. ते समाधावुपसर्गा व्युत्थाने सिद्धयः
३९. बन्धकारणशैथिल्यात्प्रचारसंवेदनाच्च चित्तस्य परशरीरावेशः
४०. उदानजयाज्जलपङ्ककण्टकादिष्वसंग उत्क्रान्तिश्च
४१. समानजयाज्ज्वलनम्
४२. श्रोत्राकाशयोः सम्बन्धसंयमाद्दिव्यं श्रोत्रम्
४३. कायाकाशयोः सम्बन्धसंयमाल्लघुतूलसमापत्तेश्चाकाशगमनम्
४४. बहिरकल्पिता वृत्तिर्महाविदेहा ततः प्रकाशावरणक्षयः
४५. स्थूलस्वरूपसूक्ष्मान्वयार्थवत्त्वसंयमाद् भूतजयः
४६. ततोऽणिमादिप्रादुर्भावः कायसम्पत्तद्धर्मानभिघातश्च
४७. रूपलावण्यबलवज्रसंहननत्वानि कायसम्पत्
४८. ग्रहणस्वरूपास्मितान्वयार्थवत्त्वसंयमादिन्द्रियजयः
४९. ततो मनोजवित्वं विकरणभावः प्रधानजयश्च
५०. सत्त्वपुरुषान्यताख्यातिमात्रस्य सर्वभावाधिष्ठातृत्वं सर्वज्ञातृत्वं च
५१. तद्वैराग्यादपि दोषबीजक्षये कैवल्यम्
५२. स्थान्युपनिमन्त्रणे संगस्मयाकरणं पुनरनिष्टप्रसङ्गात्
५३. क्षणतत्क्रमयोः संयमाद्विवेकजं ज्ञानम्
५४. जातिलक्षणदेशैरन्यतानवच्छेदात् तुल्ययोस्ततः प्रतिपत्तिः
५५. तारकं सर्वविषयं सर्वथाविषयमक्रमं चेति विवेकजं ज्ञानम्
५६. सत्त्वपुरुषयोः शुद्धिसाम्ये कैवल्यमिति

कैवल्य पाद

१. जन्मौषधिमन्त्रतपःसमाधिजाः सिद्धयः
२. जात्यन्तरपरिणामः प्रकृत्यापूरात्
३. निमित्तमप्रयोजकं प्रकृतीनां वरणभेदस्तु ततः क्षेत्रिकवत्
४. निर्माणचित्तान्यस्मितामात्रात्
५. प्रवृत्तिभेदे प्रयोजकं चित्तमेकमनेकेषाम्
६. तत्र ध्यानजमनाशयम्
७. कर्माशुक्लाकृष्णं योगिनस्त्रिविधमितरेषाम्
८. ततस्तद्विपाकानुगुणानामेवाभिव्यक्तिर्वासनानाम्
९. जातिदेशकालव्यवहितानामप्यानन्तर्यं स्मृतिसंस्कारयोरेकरूपत्वात्
१०. तासामनादित्वं चाशिषो नित्यत्वात्
११. हेतुफलाश्रयालम्बनैः संगृहीतत्वादेषामभावे तदभावः
१२. अतीतानागतं स्वरूपतोऽस्त्यध्वभेदाद्धर्माणाम्
१३. ते व्यक्तसूक्ष्मा गुणात्मानः
१४. परिणामैकत्वाद्वस्तुतत्त्वम्
१५. वस्तुसाम्ये चित्तभेदात्तयोर्विभक्तः पन्थाः
१६. न चैकचित्ततन्त्रं वस्तु तदप्रमाणकं तदा किं स्यात्
१७. तदुपरागापेक्षित्वाच्चित्तस्य वस्तु ज्ञाताज्ञातम्
१८. सदाज्ञाताश्चित्तवृत्तयस्तत्प्रभोः पुरुषस्यापरिणामित्वात्
१९. न तत्स्वाभासं दृश्यत्वात्
२०. एकसमये चोभयानवधारणम्
२१. चित्तान्तरदृश्ये बुद्धिबुद्धेरतिप्रसंगः स्मृतिसंकरश्च
२२. चित्तेरप्रतिसंक्रमायास्तदाकारापत्तौ स्वबुद्धिसंवेदनम्
२३. द्रष्टृदृश्योपरक्तं चित्तं सर्वार्थम्
२४. तदसंख्येयवासनाभिश्चित्रमपि परार्थं संहत्यकारित्वात्
२५. विशेषदर्शिनः आत्मभावभावनाविनिवृत्तिः
२६. तदा विवेकनिम्नं कैवल्यप्राग्भारं चित्तम्
२७. तच्छिद्रेषु प्रत्ययान्तराणि संस्कारेभ्यः
२८. हानमेषां क्लेशवदुक्तम्
२९. प्रसंख्यानेऽप्यकुसीदस्य सर्वथा विवेकख्यातेर्धर्ममेघः समाधिः

३०. ततः क्लेशकर्मनिवृत्तिः

३१. तदा सर्वावरणमलापेतस्य ज्ञानस्यानन्त्याज्ज्ञेयमल्पम्

३२. ततः कृतार्थानां परिणामक्रमसमाप्तिर्गुणानाम्

३३. क्षणप्रतियोगची परिणामापरान्तनिर्ग्राह्यः क्रमः

३४. पुरुषार्थशून्यानां गुणानां प्रतिप्रसवः कैवल्यं स्वरूपप्रतिष्ठा वा चित्शक्तेरिति

Appendix C

Freedom in a Nutshell

(Transliteration)

Sāmadhi Pāda

1. Atha yogānuśāsanam
2. Yogaschitta vṛtti nirodhaḥ
3. Tadā draṣṭuḥ svarūpe'vasthānam
4. Vṛtti sārūpyamitaratra
5. Vṛttayaḥ pañchatayyaḥ kliṣṭākliṣṭāḥ
6. Pramāṇa-viparyaya-vikalpa-nidrā smṛtayaḥ
7. Pratyakṣānumānāgamāḥ pramāṇāni
8. Viparyayo mithyājñānamatadrūpapratiṣṭham
9. Śabdajñānānupātī vastu-śūnyo vikalpaḥ
10. Abhāva-pratyayālambanā vṛttirnidrā
11. Anubhūtaviṣayāsampramoṣaḥ smṛtiḥ
12. Abhyāsavairāgyābhyāṃ tannirodhaḥ
13. Tatra sthitau yatno'bhyāsaḥ
14. Sa tu dīrghakāla nairantaryasatkārāsevito dṛḍhabhūmiḥ
15. Dṛṣṭānuśravika-viṣayāvitṛṣṇasya vaśīkāra-sañjñā vairāgyam
16. Tatparaṃ puruṣakhyāterguṇavaitṛṣṇyam
17. Vitarka-vichārānandāsmitānugamāt samprajñātaḥ
18. Virāmapratyayābhyāsapūrvaḥ saṃskāraśeṣo'nyaḥ
19. Bhavapratyayo videhaprakṛtilayānām
20. Śraddhāvīryasmṛtisamādhiprajñāpūrvaka itareṣām
21. Tīvrasaṃvegānāmāsannaḥ
22. Mṛdumadhyādhimātratvāt tato'pi viśeṣaḥ
23. Īśvarapraṇidhānādvā
24. Kleśakarmavipākāśayairaparāmṛṣṭaḥ puruṣaviśeṣa Īśvaraḥ

25. Tatra niratiśayaṃ sarvajñabījam
26. Pūrveṣāmapi guruḥ kālenānavachchhedāt
27. Tasya vāchakaḥ praṇavaḥ
28. Tajjapastadarthabhāvanam
29. Tataḥ pratyakchetanādhigamo'pyantarāyābhāvaścha
30. Vyādhistyānasaṃśayapramādālasyāviratibhrāntidarśanālabdhabhūmikatvānavasthitatvāni chittavikṣepāste'ntarāyāḥ
31. Duḥkhadaurmanasyāṅgamejayatvaśvāsapraśvāsā vikṣepasahabhuvaḥ
32. Tatpratiṣedhārthamekatattvābhyāsaḥ
33. Maitrīkaruṇāmuditopekṣāṇāṃ sukhaduḥkhapuṇyāpuṇyaviṣayāṇāṃ bhāvanātaśchittaprasādanam
34. Prachchhardanavidhāraṇābhyāṃ vā prāṇasya
35. Viṣayavatī vā pravṛttirutpannā manasaḥ sthitinibandhanī
36. Viśokā vā jyotiṣmatī
37. Vītarāgaviṣayaṃ vā chittam
38. Svapnanidrājñānālambanaṃ vā
39. Yathābhimatadhyānādvā
40. Paramāṇuparamamahattvānto'sya vaśīkāraḥ
41. Kṣīṇavṛtterabhijātasyeva maṇergrahītṛgrahaṇa- grāhyeṣu tatsthatadañjanatā samāpattiḥ
42. Tatra śabdārthajñānavikalpaiḥ saṅkīrṇā savitarkā samāpattiḥ
43. Smṛtipariśuddhau svarūpaśūnyevārthamātranirbhāsā nirvitarkā
44. Etayaiva savichārā nirvichārā cha sūkṣmaviṣayā vyākhyātā
45. Sūkṣmaviṣayatvaṃ chāliṅgaparyavasānam
46. Tā eva sabījaḥ samādhiḥ
47. Nirvichāravaiśāradye'dhyātmaprasādaḥ
48. Ṛtambharā tatra prajñā
49. Śrutānumānaprajñābhyāmanyaviṣayā viśeṣārthatvāt
50. Tajjaḥ saṃskāro'nyasaṃkārapratibandhī
51. Tasyāpi nirodhe sarvanirodhānnirbījaḥ samādhiḥ

Sādhanā Pāda

1. Tapaḥsvādhyāyeśvarapraṇidhānāni kriyāyogaḥ
2. Samādhibhāvanārthaḥ kleśatanūkaraṇārthaścha
3. Avidyāsmitārāgadveṣābhiniveśāḥ kleśāḥ
4. Avidyākṣetramuttareṣāṃ prasuptatanuvichchhinnodārāṇām
5. Anityāśuchiduḥkhānātmasu nityaśuchisukhātmakhyātiravidyā
6. Dṛgdarśanaśaktyorekātmatevāsmitā
7. Sukhānuśayī rāgaḥ
8. Duḥkhānuśayī dveṣaḥ
9. Svarasavāhī viduṣo'pi tathārūḍho'bhiniveśaḥ
10. Te pratiprasavaheyāḥ sūkṣmāḥ
11. Dhyānaheyāstadvṛttayaḥ
12. Kleśamūlaḥ karmāśayo dṛṣṭādṛṣṭajanmavedanīyaḥ
13. Sati mūle tadvipāko jātyāyurbhogāḥ
14. Te hlādaparitāpaphalāḥ puṇyāpuṇyahetutvāt
15. Pariṇāmatāpasaṃskāraduḥkhairguṇavṛttivirodhāchcha duḥkhameva sarvaṃ vivekinaḥ
16. Heyaṃ duḥkhamanāgatam
17. Draṣṭṛdṛśyayoḥ saṃyogo heyahetuḥ
18. Prakāśakriyāsthitiśīlaṃ bhūtendriyātmakaṃ bhogāpavargārthaṃ dṛśyam
19. Viśeṣāviśeṣaliṅgamātrāliṅgāni guṇaparvāṇi
20. Draṣṭā dṛśimātraḥ śuddho'pi pratyayānupaśyaḥ
21. Tadartha eva dṛśyasyātmā
22. Kṛtārthaṃ prati naṣṭamapyanaṣṭaṃ tadanyasādhāraṇatvāt
23. Svasvāmiśaktayoḥ svarūpopalabdhihetuḥ saṃyogaḥ
24. Tasya heturavidyā
25. Tadabhāvāt saṃyogābhāvo hānaṃ taddṛśeḥ kaivalyam
26. Vivekakhyātiraviplavā hānopāyaḥ
27. Tasya saptadhā prāntabhūmiḥ prajñā
28. Yogāṅganuṣṭhānādaśuddhikṣaye jñānadīptirāvivekakhyāteḥ

29. Yamaniyamāsanaprāṇāyāmapratyāhāradhāraṇā-dhyānasamādhayo'ṣṭāvaṅgāni
30. Ahiṃsāsatyāsteyabrahmacharyāparigrahā yamāḥ
31. Jātideśakālasamayānavachchhinnāḥ sārvabhaumā mahāvratam
32. Śauchasantoṣatapaḥsvādhyāyeśvarapraṇidhānāni niyamāḥ
33. Vitarkabādhane pratipakṣabhāvanam
34. Vitarkā hiṃsādayaḥ kṛtakāritānumoditā lobhakrodhamohapūrvakā mṛdumadhyādhimātrā duḥkhājñānānantaphalā iti pratipakṣabhāvanam
35. Ahiṃsāpratiṣṭhāyāṃ tatsaṃnidhau vairatyāgaḥ
36. Satyapratiṣṭhāyāṃ kriyāphalāśrayatvam
37. Asteya pratiṣṭhāyāṃ sarvaratnopasthānam
38. Brahmacharyapratiṣṭhāyāṃ vīryalābhaḥ
39. Aparigrahasthairye janmakathantāsambodhaḥ
40. Śauchātsvāṅgajugupsā parairasaṃsargaḥ
41. Sattvaśuddhisaumanasyaikāgryendriyajayātma-darśanayogyatvāni cha
42. Santoṣādanuttamasukhalābhaḥ
43. Kāyendriyasiddhiraśuddhikṣayāttapasaḥ
44. Svādhyāyādiṣṭadevatāsamprayogaḥ
45. Samādhisiddhirīśvarapraṇidhānāt
46. Sthirasukhamāsanam
47. Prayatnaśaithilyānantasamāpattibhyām
48. Tato dvandvānabhighātaḥ
49. Tasminsati śvāsapraśvāsayorgativichchhedaḥ prāṇāyāmaḥ
50. Bāhyābhyantarastambhavṛttirdeśakālasaṅkhyābhiḥ paridṛṣṭo dīrghasūkṣmaḥ
51. Bāhyābhyantaraviṣayākṣepī chaturthaḥ
52. Tataḥ kṣīyate prakāśāvaraṇam
53. Dhāraṇāsu cha yogyatā manasaḥ
54. Svaviṣayāsamprayoge chittasyasvarūpānukāra ivendriyāṇāṃ pratyāhāraḥ
55. Tatah paramā vaśyatendriyāṇām

Vibhūti Pāda

1. Deśabandhaśchittasya dhāraṇā
2. Tatra pratyayaikatānatā dhyānam
3. Tadevārthamātranirbhāsaṃ svarūpaśūnyamiva samādhiḥ
4. Trayamekatra saṃyamaḥ
5. Tajjayātprajñālokaḥ
6. Tasya bhūmiṣu viniyogaḥ
7. Trayamantaraṅgaṃ pūrvebhyaḥ
8. Tadapi bahiraṅgaṃ nirbījasya
9. Vyutthānanirodhasaṃskārayorabhibhava-prādurbhāvau nirodhakṣaṇachittānvayo nirodhapariṇāmaḥ
10. Tasya praśāntavāhitā saṃskārāt
11. Sarvārthataikāgratayoḥ kṣayodayau chittasya samādhipariṇāmaḥ
12. Tataḥ punaḥ śāntoditau tulyapratyayau chittasyaikāgratāpariṇāmaḥ
13. Etena bhūtendriyeṣu dharmalakṣaṇāvasthāpariṇāmāḥ vyākhyātāḥ
14. Śāntoditāvyapadeśyadharmānupātī dharmī
15. Kramānyatvaṃ pariṇāmānyatve hetuḥ
16. Pariṇāmatrayasaṃyamādatītānāgatajñānam
17. Śabdārthapratyayānāmitaretarādhyāsāt saṅkarastatpravibhāgasaṃyamāt sarvabhūtarutajñānam
18, Saṃskārasākṣātkaraṇāt pūrvajāti jñānam
19. Pratyayasya parachittajñānam
20. Na cha tat sālambanaṃ tasyāviṣayībhūtatvāt
21. Kāyarūpasaṃyamāt tadgrāhyaśaktistambhe chakṣuḥ prakāśāsamprayoge'ntardhānam
22. Etena śabdādyantardhānaṃ uktam
23. Sopakramaṃ nirupakramaṃ cha karma tatsaṃyamādaparāntajñānamariṣṭebhyo vā
24. Maitryādiṣu balāni
25. Baleṣu hastibalādīni
26. Pravṛttyālokanyāsāt sūkṣmavyavahitaviprakṛṣṭa-jñānam

27. Bhuvanajñānaṃ sūryesaṃyamāt
28. Chandre tārāvyūhajñānam
29. Dhruve tadgatijñānam
30. Nābhichakre kāyavyūhajñānam
31. Kaṇṭhakūpe kṣutpipāsā nivṛttiḥ
32. Kūrmanāḍyāṃ sthairyam
33. Mūrdhajyotiṣi siddhadarśanam
34. Pratibhād vā sarvam
35. Hṛdaye chittasaṃvit
36. Sattva puruṣayoratyantāsaṅkīrṇayoḥ pratyayāviśeṣo bhogaḥ parārthatvāt svārthasaṃyamāt puruṣajñānam
37. Tataḥ prātibhaśrāvaṇavedanādarśāsvādavārtā jāyante
38. Te samādhāvupasargā vyutthāne siddhayaḥ
39. Bandhakāraṇaśaithilyātprachārasaṃvedanāchcha chittasya paraśarīrāveśaḥ
40. Udānajayājjalapaṅkakaṇṭakādiṣvasaṅga utkrāntiścha
41. Samānajayājjvalanam
42. Śrotrākāśayoḥ sambandhasaṃyamāddivyaṃ śrotram
43. Kāyākāśayoḥ sambandhasaṃyamāllaghutūla-samāpatteśchākāśagamanam
44. Bahirakalpitā vṛttirmahāvidehā tataḥ prakāśāvaraṇakṣayaḥ
45. Sthūlasvarūpasūkṣmānvayārthavattvasaṃyamād bhūtajayaḥ
46. Tato'ṇimādiprādurbhāvaḥ kāyasampattaddharmānabhighātaścha
47. Rūpalāvaṇyabalavajrasaṃhananatvāni kāyasampat
48. Grahaṇasvarūpāsmitānvayārthavattvasaṃyamād-indriyajayaḥ
49. Tato manojavitvaṃ vikaraṇabhāvaḥ pradhānajayaścha
50. Sattvapuruṣānyatākhyātimātrasya sarvabhāvādhiṣṭhātṛtvaṃ sarvajñātṛtvaṃ cha
51. Tadvairāgyādapi doṣabījakṣaye kaivalyam
52. Sthānyupanimantraṇe saṅgasmayākaraṇaṃ punaraniṣṭaprasaṅgāt
53. Kṣaṇatatkramayoḥ saṃyamādvivekajaṃ jñānam

54. Jātilakṣaṇadeśairanyatānavachchhedāt tulyayostataḥ pratipattiḥ
55. Tārakaṃ sarvaviṣayaṃ sarvathāviṣayamakramaṃ cheti vivekajaṃ jñānam
56. Sattvapuruṣayoḥ śuddhisāmye kaivalyamiti

Kaivalya Pāda

1. Janmauṣadhimantratapaḥsamādhijāḥ siddhayaḥ
2. Jātyantarapariṇāmaḥ prakṛtyāpūrāt
3. Nimittamaprayojakaṃ prakṛtīnāṃ varaṇabhedastu tataḥ kṣetrikavat
4. Nirmāṇachittānyasmitāmātrāt
5. Pravṛttibhede prayojakaṃ chittamekamanekeṣām
6. Tatra dhyānajamanāśayam
7. Karmāśuklākṛṣṇaṃ yoginastrividhamitareṣām
8. Tatastadvipākānuguṇānāmevābhivyaktirvāsanānām
9. Jātideśakālavyavahitānāmapyānantaryaṃ smṛtisaṃskārayorekarūpatvāt
10. Tāsāmanāditvaṃ chāśiṣo nityatvāt
11. Hetuphalāśrayālambanaiḥ saṅgṛhītatvādeṣāmabhāve tadabhāvaḥ
12. Atītānāgataṃ svarūpato'styadhvabhedād-dharmāṇām
13. Te vyaktasūkṣmā guṇātmānaḥ
14. Pariṇāmaikatvādvastutattvam
15. Vastusāmye chittabhedāttayorvibhaktaḥ panthāḥ
16. Na chaika chittatantraṃ vastu tadapramāṇakaṃ tadā kiṃ syāt
17. Taduparāgāpekṣitvāchchittasya vastu jñātājñātam
18. Sadā jñātāśchittavṛttayastatprabhoḥ puruṣasyāpariṇāmitvāt
19. Na tatsvābhāsaṃ dṛśyatvāt
20. Ekasamaye chobhayānavadhāraṇam
21. Chittāntaradṛśye buddhibuddheratiprasaṅgaḥ smṛtisaṅkaraścha

22. Chitterapratisaṅkramāyāstadākārāpattau svabuddhisamvedanam
23. Draṣṭṛdṛśyoparaktaṃ chittaṃ sarvārtham
24. Tadasaṅkhyeyavāsanābhiśchitramapi parārthaṃ saṃhatyakāritvāt
25. Viśeṣadarśinaḥ ātmabhāvabhāvanāvinivṛttiḥ
26. Tadā vivekanimnaṃ kaivalyaprāgbhāraṃ chittam
27. Tachchhidreṣu pratyayāntarāṇi saṃskārebhyaḥ
28. Hānameṣāṃ kleśavaduktam
29. Prasaṅkhyāne'pyakusīdasya sarvathā vivekakhyāterdharmameghaḥ samādhiḥ
30. Tataḥ kleśakarmanivṛttiḥ
31. Tadā sarvāvaraṇamalāpetasya jñānasyānantyājjñeyamalpam
32. Tataḥ kṛtārthānāṃ pariṇāmakramasamāptirguṇānām
33. Kṣaṇapratiyogī pariṇāmāparāntanirgrāhyaḥ kramaḥ
34. Puruṣārthaśūnyānāṃ guṇānāṃ pratiprasavaḥ kaivalyaṃ svarūpapratiṣṭhā vā chitśakteriti

Glossary

A – अ

abhāva(ḥ)	absence
abhibhava	suppression
abhijātasya	well-polished; purified
abhimata	desired; agreeable
abhiniveśa(ḥ)	fear of death
abhivyaktih	manifestation
abhyāsa(ḥ)	repeated practice; practice
abhyantara	internal
adhiṣṭhātṛtvam	supremacy
adhigama	attainment
adhimātra	extremely strong
adhyātma	spiritual
ahiṃsā	non-violence (one of the yamas)
ajñāna	ignorance
ajñātam	unknown
akalpitā	unimaginable
akliṣṭāh	without pain
akusīdasya	one who has no interest
alabdhabhūmikatva	inability to achieve a finer state
aliṅga	prakriti; without mark or symbol
alpam	but little
anāditvaṃ	beginninglessness
anāgatah	future
anātmaṣu	non-self

ananta	endless; serpent symbolizing eternity
anantaryaṃ	sequence
anantyāt	infinity
anaṣṭaṃ	not destroyed
anavachchhinnā(ḥ)	unconditioned; unlimited
anavachhedāt	unlimited by time
anavadhāraṇam	non-comprehension
anavasthitatva	instability
aṅgamejayatva	shaking of the body
aṇima	atom-sized (siddhi)
anitya	not eternal; ephemeral
antah	ending
antarāya	obstacles; hindrances
antaraṅga	internal; limbs of Patanjali Yoga
antardhānam	being invisible
anuśāsanam	complete instructions
anuśravika	heard
anubhūta	experienced
anugamāt	by association
anumāna	inference
anupātī	common; following upon
anyah	other
anyatā	difference
aparāmṛṣṭah	untouched
aparānta	death; in the end; finally
aparigrahā	non-covetousness; non-acquisitiveness; non-possessivness
apariṇāmitvāt	because of changelessness
apavarga	liberation
apekṣāṇām	indifference
apekṣitvāt	due to necessity
api	also; even
apramāṇakam	non-perception
apuṇya	vice; sin; demerit
ariṣṭebhyah	by omens
artha	meaning; object; purpose
asaṅkhyeya	countless

asamprajñāta	samadhi which occurs between successive stages of samprajnata samadhi
asampramoṣaḥ	not letting escape
asamprayoge	absence of contact
aśuchi	impure
aśuddhi	impurity
aṣṭa	eight
asmitā	ego, feeling of 'I-ness'
asteya	honesty (one of the yamas)
asya	of his
atīta	past
atat	not its own
atha	now therefore
atiprasaṅgaḥ	absurd; superfluous
atyanta	extremely
auṣadhi	herbs
avasthānam	establishment; settled; fixed; condition
aviśeṣa	without difference
avidyā	ignorance
avirati	craving for enjoyment
avyapadeśa	unmanifest

Ā – आ

ādarśa	visualization
āgama	testimony; revelation
ākāśa	ether; space
ākṣepī	transcending
ālambana	support; object
ālasya	laziness
ālokaḥ	illumination
ānanda	bliss; beautitude
āpattau	having achieved
āpūrāt	compensating; overflowing
āsana	fixed sitting position
āsannaḥ	quite near
āsevita(ḥ)	practised
āśaya	store of the traces of past karma

āśiṣah	will to live
āśraya	support
āśrayatvam	basis
āsvāda	taste perception
ātma(n)	pure awareness; the self
ātmabhāva	awareness of the self
āvaraṇa(ṃ	covering; veil

B – ब्

bāhya	outer; external
bahiraṅga	external limbs of Patanjali Yoga
balāni	powers
bala	strength
bandha	binding; bondage
bījam	principle; seed
brahmacharya	celibacy; sexual abstinence (one of the yamas)
buddhi	mental faculty of intelligence
buddhibuddheh	perception of perceptions

Bh – भ्

bhāva	states of existence
bhāvanā(ṃ)	dwelling upon mentally; feeling
bhāvanāta(ḥ)	attitude
bhakti yoga	yogic path of devotion
bhavapratyayah	birth is the cause
bhedah	removal, piercing, difference
bhoga	worldly experience
Bhoja	famous commentator on Patanjali's text
bhrāntidarśana	erroneous perception
bhuvana	solar system
bhūmih	ground
bhūta	elements
bhūtajaya(ḥ)	mastery over the elements

Ch – च्

chakṣuh	eye
chandra	moon
chaturtha	fourth (state of consciousness and pranayama)
chetanā	consciousness
chītśakteḥ	consciousness
chitram	coloured; variegated
chittāni	minds
chitta	individual consciousness which includes the conscious, subconscious and unconscious levels of mind
chittabhedāt	because of differences of mind
chittāntaradṛśye	cognition of one mind by another
chittasaṃvit	knowledge of mind
chittasya	of the mind; mental
chittavikṣepāḥ	mental obstacles

D – द्

darśana	cognition; spiritual vision
darśanaśakti	power of expression (vehicles of consciousness)
darśinaḥ	one who sees
daurmanasya	depression
deśa	country; place
dīrgha	long
divya(m)	divine
doṣa	defect
dṛḍha	firm
draṣṭuḥ; draṣṭā; draṣṭṛ	seer
dṛśimātra	only pure consciousness
dṛśyatvāt	due to cognition
dṛṣṭa; dṛśya(m)	seen
dṛg	consciousness
dṛgśakti	power of cognition
duḥkha	pain; frustration; misery
dvandva	pairs of opposites; conflicts

dveṣa	aversion; dislike

Dh – ध्

dhāraṇā	concentration
dharma	quality; property; righteous path and acts
dharmameghah	showering of sat-chit-ananda (truth, consciousness and bliss)
dharmi	substratum of properties
dhruva	pole star
dhyānajam	born of meditation

E – ए

ekāgratā	one-pointedness of mind
eka	one; single
ekasamaye	simultaneously
ekatra	together
ekatvāt	due to oneness
etaya	by this
eva	as if; only

G – ग्

gati	movement
grāhyeṣu	object of cognition
grahaṇa	senses; means of cognizing; power of perception
grahitā	cognizer; seer
guṇānām	of the gunas
guṇātmānaḥ	comprised of gunas
guṇa	the threefold aspects of nature; see sattwa, rajas and tamas
guṇavaitṛṣṇyaṃ	freedom from desire for the gunas
guru(ḥ)	greater; teacher; preceptor

H – ह्

hānam	destruction
hṛdaya	heart

I – इ

indriya	sense organs
indriyajaya	mastery over the senses
iśitva	power to wilfully create and destroy (siddhi)
iṣṭadevatā	personal deity
itaratra	in other state
itareṣām	of others
iva	just like

Ī – ई

īśvara	Lord; God; pure awareness
īśvara praṇidhāna	surrender to God (one of the niyamas)

J – ज्

jāti	class, caste, type, species
jala	water
janma	birth
japa	repetition of a mantra
jyotiṣmatī	luminous; full of light
jyotiṣmati	supersensory perception

Jñ – ज्ञ्

jñāna(m)	knowledge; cognition
jñānasya	pertaining to knowledge
jñāta	known
jñeya	knowable

K – क्

kāla	time
kālena	by time
kāmāvaśitva	fulfilment of every wish
kāraṇa	cause
kāyā	body
kaivalya(m)	liberation; onlyness; oneness; non-duality
kaivalya-prāgbhāram	inclined towards oneness

karmāśaya	reservoir of karma (from previous births)
karma	action
karma yoga	yogic path of action
karmavipāka	fruits of past acts
karuṇā	compassion
khyāti	knowledge; awareness
kleśa	affliction; tension
kliṣṭā	painful; hard; difficult
krama(ḥ)	order; sequence; process
kṛtārthānāṃ	having completed their purpose
kṛtārtha(ṃ)	a person whose pupose is fulfilled
kriyā	activity; action
kriyā yoga	practical yoga; preparatory yoga
krodha	anger
kūrma-nāḍyām	kurma, psychic pathway in the throat

Kṣ – क्ष्

kṣaṇa	moment in time
kṣayāt	through destruction
kṣetram	field
kṣipt(a)	disturbed state of mind
kṣīṇavṛtti	a person who has weakened the modifications (vrittis) of the mind
kṣut	hunger

Kh – ख्

khyāti	awareness

L – ल्

lābha(ḥ)	gain; benefit
laghimā	lightness (siddhi)
laghu	light
lakṣaṇa	characteristic
liṅgamātra	with mark or symbol
lobha	greed

M – म्

mātra	only
madhya	medium
mahāvideha	disembodied existence
mahāvratam	great vow or discipline
mahimā	immensity of body (siddhi)
maitrī	friendliness
mala	impurity
manasaḥ	of the mind
maṇeḥ	of a crystal or jewel
manojavitvaṃ	speed of mind
mantra	incantation; psychic sound
mithyā	false
moha	confusion
mṛdu	mild
muditā	gladness
mūḍha	dull state of mind
mūla(ḥ)	root
mūrdhā	crown of the head

N – न्

nābhi	navel
na	not
naṣṭam	destroyed
nairantarya	without interruption
nibandhanī	that which binds
nidrā	sleep
nimitta(ṃ)	instrument
niratiśayam	limitless
nirbhāsa	shining
nirbīja	without seed (in samadhi)
nirgrāhyaḥ	completely comprehensible
nirguṇopāsanā	practice or worship without objective point of concentration
nirmāṇa	creation
nirodha(ḥ)	blocking; stopping; state of mind beyond the three gunas

nirodhakṣaṇa	moment of suppression
nirvichāra	without reflection
nirvitarka	without confusion of sense; mental and true knowledge
nitya	eternal
nivṛtti(ḥ)	retirement; cessation; return
niyama	fixed observation or rules

P – प्

pañchatayaḥ	fivefold
panthāḥ	path of manifestation
parārthaṃ	for the sake of consciousness
parāvairāgya	detachment arising from direct experience of underlying consciousness
parama	highest
paramāṇu	infinitesimal atom
paramamahattva	ultimate largeness
pari	complete
pariṇāmā(ḥ)	consequence; result, transformation
paryavasānam	extension
pipāsā	thirst
prāṇasya	of breath
prākāmya	certain fulfilment of desire
prāṇāyāma	breath and prana control
prāpti	ability to reach everywhere (siddhi)
prachchhardana	exhalation (rechaka)
prajñā	intuition; revelation
prakāśa	light; illumination
prakṛti	nature; the manifested universe
prakṛtilayānām	yogis who are merged in prakriti
pramāṇāni	sources of right knowledge
pramāṇa	right relative knowledge
pramāda	procrastination
praṇavaḥ	aum
praṇidhānāt	devotion
prasādanam	purification; making peaceful; grace
prasaṅkhyāne	in the highest meditation

praśānta	peaceful
prasupta	dormant
prati	towards
pratibhā	intuition
pratipakṣa	opposite
pratipattiḥ	knowledge
pratiprasava	involution
pratiprasavaḥ	involution
pratiṣedhārtham	for removal
pratiṣṭha(m)	based; established
pratiyogi	corresponding
pratyāhāra	sense withdrawal
pratyabhijña	illumined knowledge
pratyak	reversed; turned inwards
pratyakṣa	direct perception; sense perception
pratyaya	content of the mind
pravibhāga	separate
pravṛttih	functioning; activity
prayatna	effort
punaḥ	again
puṇya	virtue, merit
puruṣārtha	purpose of the consciousness
puruṣa	pure consciousness
puruṣajñānam	knowledge of purusha
puruṣakhyāteh	true knowledge of the purusha
puruṣaviśeṣa	special kind of soul
pūrva(ḥ)	coming before
pūrvaka	preceded by
pūrveṣām	of those who come before

Ph – फ्

phala(m)	fruits; result

R – र्

rāga	liking, attachtment
rajas	the active and fluctuating state of mind and nature

ṛtam	ultimate truth
ṛtambharā	full of experience; cosmic harmony
ruta	speech
rūpa	form

S – स्

sādhaka	yogic or spiritual aspirant
sādhanā	continous yogic practice and effort
sākṣātkaraṇāt	by direct perception
sārūpyam	identification
sārvabhauma	universal
sabīja	with seed (in samadhi)
sadā	always
saguṇopāsanā	practice or worship with object or deity
sah	that
sahabhuvah	accompanying symptoms
samādhiprajñā	intelligence arising from experience of samadhi
samāna	specific prana of the body
samāpattiḥ	complete absorption; complete acceptance
samāptih	end; culmination
samaśaya	doubt
samaya	circumstances
saṃbandha	relationship
sambodha(ḥ)	knowledge
samprajñāta(ḥ)	samadhi with illumination
samprayoga(ḥ)	communion
saṃskāra	latent mental impression; seed of consciousness
saṃskāraśeṣa	in which only traces of mental impressions remain
saṃvedanam	knowing about
saṃvega	urge
saṃyama	the threefold process of dharana, dhyana and samadhi
samyoga	union; coming together

saṅga	attachment
sanjñā	awareness
saṅkara(h)	confusion
saṅkīrṇa	confused; mixed up
santoṣa	contentment (one of niyamas)
sarvārtham	all inclusive; all apprehending
sarva(ṃ)	everything
sarvabhūta	all living things
sarvajñātṛtvaṃ	omniscience
sarvajña	omniscient
satkāra	reverence
sattva	pure and calm state of mind or nature
satya	truthfulness (one of the yamas)
satyam	relative truth
savichāra	with reflection
savikalpa	combined with sense, verbal and true knowledge
savitarka	combined with worded thinking
siddha	adept
siddhi	perfection; psychic power
smṛtayaḥ; smṛti	memory
smaya	pride
stambhe	suspension
sthāni	deities; devatas; gods
sthūla	gross
sthira	steady
sthiti	steadiness
sthitau	being fixed
styāna	dullness
sukha	happiness
sūkṣma	subtle
sūrye	sun
svābhāsaṃ	self-illumined
svādhyāya	self-study; study of the scriptures
sva	of one's own
svabuddhi	self-perception
svapna	dream state

svarūpa	one's own essential nature
svādhyāya	self-study (one of the niyamas)
swāmi, svāmi	master of one's self

Ś – श्

śabda	word; sound; mantra
śaithilya	looseness
śakti	power
śarīra	body
śaucha	cleaniness (one of the niyamas)
śilam	qualities
śraddhā	faith
śravana	faculty of hearing
śrotra(m)	ear
śruta	heard
śuchi	pure
śuddhau	purification
śūnyanaṃ	devoid of; empty of
śūnya(ḥ)	empty; void
śvāsapraśvāsa	inhalations and exhalations of breath

T – त्

tārā	stars
tāraka	transcendental
tadā	then
tadākāra	form of that
tadañjanatā	assuming the colour of something
taduparāga	object reflected in mind
tamas	the dull, inert state of mind and nature
tantram	dependent
tanu	thin
tapa(h)	austerity; elimination of mental impurities; acute suffering (also a niyama)
tasya	of it
tat	that
tatah	from that
tatprabhoh	on its master

tatra	there; of the two; in that state
tatstha	on which it rests
tattva chintana	contemplation and reflection
tattva darshana	direct perception
tattva(m)	principle; essence
tīvra	intense
tṛṣnā	craving; desire
tulya	equal
turīya	fourth state of consciousness; the unmanifested state of purusha
tvāt	due to
tyāga(ḥ)	abandonment; renunciation

Tra – त्

traya(ṃ)	three; group of three

U – उ

ubhaya	both
udāna	type of prana in the body
udārāṇām	expanded
udita	manifest
uktam	is said
uparaktaṃ	coloured
upasargā	obstacles
utkrāntih	levitation
utpanna	arisen

V – व्

vāchakaḥ	designator; indicator
vāhita	flow
vārtā	smell
vāsanām	desires
vāsanānām	of potential desires
vairāgyābhyāṃ	by detachment
vairāgya(m)	absence of craving; desirelessness
vairatyāgah	abandonment of aggression
vaiśāradye	after gaining perfect mastery

varaṇa	obstacles; veiling
vaśīkāra(ḥ)	control; mastery
vaśitva	control over objects (siddhi)
vastu	object
vastusāmye	sameness of an object
vedanā	touch perception
vibhaktah	separate; different
vichchhedaḥ	break; cessation
vichchhinna	scattered
videha	disembodied yogi
vidhāraṇābhyāṃ	holding of breath (kumbhaka)
vīchāra	reflection
vītarāga	desireless and passionless person
Vijñāna Bhikṣu	another commentator of Patanjali's text who wrote Yogasara Sangraha
vikalpa(ḥ)	fancy; imagination
vikaraṇabhāvaḥ	freedom from sense distractions
vikṣepa	distraction of the mind
vikṣipta	an oscillating state of mind changing from steadiness to distraction
vinivṛttiḥ	complete cessation
viparyaya(ḥ)	wrong knowledge; misconception
virāma	stopping
vīrya	energy; strong will; courage
viśeṣa(ḥ)	special; peculiar; with difference
viśokā	without sorrow
viṣaya(ḥ)	objects of sense perception
viṣayavatī	sensuous; of the senses
vitarka	reasoning; thoughts; passions
vitriṣṇasya	of one who is free of desire
viveka	discrimination
vivekakhyāti	discriminative awareness
vivekanimnaṃ	inclined towards discrimination
vṛttayah	pattern of the mind
vṛtti	pattern or circular patterns of consciousness ; modification
vyādhi	disease

vyākhyātā	explained
Vyāsa	commentator on Patanjali's work who wrote Yogabhasya
vyakta	manifest
vyūha	arrangements

Y – य्

yama	self-restraints
yatnah	effort
yogāṅga	limb or stage of yoga practice
yoga	union; the practice and process of yoga as explained by Patanjali
yogyatā	fitness; competence

Index

INTERNATIONAL YOGA FELLOWSHIP MOVEMENT (IYFM)

The IYFM is a charitable and philosophical movement founded by Swami Satyananda at Rajnandgaon in 1956 to disseminate the yogic tradition throughout the world. It forms the medium to convey the teachings of Swami Satyananda through its affiliated centres around the world. Swami Niranjanananda is the first Paramacharya of the International Yoga Fellowship Movement.

The IYFM provides guidance, systematized yoga training programs and sets teaching standards for all the affiliated yoga teachers, centres and ashrams. A Yoga Charter to consolidate and unify the humanitarian efforts of all sannyasin disciples, yoga teachers, spiritual seekers and well-wishers was introduced during the World Yoga Convention in 1993. Affiliation to this Yoga Charter enables the person to become a messenger of goodwill and peace in the world, through active involvement in various far-reaching yoga-related projects.

BIHAR SCHOOL OF YOGA (BSY)

The Bihar School of Yoga is a charitable and educational institution founded by Swami Satyananda at Munger in 1963, with the aim of imparting yogic training to all nationalities and to provide a focal point for a mass return to the ancient science of yoga. The Chief Patron of Bihar School of Yoga is Swami Niranjanananda. The original school, Sivanandashram, is the centre for the Munger locality. Ganga Darshan, the new school established in 1981, is situated on a historic hill with panoramic views of the river Ganges.

Yoga Health Management, Teacher Training, Sadhana, Kriya Yoga and other specialized courses are held throughout the year. BSY is also renowned for its sannyasa training and the initiation of female and foreign sannyasins.

BSY provides trained sannyasins and teachers for conducting yoga conventions, seminars and lectures tours around the world. It also contains a comprehensive research library and scientific research centre.

SIVANANDA MATH (SM)

Sivananda Math is a social and charitable institution founded by Swami Satyananda at Munger in 1984, in memory of his guru, Swami Sivananda Saraswati of Rishikesh. The Head Office is now situated at Rikhia in Deoghar district, Bihar. Swami Niranjanananda is the Chief Patron.

Sivananda Math aims to facilitate the growth of the weaker and underprivileged sections of society, especially rural communities. Its activities include: distribution of free scholarships, clothing, farm animals and food, the digging of tube-wells and construction of houses for the needy, assistance to farmers in ploughing and watering their fields. The Rikhia complex also houses a satellite dish system for providing global information to the villagers.

A medical clinic has been established for the provision of medical treatment, advice and education. Veterinary services are also provided. All services are provided free and universally to everyone, regardless of caste and creed.

YOGA RESEARCH FOUNDATION (YRF)

The Yoga Research Foundation is a scientific, research-oriented institution founded by Swami Satyananda at Munger in 1984. Swami Niranjanananda is the Chief Patron of the foundation.

YRF aims to provide an accurate assessment of the practices of different branches of yoga within a scientific framework, and to establish yoga as an essential science for the development of mankind. At present the foundation is working on projects in the areas of fundamental research and clinical research. It is also studying the effects of yoga on proficiency improvement in various social projects, e.g. army, prisoners, children. These projects are being carried out in affiliated centres worldwide.

YRF's future plans include literary, scriptural, medical and scientific investigations into other little-known aspects of yoga for physical health, mental well-being and spiritual upliftment.

SRI PANCHDASHNAM PARAMAHAMSA ALAKH BARA

SRI PANCHDASHNAM PARAMAHAMSA ALAKH BARA (PPAB)

Sri Panchdashnam Paramahamsa Alakh Bara was established in 1990 by Swami Satyananda at Rikhia, Deoghar, Bihar. It is a charitable, educational and non-profit making institution aiming to uphold and propagate the highest tradition of sannyasa, namely vairagya (dispassion), tyaga (renunciation) and tapasya (austerity). It propounds the tapovan style of living adopted by the rishis and munis of the vedic era and is intended only for sannyasins, renunciates, ascetics, tapasvis and paramahamsas. The Alakh Bara does not conduct any activities such as yoga teaching or preaching of any religion or religious concepts. The guidelines set down for the Alakh Bara are based on the classical vedic tradition of sadhana, tapasya and swadhyaya, or atma chintan.

Swami Satyananda, who resides permanently at the Alakh Bara, has performed the Panchagni Vidya and other vedic sadhanas, thus paving the way for future paramahamsas to uphold their tradition.

बिहार योग भारती
BIHAR YOGA BHARATI

BIHAR YOGA BHARATI (BYB)

Bihar Yoga Bharati was founded by Swami Niranjanananda in 1994 as an educational and charitable institution for advanced studies in yogic sciences. It is the culmination of the vision of Swami Sivananda and Swami Satyananda. BYB is the world's first government accredited university wholly devoted to teaching yoga. A comprehensive yogic education is imparted with provision to grant higher degrees in yogic studies such as MA, MSc, MPhil, DLitt, and PhD to the students. It offers a complete scientific and yogic education according to the needs of today, through the faculties of Yoga Philosophy, Yoga Psychology, Applied Yogic Science and Yogic Ecology.

Residential courses of four months to two years are conducted in a gurukul environment, so that along with yoga education, the spirit of seva (selfless service), samarpan (dedication) and karuna (compassion) for humankind is also imbibed by the students.

YOGA PUBLICATIONS TRUST (YPT)

Yoga Publications Trust (YPT) was established by Swami Niranjanananda in 2000. It is an organization devoted to the dissemination and promotion of yogic and allied knowledge – psychology (ancient and modern), ecology, medicine, vedic, upanishadic, tantric darshanas, philosophies (Eastern and Western), mysticism and spirituality – nationally and internationally through the distribution of books, magazines, audio and video cassettes and multimedia.

YPT is primarily concerned with publishing textbooks in the areas of yoga philosophy, psychology and applied yogic science, research materials, practice texts and the inspiring talks of eminent spiritual personalities and authors aimed at the upliftment of humanity by means of the eternal yogic knowledge, lifestyle and practice.